Japanese Schooling

Japanese Schooling

Patterns of Socialization, Equality, and Political Control

Edited by James J. Shields, Jr.

The Pennsylvania State University Press
University Park and London

Library of Congress Cataloging-in-Publication Data

Japanese schooling.

   1. School environment—Japan. 2. Education—Social
aspects—Japan. 3. Socialization. 4. Education—
Japan—Aims and objectives. I. Shields, James J.
LC210.8.J3J37 1989   370.19′0952   88–25393
ISBN 0–271–00658–7

Contents

Part I

Patterns of Socialization in the Family and at School

Introduction

James J. Shields, Jr.

There is a growing interest, particularly in the United States, in the impact of the home and cultural values on pupil achievement. The focus is turning away from the school and toward family culture as the primary root of educational quality. As a result, there has been a shift away from those 1970s paradigms, which gave very little attention in school reform plans to the role that families play in academic success and failure.

In the recent past, those who have tried to connect school failure to home and family culture often were attacked for "blaming the victim." Currently, however, conservative ideologues have created a climate in which it is acceptable to locate the problem in family neglect of character development. Increasingly, school failure is being identified as a byproduct of family pathology.

In a study released by the U.S. Department of Education in 1986, "Gaining Ground, Values and High School Success," it was reported that students whose parents inculcate values commonly described as the "Protestant work ethic" are significantly more likely to attain high grades than others.

The authors indicated that their study was prompted by recent research on the academic success of immigrants from Vietnam and other Asian countries whose families place a high value on school achievement. The irony is that the authors found it necessary to turn to pupils from non-Western and non-Protestant cultures to demonstrate the relationship between school success and character development that they had defined from a Protestant perspective.

The awareness among U.S. educational leaders of the role of the family in school effectiveness has generated considerable interest in Japanese child-rearing patterns. From the earliest years, Japanese schools and families are closely united in their mutually respected goals of imprinting disciplined work habits and cooperative attitudes in children.

The essays in this section focus on conceptual issues within the context of the home and school learning from nursery through the secondary level. Primarily the emphasis is on the way Japanese patterns of socialization translate into strong pupil motivation in school. On the most fundamental level, early childhood education in the home and in the school in Japan is a matter of character formation and moral development.

Beyond their social science credentials, the authors integrate into their essays rich personal experiences in Japanese families and schools both as parents and as teachers. For instance, not only did John Singleton's children attend Japanese schools in the early 1960s, but also his son, twenty years later, became an apprentice potter in a traditional Japanese workshop. Anne Imamura is a foreign wife with a Japanese husband and a child who attended a school in Japan. Hiroshi Iwama speaks from his teaching experience in Japanese schools. Each, from quite different cultural perspectives, offers important insights into the contradictions and problems, as well as the strengths, in the complex interplay between home and school in Japan. The rich blend of authors in this section gives it a special and rich authenticity.

What comes across in these essays is that many Japanese mothers work very hard at seeing to it that their children succeed in school. They spend a good deal of time making things for their children to use in school, preparing elaborate lunches, and attending school functions faithfully.

In addition, they are consistent and clear about the values and behaviors they reinforce in their children. In particular, they stress persistence (*gambaru*) and exact, correct forms of behavior in public. Over the twenty-year period Singleton has observed Japan, he has found no change in the definition of a good child as one who persists, hangs on, does his best always, and applies elbow grease. In a word, good children are tenacious.

Related to this is the assumption that ability is not inherited, but acquired through effort. The prerequisite for academic achievement is seen as severe discipline, self-imposed through the dedication of the learner and reinforced by parents and teachers. From the earliest years, a child learns that the big tests are not of knowledge and skills alone, but of motivation, loyalty, sincerity, and devotion to self-conquest.

As Harold Stevenson indicates, lack of achievement in Japan is attributed to the failure to work hard rather than to the lack of ability or to personal or environmental obstacles. The remarkable success of Japanese children in elementary school in such areas as mathematics, he claims, is due in part to the renunciation of the view that children of low ability will not achieve regardless of how hard they work and that children of high ability need not work hard.

Mothers in Japan are very indulgent with their children. Because of this, many observers find themselves mystified by the relative ease of the transition of most pupils from the one-on-one, highly indulgent home to the one-in-forty, demanding classroom environment. On the matter of class size alone, teaching conditions in Japan appear less than desirable by U.S. standards. But as Joseph Tobin, David Wu, and Dana Davidson inform us, large class size in Japanese schools has become an important strategy for promoting traditional cultural values. Overall, their research in Japanese preschools challenges us to rethink the issues of class size and teacher/pupil ratios in a much different way.

The traditional *uchi/soto* (intimate/public behavior) discrepancy, so well documented in literature on Japanese culture, probably has a lot to do with neutralizing the transition children must make from the sharply different environments of the home and the school. On all levels, Japanese behavior tends to be highly situational and embraces huge differences in public and private settings.

Moving on to the realm of teaching pedagogy, we find that Japanese teachers rarely use overt pressure to develop classroom discipline. This is contrary to what might be expected given the large pupil/teacher ratios and the high degree of conformity. As Catherine C. Lewis points out in her prizewinning essay, the philosophy of teachers in Japan is to promote strong internalization of pupil behavioral responses through peer and group pressure rather than through adult imposition of rules.

What comes across in all the essays is that peers, not teachers, carry considerable responsibility for eliciting proper school behavior. Teachers seldom address individual children in nursery school or single them out from the group. A child's behavior, whether positive or negative, rarely elicits a direct response from a teacher.

Appropriate behavior from nursery school through the university is attained implicitly rather than explicitly by means of a strict adherence to established routines, strong group identification, and almost no focus on the individual as a distinct entity. The Iwama essay provides an anecdotal record by a Japanese educator of how personal goals are subordinated to those of the group on the secondary and university levels in both teaching methodology and school management. Not unexpectedly, the price for those who choose to behave differently is severe.

What if anything can be learned from Japanese patterns of socialization in the home and in school for improving academic performance in other settings? Beyond specific practices, there are a number of broad principles highlighted in the essays that could prove helpful for educators in quite different cultural contexts.

As school systems grow larger and more complex, they often lose touch with many of the basic human understandings upon which they are built. The Japanese have stayed closer to these understandings than have many other modern societies. They do not leave the careful socialization or academic development of their children entirely to professional educators in state school systems. The intense involvement of Japanese mothers, even working mothers, with their children's education should serve to remind us that schooling is but one element in a much earlier and more comprehensive out-of-school socialization process that all individuals experience.

Teachers can build upon, but can rarely create, the foundations upon which classroom learning takes place. Few children in the United States spend more than one-third of any given day in school. Obviously, the amount of school-enhancing support children receive from parents and others in the balance of the day has a big impact on how they progress in school. Clearly, the Japanese experience provides a strong message on the importance of adding parental responsibility and family culture to the list of variables that must be considered in formulating plans for improving academic achievement.

A second broad principle is related to the moral dimension of learning. Teenage pregnancy, dropouts, violence in the streets, drugs, and suicides have stimulated a readiness in many Western nations to find a way to articulate a sense of morality and character development in child-rearing and schooling. The emphasis that

Japanese parents and teachers place on an exact behavior in public and on effort and discipline provide a good basis for understanding the characterological as well as cognitive roots of school failure and other antisocial behavior.

In stressing effort over ability as the foundation of academic achievement, the Japanese present an implicit challenge to other educational systems, such as that in the United States, where ability as measured by so-called scientific tests is considered primary. Ability testing as a kind of academic predestination theory has had the unplanned effect of downplaying personal effort as a positive trait. Those who attain higher academic standing than their test scores predict, for instance, are given the rather negative label of "overachiever." Conversely, in Japan, where the emphasis is on effort, there is a better sense not only that all children can change their world but also that having a method or strategy for doing so is a sign of good character.

A third principle is reflected in the way a child, his peers, and groups are employed to help internalize acceptable rules of behavior. In place of the direct and overt imposition of rules by adults, an important role is given to pupils disciplining and governing themselves in peer-group situations. This helps teach children a great deal about interdependence and cooperation. However, on the negative side, it can lead to a deeply submerged sense of self and a tyranny of peers in the face of individual differences that is more oppressive than that of adults.

In the concluding essay, Harold Stevenson speaks directly to the question of why American children are falling behind those in other countries, including Japan, in such areas as mathematics skills. In doing so, he provides an excellent summary of the critical differences in pedagogical and socialization patterns in the United States and Japan. These include: dramatically less time spent in classes and later introduction of concepts in the United States; complacency resulting from overly positive appraisals of achievement levels and less emphasis on the importance of hard work and effort in the United States; and more out-of-class time available to Japanese teachers for lesson preparation and work with individual children.

1

Gambaru: A Japanese Cultural Theory of Learning

John Singleton

There are, in every social setting and society, unstated assumptions about people and how they learn, which act as a set of self-fulfilling prophecies that invisibly guide whatever educational processes may occur there. They act as a kind of unintentional "hidden curriculum," or what an anthropologist might call a "cultural theory of learning." It is these cultural assumptions in Japan about education, whether intentional or incidental, that I will describe here. These are, of course, the product of cross-cultural comparative observations and reflect the observer's cultural baggage as well as Japanese culture. Cultural differences are what are observed. Where we think alike, there is nothing to stand out in cross-cultural observation. I have been specifically impressed by a Japanese emphasis on *gambaru* (persistence) in explaining and organizing education. This contrasts with an American emphasis on ability (that is, IQ, intelligence, talent) and is an underlying assumption of a Japanese cultural theory of learning.

The data here come from ethnographic observations of a Japanese junior high school and from observations as a parent of my own, American, children's experiences in Japanese educational settings. Over the years, there have been four major settings for parental observation. They included the home in the Japanese countryside where our landlady became a grandmother to my infant son when my wife and I moved into her household in 1962; the kindergartens where my two older sons learned to fold *origami* and participate enthusiastically in group-oriented cooperative activities; a country elementary school where my oldest son, a new first-grader, learned in less than six months to read and write in the Japanese *kana* syllabary before he had instruction in English literacy; and, more than twenty years later, a rural potter's household where my second son, then aged twenty-six, lived in 1982–83 for more than a year as a traditional potter's apprentice.[1]

My formal ethnographic observations of Japanese education, separated from the situations in which I watched my own children, were made in a Japanese public junior high school during 1962–63. I was there able to watch the processes of school and community concern about educational advancement for a cohort of ninth grade students as they prepared for their first major examination ordeal—the entrance exams for senior high school. Both teachers and parents helped me understand their problems and purposes as they made educational choices with, and for, their children.

Twenty years later, as director of a study-abroad program for thirty-three American university students, I was able to observe the educational and social worlds of a private Japanese university. While I thought of this experience as a chance to learn about Japanese higher education, the observations of my American students in their urban Japanese host families gave me key data for a more general understanding of Japanese education.

That was, for instance, my second experience with Japanese *kyōiku mama* (education-obsessed mother). A constant topic of conversation among the host family "mothers" was the scores that their visiting "children" received on their most recent class quizzes. Most talkative were those whose guest students had received the highest grades. I should have expected this intense motherly interest and competition—but even I was surprised by the enthusiastic way in which the "mothers" joined in the school game of their temporarily adopted children.

While my school observations were separated by twenty years, my return trip convinced me that the major changes in Japanese schooling were more related to national wealth and new school buildings than to the cultural assumptions underlying what went on inside those buildings. As I became familiar with a private school system associated with my Japanese university, the continuity with my earlier public school observations was dramatic.

There is an outwardly gentle, but relentless, school career progression. It begins with the delightful, usually nonacademic, *yochien* (kindergarten) experience where three-to-five-year-old children learn group routines for group activity. The separate six-year elementary school is where learning, at least in the early years, is fun. In the junior high school, educational endeavor becomes real and earnest in preparation for senior high school entrance exams. Senior high school is usually the first separation into ability-graded career tracks. The university, representing very thin academic status strata determined by their entrance examinations, allows most students to relax for the first time since they were elementary students and to put their energies into intensive student club activities—whose demands often take precedence over class attendance.

Underlying all understandings and anticipations of this schooling, the related tutoring, and even the learning of non-school-connected arts and skills is the principle of *gambaru*. It is a critical cultural assumption that distinguishes a contemporary Japanese theory of learning. Literally, *gambaru* is a verb that means "to persist, hang on, or do one's best." In its imperative form, *gambare*, it is "used among members of a group to encourage each other in cooperative activities."[2]

I first had to look up the term in my pocket dictionary when I was tagging along with the junior high school teachers on their annual home visits with parents of the children in their ninth grade homeroom classes. At each home conference, the teacher and one or both parents would confer about the child of the household. During the conference, the most important topic was usually the child's chances for admission to one of the seven or eight hierarchically graded and specialized public high schools within commuting distance of the junior high school district. There were often fine calculations of the chances for entrance to a particular academic level of high school. Most of the conferences concluded with a stock phrase from the teacher in response to the parents' concern about what might be done to help the child achieve the best possible entrance exam results: "*Mō sukoshi gambaru hō ga ii to omoimasu.*" (I think a little more persistence would be good.) Whether talking about the top student in the class or the bottom, the laziest or the most diligent, the answer never changed.

I then began to follow up on these students and talked with the teachers privately about the students' academic records and characteristics. The teachers had no problems reciting the students' school grades, scores on their last "practice" entrance exam, their study habits, and other details. When I asked about their IQ, even in rough terms, however, they inevitably referred me to the student files that were kept in the school office. They knew that the IQ scores were on file, but the scores themselves were not an item of teacher interest or concern. They would not assess children as "underachievers" or "overachievers." *Gambaru* could be measured by test scores achieved. Comparison with IQ scores was irrelevant. Persistence is the secret; effort, not IQ, is the Japanese explanation for educational achievement.

While this persistence explains educational achievement, the important cultural curriculum has nothing to do with the conventional government-prescribed course of study. The formal curriculum is only a means to other goals. The real content of any educational process is *seishin* (individual spirit and character development) and *shūdan ishiki* (group consciousness, belongingness) or *dantai ishiki* (organizational consciousness). This holds not only in schools but in the society at large. It underlies the wide public and government support for school-based moral education and guides the corporate training programs for new employees.

Junior and senior high schools are model experiences for such training. It is not the content of the entrance exams but the intense experience of exam preparation that is believed to strengthen an individual's character and moral fiber. In cooperative endeavor with one's peers and coaches (teachers, tutors, and parents) one prepares for the time of individual ordeal. One's coaches and peers can help only in preparation for the lonely trial. It cannot be taken collectively, though collective support and encouragement for the individual is assured, at least within the family.

To understand the nature of this moral training from a Western perspective, there is no better description than that by the German philosopher Eugen Herrigel.[3] He describes his frustrations in attempting to learn Zen philosophy through training in the "art of archery." He learns from the experience of unfathomable contradictions; conquering difficult tasks and developing selfless perfection in particular skills. The learning style is consistent with that encountered in preparation for entrance examinations.

Relentless tutoring in the answers to objective multiple-choice questions about esoteric facts is much of what goes on in the junior and senior high schools and associated tutoring. The students do manage to gain broad understandings of mathematics, science, history, and even English grammar in the process. The self-discipline required is not unlike that of the Zen novice who must sit in uncomfortable positions for long hours of quiet meditation or the potter's apprentice who must spend many months, or even years, at the wheel making exact copies of a single basic and ordinary pot form. "Through intense application, strict obedience, and long apprenticeship, the pupil may one day hope to approach the level of competence that will wring a word of praise from the teacher."[4]

Much like John Dewey, direct experience is seen by the Japanese teachers as the most powerful educational strategy. Carefully constructed experience is more powerful than lecturing or telling. One learns from the experience of hardships, conquering difficult tasks, developing perfection in particular skills.

At the same time, the family, neighborhood, schools, corporations, and university student clubs, especially the sports clubs, convey the messages of *shūdan ishiki* (group consciousness). Exclusive group solidarity and commitment is a part of the real (or hidden) curriculum of most educational process. The assumption is that commitment to exclusive groups is a necessary individual choice. Commitment, solidarity, achievement, egalitarianism—within the same age or status group, and the complementary hierarchy of *sempai-kohai* relations (junior to senior obligations and privileges) are all important values related to one's group membership. Open, interpersonal competition within the group is seen as destructive of group harmony and, therefore, of individual learning.

> Modern Japanese institutions tend even today to be bound together by an intensity of commitment that is quite unfamiliar to their American counterparts. . . . Since the Japanese family is an institution that binds the individual for life, he is encouraged to view his relationship with other family members as one of continuing mutual support and participation in common goals. . . . The classroom situation parallels the family. Just as the child's relationship with his family is strong and permanent, so his relationships with classmates tend to be strong and permanent also. . . . The American classroom resembles a competitive arena, whereas the Japanese classroom resembles the training ground of a single team, learning how to play the game for life cooperatively.[5]

Kindergarten and elementary school teachers consciously teach group identity. Because school is a time for developing peer solidarity, absolute social promotion is the norm. Failing or jumping grades is unthinkable. In-school ability grouping is avoided in almost every situation. Upper secondary schools, universities, and schools within a university are rigidly ability-graded (but by group rather than by individual rankings). Heterogeneous grouping for learning in large groups is practiced in most schooling. Large groups allow for peer cooperation in learning.

All groups provide numerous occasions for reinforcing individual identity with the group. Social promotion continues through schooling and even into corporate career life.

An organizational principle that supports this development of group identity is the institutional segregation of strict (*kibishii*) and indulgent (*amai*) discipline (*shitsuke*). Parents repeatedly encouraged teachers to be more *kibishii* in their relations with junior high school students but resisted any suggestion that they could be more *kibishii* with their own children. I once commented that a junior high school student whose uncle was a professional tutor had a special advantage in preparing for the high school entrance examinations. Her mother corrected me by saying, "But he's a member of the family." She implied that one who is a family member cannot be sufficiently *kibishii* to be an effective tutor.

When I inquired about the principle of sending one's child off to another household to learn the craft on which the family business was built, I would be told, *"Tanin no meshi o kuu"* (You have to eat someone else's rice). You have to experience dependence on a stern disciplinarian to be able to develop the strength of character that is necessary to learn an adult skill—so families often send sons who will be inheriting a family business to another household for their apprenticeship in the family trade. In the same way, new bank employees are taken for a short period of military "boot camp" training at a Self-Defense Forces base camp.[6]

In thinking about "discipline" as the use of punishment for correction and training, it is seen as a job for a person outside of the group within which "good feelings" must be maintained. This is also implied by the justification for some drinking parties and other social activities I observed in the junior high school, "We do it in order to promote good human feelings" (*ii kimochi no tame ni*). It is the idea that indulgence will reinforce human relationships within the group. How else could one maintain the unending commitment to one's family, group, or organization? Empathy and responsibility are the requirements for all group members.[7]

The separation of entrance examinations from the schools in which children study promotes the same kind of separation between strictness and indulgence. The teachers can even be seen as indulgent coaches separate from the strict examination system that distributes the real rewards and punishments: "By means of the entrance examination system, competition is taken out of the class-room into an impersonal setting in which contact and communication between competitors is minimized."[8]

Inside the family, kindergarten, and the elementary school there are many reinforcements for a "good child" identity. Underlying this approach is the assumption that a child is basically good. A positive self-image is encouraged by parents, grandmothers, and kindergarten and elementary school teachers who would never accuse a child of willful mischief. The child just "doesn't understand" what is proper. Even when my boys were deliberately poking holes in the paper *shoji* doors of our house, "grandmother" would say *"Ii ko ne"* (You're a good child, aren't you?) while I was saying sharply, "Stop that!"—and thinking of them as willfully mischievous.

At the same time, the children tend to enjoy their school experience, at least in kindergarten, elementary school, and in the university, though they too sometimes develop "school phobia," refuse to go go school, and are referred to psychiatrists or counsellors to see if their "character" can be improved. If nothing else, the Japanese educational system in the school and home demonstrates the extent to which children can be pushed to learn those skills that the modern school can teach and to adapt to the arbitrary authoritarian structures of modern schooling.

It is in the assumptions about learning, and about the teaching strategies that would lead to desired learning goals, that we can begin to understand the rationale for organizing education in a Japanese way—in schools and in other social settings and institutions. American preoccupations with technical pedagogical differences, for example, "time in school" and "time on task," overlook a simple cultural explanation of differences in our national systems. The Japanese think about schooling and education differently than we do. How we think about teaching and learning—our cultural theory of learning—makes an important difference in what can be accomplished in school or other educational institutions. Social promotion and heterogenous grouping may be more important than a longer school year. The assumption that effort, not intelligence, is what leads to school success may be the most important contribution that comparative studies of Japanese education can make to American schools.[9]

Notes

1. John Singleton, *Nichu: A Japanese School; Case Studies in Education and Culture* (New York: Holt, Rinehart, and Winston, 1967: Reprinted 1982 by Irvington Publishers, New York), and "The Way of the Potter" (with Willi Singleton), in "The Sociology of Craft: Japan 1984," ed. John Mock, Special issue of *Craft International* 3(2) (January–March, 1984): 14–17.

2. Hiroshi Wagatsuma, *"Gambaru," Japan Encyclopedia* (Tokyo: Kodansha, 1983).

3. Eugen Herrigel, *Zen in the Art of Archery* (New York: Random House, Vintage Books, 1971).

4. Robert J. Smith, *Japanese Society: Tradition, Self and the Social Order* (Cambridge: Cambridge University Press, 1983).

5. Christie W. Kiefer, "The Psychological Interdependence of Family, School, and Bureaucracy in Japan," *American Anthropologist* 72 (1970): 66–75.

6. Thomas P. Rohlen, *"Seishin Nyoiku* in a Japanese Bank," *Anthropology and Education Quarterly* 15 (1984): 17–28.

7. Nathan Glazer, "Social and Cultural Factors in Japanese Economic Growth," in *Asia's New Giant: How the Japanese Economy Works,* ed. Hugh Patrick and Henry Rosovsky (Washington, D.C.: The Brookings Institution, 1976).

8. Christie W. Kiefer.

9. Several publications since this paper was written in 1984 have paid similar attention to the importance of *gambaru* in understanding Japanese educational practice and theory. See, for example, Benjamin Duke, chapter 5, in *The Japanese School: Lessons for Industrial America* (New York: Praeger, 1986); Harumi Befu, *"The Social and Cultural Background of Child Development in Japan and the United States,"* in Harold Stevenson, Hiroshi Azuma, and Kenji Hakuta, eds., *Child Development and Education in Japan* (New York: W. H. Freeman, 1986); and Merry White, *The Japanese Educational Challenge: A Commitment to Children* (New York: The Free Press, 1987).

2

Interdependence of Family and Education: Reactions of Foreign Wives of Japanese to the School System

Anne E. Imamura

The Japanese education system is a focus of debate both in Japan and abroad. American observers recognize the success of the system in providing Japan with well-educated citizens who form an invaluable base for Japanese productivity and Japan's relatively low level of violence. At the same time, they are reluctant to adopt the Japanese system either because they doubt the uniformity and centralized control would be acceptable in America or because the long hours and regimentation required on the part of students goes against American concepts of childhood and individual freedom. As foreigners, Americans of course are able to maintain a distance from the Japanese system and pick and choose what if anything they will adopt.

Japanese, on the other hand, recognize the deficiencies of their system. However, since success in that system is so tied to employment opportunity, few individual Japanese are willing to chance their children's futures by either choosing an alternate form of education or by not sending their children to prep school (*juku*). For most Japanese also the only other model of education with which they are familiar is their own rigid prewar system.

There is a third position vis-à-vis the education system, that of the foreign wives of Japanese residents in Japan. As foreigners, they have personally experienced different systems of education. This experience gives them other models and a basis from which to evaluate the pros and cons of both their own and the Japanese systems.

In one sense these foreign wives are quintessential "strangers . . . who come(s) today and stay(s) tomorrow" with an objectivity "composed of distance and nearness, indifference and involvement."[1] This makes their criticisms particularly salient and useful in debunking stereotypes held by either foreigners or by Japanese.

Foreign wives who are also mothers must deal with the issue of educating their children and with the choices available to them in Japan. As mothers, they must meet three demands: the preservation, growth, and acceptability of the child(ren).[2] For the foreign mother this raises the issues of acceptability by whom? How is she to accomplish this in a foreign society? To the extent that "parents, and particularly mothers, importantly inform the nature of various symbolic markers that children use to organize social life" how will such mothers be able to prepare their children for a school system with which they are unfamiliar and whose values may differ from their own?[3]

The issue is more than the sum of experiences of individual mothers and children. It involves the nature of familial and educational institutions. The interdependence of family and education is recognized both in the West and Japan. At the same time, family systems differ throughout the world on a number of dimensions including family roles in the education process. Comparing Japan to America, Kiefer points out three such differences: (1) the Japanese middle-class mother is more solely responsible for children's education than the American; (2) the Japanese mother-child (especially mother-son) tie is more intense than the American; (3) the Japanese individual is bound by the family for life and learns to consider the effect of all his actions on the family. The American child makes more distinction between family controlled areas and those outside the family.[4]

In addition to differing family roles, societies may desire different products in terms of the acceptable child. Along these lines, White points out the characteristics of a "good child," that is, an acceptable one, in Japan. The child is *otonashii* (mild or gentle), *sunao* (compliant, obedient, and cooperative) *akarui* (bright, alert), and *genki* (energetic and spirited). White argues: "The basic principle of child rearing seems to be: Never go against the child. *Wakaraseru* (getting the child to understand) is often a long-term process that ultimately engages the child in the mother's goals, and makes her goals the child's own. . . . The distinction between external social expectations and the child's own personal goals becomes blurred." The underlying assumption is, of course, that the goals of the mother and external social expectations are the same.[5]

Foreign mothers are in a unique position to evaluate the Japanese education system. Although they are living more or less permanently in Japan and are able to distance themselves somewhat from the society, they also have the responsibility of raising "acceptable" children. Their evaluations present an important contribution on two levels. First, they shed light on the Japanese system of education from a third standpoint, which should help to illuminate strengths and weaknesses of that system. Second, on the broader theoretical level, they point to the importance of considering differences in family systems in comparative studies in education. To shed light on both these levels, this paper examines the views foreign mothers hold on the Japanese system of education.

Data come from in-depth interviews with foreign wives of Japanese living in Japan. All interviews were done by the author in the fall of 1983. A total of fifty-five women were interviewed, forty individually and fifteen in group contexts. Interviewees were selected through introductions to include members of the Association of Foreign Wives of Japanese (AFWJ), nonmembers, recent arrivals in Japan, long-term residents, English speakers and non-English speakers, and wives who looked Asian and those who were obviously foreign. Interviewees resided in or near Tokyo, Kansai (the greater Kobe, Kyoto, Nara and Osaka area), and Hokkaido (within two hours of Sapporo). Wives tended to be highly educated. Those under forty were predominantly university graduates whereas older wives had at least a high school education. Their husbands were almost all university (or above) educated business or professional men. At the time of the interview these wives had a total of forty-two school-aged children. Of these, thirty-two were attending Japanese schools and ten were in international or foreign schools.

How Foreign Mothers View the Education System

The System Overall: Is It Good for Children in General?

On the positive side, respondents identify several ways the Japanese school system is good for children. Japanese schools, and society in general, are considered safer than abroad. Children are kept from "growing up too soon" and foreign mothers agree there are almost no real worries about drugs and sex: "There are problems in the international high schools that I don't want to have to deal with yet: sex, drugs, bad language, discipline—you know the Japanese are rather different in this respect."[6]

Foreign mothers also acknowledge that the level of elementary academic education is probably higher than abroad; children learn a sense of responsibility by cleaning the classrooms themselves and develop a higher respect for teachers. As children get into the upper grades, club activity after school makes for a long day but keeps children busy, and mothers know where their children are.

On the con side, they criticize the system generally because it inculcates too much competition at too early an age. Childhood, they argue, should be more than study and prep school. And the system begins so early that even kindergarten-age children can be made to feel they are failures: "She [daughter] failed the interview [for private kindergarten]. . . . There was another kindergarten which because of lottery only took one out of three kids. And she lost out on the lottery . . . but it hurt her very much. . . . They make the kids go . . . they make the kids pick the paper that says you've lost." [American mother]

A second general objection is raised along the lines of moral/social education. Related to the interdependence of family and school, mothers hope for "principles of morality" more generalizable than "cooperation." This relates especially to the definition of a "good child" mentioned above. Mothers seeking more abstract principles continue to be disappointed.

Related to this is the objection that Japanese schools can undermine the informal curriculum at home. This objection is in direct contrast to the position of the Japanese mother who becomes the "agent or delegate of a school" who "seems to have renounced her privilege of being a home educator juxtaposed with school teachers."[7] Whereas the Japanese mother will accommodate to the principles of the school, the foreign mother may deliberately work to undermine principles with which she does not agree. In referring to the informal curriculum, foreign mothers specifically mean that Japanese schools enforce gender role behavior opposite to expectations at home. After entering elementary school, boys stopped helping mothers around the house, and girls became less independent. One American mother of sons says she is relieved she does not have a daughter because Japanese society trains girls to be "shallow and vindictive." An American mother of both a son and a daughter, comments thus on the life of Japanese women today:

> It's pretty bad; that's why I don't want my daughter to stay there. Japanese women have, I guess, no core, they don't have anything that's themselves. They have no privacy in the home, no place that's their own . . . no high hopes from the very beginning. They are just trained to be second place . . . when they go to school. The girl can never be *hancho* [president]. She's always *fukuhancho* [vice-president].

Mothers also question the lack of individualism in the schools. Both gifted children and those in need of remedial work suffer from the lack of special instruction. Memorization, not learning, is the goal, and these mothers argue children become bored with school.

> You're not allowed to have any strong points and weak points, you have to be just the same. You can't ask questions. . . . I don't like the way they have to march to and from school and always be in groups. [American mother quoted above]

> It may just be that my luck has not been too good. I mean the teachers that he's gotten have not been concerned or caring. . . . They've all been overworked. . . . It seems like they just want to treat the class as a whole, and they can't treat the individual children in the class. [American mother of junior high school aged son]

> The system seems too strict . . . based too much on memorization and not creativity. I want my child to grow up creative . . . be someone who can think for themselves [*sic*] . . . have strong opinions. [American, no children yet]

Whereas their opinions are more or less united on issues of streaming and special education, not all mothers agree on the lack of creativity.

> After all a child is a child, he has a naturally questioning mind. The cultural overlay is there as so it may look on the surface as though they're all robots, but Japan wouldn't be where it is today if what you said was true. There are thinkers; there are doers. But I feel comfort in that the child is taught a good basic education. At the other extreme, in the American system, the students seem to be so preoccupied with themselves, always wanting to be talking about what they think and what they feel—yet they might not be able to read or write that well or have such knowledge about anything.[8]

The Role of Mother in the Education System

It can be argued that in the West the mother bears more of the burden for children's education than the father. However, in Japan, she is virtually totally responsible for seeing that her children succeed in school.[9] Foreign mothers are critical of this expectation. They argue that the society is too child-centered and that Japanese mothers worry too much about their children's education.

In one sense, at the elementary school level, the mother's involvement is structured by the high number of pupils per teacher. "My child's class has forty-two children; I think there are too many pupils. The teacher doesn't know if all the children understand, and if the children have something they don't understand about the lessons, I don't think the teacher can explain to them individually. Therefore, it's important that the mother supervise studying, only the mother can teach the child what she or he couldn't do or understand at school."[10]

While few foreign mothers disagree with the principle that the mother should help her children with their studies, many object to the type of participation demands placed on the mother. They consider many of the activities to be either irrelevant to education, or even counterproductive. "They (school) really expect a lot and there's so much competition among the women to produce. I was really surprised. The first six months of his kindergarten this year I was really surprised at the way the women have dedicated themselves body and soul to the kindergarten" [American mother of two sons]

The Specific Situation of Children of International Marriages

Before children enter school, mothers are fairly free to raise them as they would in their own culture. However, when school starts parents must choose a system of education. For most, this means Japanese schools.

Why do they choose Japanese schools? On the practical side, international education may not be available, or it may be too expensive or require a long daily commute. There is also the issue that a Japanese university education is a virtual prerequisite for good employment, and this is particularly important for boys who expect to remain in Japan. Children who attend international schools "will graduate well-equipped to fit into an international environment but will be trained for little else."[11] Japanese schools provide the "only way" these children will really be competent in Japan and also teach them how to deal socially in a Japanese environment. They make friends who may form the bases of lifelong networks. In the international schools they are likely to meet Japanese who are "people with their own family company, or artists, or people who in some way do not need to be a typical product of a Japanese school."[12]

In a variety of ways, Japanese schools offer the specific benefit a foreign mother cannot provide—integration into local society.

> I still don't know if I did choose right . . . but we are intending to stay here . . . and . . . also I considered my children-
> .. . . they do have Japanese nationality. . . . I wouldn't like them to feel foreign here in Japan . . . they must feel completely at home here. . . . I thought if we choose international education they will be sort of more foreigners in Japan. [Dutch mother of two]

Choosing a system of education is not easy. The AFWJ has run workshops and collected data from families that are proponents of one or the other systems and issued some summary points on the topic. Among the recommendations are: (1) choose a system of education early and stick with it; (2) if children have only Japaese citizenship, that is a compelling reason for choosing Japanese education; (3) it's better if the father can communicate in the foreign language if international education is chosen; and (4) international education may limit the child's possibilities in Japan, for example, what if the child wishes to become a doctor and must be certified in Japan?[13]

One foreign mother who has long experience teaching in international schools argues that in the international marriage one parent inevitably suffers a sense of loss when the child is not educated in that parent's system. For the foreign mother, this is related to her own feelings about passing on Japanese culture.

> Do I want my children to be Japanese? At this point, no . . . they'll be mixed. . . . I want them to . . . speak Japanese because their father will be Japanese . . . but I also want them to know other things. . . . I want to give them my Americanism. . . . if I were here and my children were in Japanese school and I were speaking only Japanese to them, I believe there would be a big anxiety point of—are these children really mine? [American, no children yet]

> I would prefer that [son] grow up in an American culture. . . . I have no intention to . . . have him be just a kind of Japanese kid that happens to have a foreign mother. . . . I want him to be more . . . as much as possible equally attuned to American culture. [American mother of one]

There is some debate as to what extent the "losing" parent can pass his or her culture on to the child. On the one hand, some mothers feel they cannot obtain or afford enough materials or contacts with their own culture to make it real and living to the children. On the other, some argue that they leave Japanese culture up to the schools and keep their homes mostly foreign, speaking their own languages and celebrating their own holidays.

> I keep English in the home because everything else they do is Japanese . . . everything in their lives except Mama. So we decided we would keep English as the family language when we are just together . . . of course when there are other people there . . . outside in public we speak Japanese. . . . The oldest boy . . . he really feels he can pick up the English newspaper, he can pick up the Japanese newspaper . . . and he said, "I'm very glad about that." What I like about living in Japan with the Japanese school system is that I'm free to be as American as possible without the feeling I'm in any

way interfering with their absorbing Japanese culture. [American mother of three]

Since husbands are for the most part too busy, or define education as the mother's role, few foreign mothers can expect husbands to spend much time on children's education. Foreign mothers need networks. To some extent, other foreign wives may suffice, but unless they have children in exactly the same school, they will be insufficient.

The first major area to contend with is language. Can the wife deal with school-home communication herself? A lot of this involves reading and writing in a "communication book" that goes back and forth between home and school. Whereas respondents indicate increasing competence in spoken Japanese, and some use tape recorders so that husbands can tape questions for teachers and teachers can record comments for husbands, written competence is extremely difficult.

When my husband is gone the teacher explains things to me on the telephone [in Japanese]. I couldn't read or write the Japanese syllabary when my children started school ten years earlier, but I learned because of the memos from school. My eldest child brought lots of papers home—I read them and read them—I couldn't at first understand them . . . the communication was very hard. [Spanish-speaking mother of two]

Second, mothers need advice on matters husbands know little of. They need to know what to wear to school activities, what to do, how to find all the items their children must bring, and what are the real norms as opposed to the ideal.

Third, for the child of a foreign mother the teacher is especially important. Several mothers identify teachers who either expect their children to be authorities on English or refuse to believe their children can learn Japanese. For example, one teacher refused to give a child advanced *kanji* (Chinese character) tests because she did not believe the child could pass them. She told the mother not to worry, the child was making great progress "for a foreigner." The mother's retort was that indeed, the child had only been raised in Japan, had Japanese citizenship and was not very competent in English. So why shouldn't she do the same in Japanese as any other Japanese child?

Along these lines, some mothers feel their children were discriminated against by private schools, not given the same treatment in entrance interviews, and rejected out of hand. There are also many cases of children taunted as foreigners by classmates. This latter situation appears to reverse itself in the upper grades if the child has a good knowledge of English and, therefore, does not have to study as hard as his classmates. Foreignness also appears to lose its salience when the child has other outstanding qualities such as becoming a star runner on the track team. In a few cases, parents actually spoke to teachers and principals to have the situation corrected.

Foreign mothers have relatively few role models of mixed children grown to adulthood and living in Japan successfully. Among children of respondents there were four sons working for Japanese companies, one working abroad, and two daughters married to Japanese men. There is, however, some ambivalence as to how major companies view such children as future employees. Considering this, and considering gender roles in Japan, an oft-heard comment among respondents was that for their children, and for their daughters in particular, it would be especially beneficial to become physicians or dentists. The status of the profession, it was felt, would take precedence over the detriments of being "foreign" and/or female.

Discussion and Conclusions

Foreign mothers bridge the gap between foreign and Japanese evaluations of the education system. While maintaining a kind of emotional distance, they are able to view the system instrumentally. On the one hand, this can lead to an overly critical lack of objectivity. On the other, it can provide a powerful pool of data for the analysis of the extent of home-school interdependence.

At present adult children of Japanese-foreign marriages are primarily from two different backgrounds. By far, the largest number come from Japanese mother/foreign father homes and many of these are children of the Occupation Forces. This group tends to have had a less than middle class upbringing and has been viewed pejoratively because of their parentage. It is highly unlikely that the majority of these children will find their way into mainstream occupations. Also, because their mothers are Japanese, the position vis-à-vis the education system should be different from the foreign mother.

The second, smaller, group of adult children comes from foreign mother/Japanese father families. In cases of those married long enough to have adult children, the Japanese father is likely to have some kind of elite status. The mere fact that he was in a position to meet and marry a foreigner meant for the older husband that he was part of a small highly educated internationally oriented elite. His children can benefit from his name and connections in entering Japanese society.

International marriages today appear to be predominantly middle class. Most husbands are salaried workers whose children, if they had married Japanese women, could have been expected to compete for positions in ranking universities and Japanese companies. In five or so years' time, the first adult children of these postwar marriages should be entering the job/marriage market. These children should provide a rich data pool for testing hypotheses on the interdependence of family and school. To this end, future comparisons of adult children of international marriages and adult children of Japanese parents who have been partially educated outside of Japan should prove particularly fruitful.

The theoretical implications of this research go far beyond questions surrounding international marriage. They point to the importance of looking at the family system in all comparative work on education. To isolate education systems or to judge them only in terms of product, for example, international comparisons on mathematics or science examinations, leads to a false understanding of the exportability or desirability of different systems. Long before any direct experience with the school systems takes place, the family system is at work in shaping the child and continues to do so after the child enters school. As a result, before any meaningful comparative work on systems of education can be accomplished, the study of family and school interrelationships must move into the forefront of research agendas.

Notes

1. Georg Simmel, *The Sociology of Georg Simmel,* ed. and tr. Kurt H. Wolff (New York: The Free Press, 1950), 402–4.

2. Sara Ruddick, "Maternal Thinking," in Barrie Thorne and Marilyn Yalom, eds., *Rethinking the Family: Some Feminist Questions* (New York and London: Longman, 1982), 78–79.

3. Barbara Finkelstein, "Family Studies," *Encyclopedia of Educational Research* (New York: Macmillan, 1983), 662.

4. Christie W. Kiefer, "The Psychological Interdependence of Family, School, and Bureaucracy," in *Japanese Culture and Behavior; Selected Readings* (Honolulu: University of Hawaii Press, 1974), 346.

5. Merry White, "Japanese Education: How Do They Do It?", *Bulletin The Japan-American Society of Washington* (December 1984): 3–6.

6. "School Life in Japan," *A.F.W.J. National Newsletter* (February 1982): 27.

7. Takie Sugiyama Lebra, *Japanese Women: Constraint and Fulfillment* (Honolulu: University of Hawaii Press, 1984), 193ff.

8. "School Life in Japan."

9. George A. De Vos et al., *Socialization for Achievement: Essays on the Cultural Psychology of the Japanese* (Berkeley: University of California Press, 1973), and Suzanne H. Vogel, "Professional Housewife: The Career of Urban Middle Class Japanese Women," *Japan Interpreter* 12, no. 1 (1978): 16–43.

10. "Aoi Me no Ikuji Ko" (Foreign Views on Child Rearing), interview with Jennifer Ukawa, *Shogakusei no Okaasan* (Mothers of elementary school children) February 1981.

11. Barbara Fisher, "Gaijin Wives-Gaijin Therapist: Therapeutic Implications" (n.d.), 7.

12. "School Life in Japan."

13. Ibid.

3

Cooperation and Control in Japanese Nursery Schools

Catherine C. Lewis

Phenomena as diverse as nonverbal communication and commitment to permanent employment have been attributed to Japanese child rearing. Yet, there is remarkably little English-language evidence on early socialization in Japan. This article provides observational data from fifteen Japanese nursery schools. It is not my intention here to draw generalizations about Japanese nursery schools or to demonstrate differences between Japanese and American schools. The substantial variability in nursery schools within each country makes such systematic comparison an ambitious undertaking. Rather, the behavioral and ethnopsychological data of the present paper are intended to identify potentially interesting areas for future research on nursery school socialization and to stimulate American thinking about two aspects of early education: school practices which influence the development of cooperative behavior in children and adult strategies for controlling children's behavior.

An earlier version of this essay was published in *Comparative Education Review,* Vol. 28, No. 1 (February 1984). Copyright © 1984 by the Comparative and International Education Society. Reprinted by permission of the University of Chicago Press.

Japanese Early Education

Nearly two-thirds of the five-year-olds in Japan attend nursery school (*yochien*).[1] Researchers have studied the early Japanese parent-child relationship and the socialization of values by Japanese elementary and secondary schools.[2] Studies seeking the roots of Japanese educational achievement have investigated the period between ages two and a half and six,[3] but social development during this period remains largely unstudied. This is a tantalizing gap. Accounts suggest that Japanese children must make a transition from the undisciplined, "indulgent" child-rearing of the home[4] to an elementary school classroom where forty to fifty children share one teacher and where subordination of personal needs to group goals is the dominant norm.[5] For most Japanese children, nursery school is that transition. Nursery school generally commences at age three or four and continues until age six, when elementary school begins. Of the almost 15,000 nursery schools in Japan, approximately 60 percent are private, 40 percent public, and fewer than 1 percent national.[6] Of the fifteen schools in the present study, six were private, seven public, and two national.

The Development of Cooperative Behavior: A Brief Review of Literature

The reader is referred elsewhere for an extensive discussion of theoretical and operational definitions of cooperation.[7] In this article, cooperation refers to an orientation to seek mutual benefit rather than individual benefit when the two conflict. Japan presents an interesting arena for studying socialization to cooperate. In Japan, as in other highly industrialized countries, a large number of individuals compete on objective examinations for a limited number of educational and occupational opportunities.[8] Yet, contemporary Japanese institutions often preserve traditional sanctions against face-to-face interpersonal competition.[9] For example, Japanese workers' willingness to subordinate individual goals to group goals is frequently cited as a reason for the success of Japanese work groups.[10]

Numerous studies employing various cooperative board games and tasks have documented large, replicable cross-cultural and sub-cultural differences in cooperative behavior.[11] These studies demonstrate, for example, that while Mexican or Israeli kibbutz children quickly work out a cooperative style which allows all children to win prizes in a board game, American children maladaptively compete in a way that prevents all children from winning prizes. While cross-cultural differences in cooperation as early as age five are well-documented, we know very little about why these cultural differences emerge. What aspects of early education promote in children a willingness to cooperate? While the research and theoretical literature is sparse, it suggests several hypotheses.

The Opportunity to Learn the Rewards of Competition

In the framework of learning theory, cooperation may be viewed as a behavior which is elicited and reinforced within the classroom. Experiences of shared positive arousal, such as sharing a group reward or a sense of accomplishment, may condition empathy among children who cooperate. Empathy, in turn, may promote cooperation in a circular process. Research designed as a laboratory analogue of empathy conditioning has been carried out.[12] Classrooms may differ in the extent to which cooperation is elicited and reinforced. Competitive situations may decrease children's opportunities to learn an association between positive affect and cooperation. Research suggests that competitive situations that focus children's attention on individual rewards tend to undermine, for example, children's attention to creative aspects of a task.[13] Other research suggests that a seemingly trivial manipulation of game instructions (for example, describing a game goal using the word "we" versus "I") significantly influences cooperation. These various findings suggest that children's tendency to cooperate may be increased by providing classroom activities that elicit cooperation and enable children to learn associated positive rewards and reducing competitive activities which focus children's attention on individual achievement and consequently undermine attention to cooperative aspects of tasks.

The Use of Small Constant-Membership Groups

A single experimental study found that children who learned to perform a cooperative block-building task in groups of constant (rather than changing) membership were subsequently more cooperative when paired with new children.[14] The authors of the study speculate that membership in a constant group may facilitate children's ability to recognize and avert maladaptive competition.

Competition for the Teacher as a Resource and for Other Classroom Resources

As anyone will attest who has observed frantic hand waving by children seeking a teacher's attention, competition for the teacher's recognition can be a major classroom force. It stands to reason that minimizing competition for the teacher's attention (either by having the teacher interact with the class as a whole or by having a high adult-child ratio) would reduce classroom competition. Similarly, reducing competition for symbols of the teacher's attention (honors, awards, conferred positions) and for classroom resources may increase children's attention to the cooperative and interpersonal aspects of tasks.

A shortcoming of experimental studies of cooperation is the questionable ecological validity of the tasks (for example, board games) used to study cooperation, particularly with respect to cross-cultural comparisons. This article provides some data on the natural contexts in which cooperation may be socialized (and studied) in the classroom.

Adult Strategies for Controlling Children's Behavior: A Brief Literature Review

Until recently, psychologists widely accepted the view that firm control by parents (that is, consistent enforcement of clear rules) promotes internalization of values by children.[15] Accounts of Japanese child-rearing challenge this American view of firm control. Japanese mothers apparently do not make explicit demands on their children and do not enforce rules when children resist;[16] yet, diverse accounts suggest that Japanese children strongly internalize parental, group, and institutional values.[17] The nursery school observations reported in this article were designed to stimulate American thinking about firm control by providing preliminary data on Japanese teachers' control strategies and beliefs regarding control.

Recent psychological research suggests that children are most likely to internalize rules when they receive the least external pressure in the course of obeying these rules.[18] Presumably, children who obey rules under strong external pressure can "attribute" their obedience to the external pressure, while children who obey rules without salient external pressure must "attribute" their obedience to some internal factor, such as believing in the rules or being a good child. According to this attribution theory, control strategies will maximize children's internalization of rules if they minimize the external pressure necessary to exact children's compliance, and reinforce the "good child" identity, that is, the child's tendency to think of himself or herself as someone who obeys rules.

Method

Observations of fifteen Japanese nursery schools were conducted during May through July of 1979. At each school, one class of five-year-olds was observed for two days. During the first day, the author noted the materials and equipment in view at the school, the schedule of activities engaged in by the children, and any incidents related to control or cooperation. Initially, the major purpose of the first day's observation was simply to accustom children and teachers to the presence of a foreigner in the classroom. However, these unstructured observations, and teachers' subsequent interpretations of what occurred, proved remarkably interesting and are the primary data of this report. On the second day, the author conducted spot observations every twenty minutes, noting the locations and activities of all children and teachers. In addition, a ten-minute running account of teachers' behavior was dictated into a small hand-held tape recorder every twenty minutes. After observations on both days one and two, teachers were interviewed about specific incidents which had been observed, about usual classroom practices, and about the concepts of child development which lay behind teachers' practices.

Observations

Setting. The teacher-child ratio was noteworthy: almost all classrooms contained one teacher and thirty to forty children. In only two of fifteen schools was a second adult (a student teacher) present. All fifteen teachers observed were female. No schools permitted parents to visit the nursery school classroom, except for special parent programs which occurred several times a year. In the nursery schools studied, children attended school between two and a half and five and a half hours per day.

The sections which follow topically organize information from the unstructured observations, interviews with teachers and school directors, spot observations, and transcribed dictations of teacher behavior. Since interview questions and observational categories were added to the original format in the course of the observations, data from fewer than fifteen schools are sometimes reported.

Small Groups Within the Classroom. Small fixed-membership groups were a striking feature of most nursery schools visited; thirteen of fifteen classrooms had such groups. Groups had their own tables and were frequently the units for chores, teacher-initiated special projects, lunch, and children's own informal play. Groups of six to eight children were most common, with group size ranging from four to ten. Teachers selected the groups. Nine of eleven teachers reported that they based the groups on children's own friendships, choosing as a core for each group children who "played well together." Only one of eleven teachers mentioned that best friends were split up in constructing groups. Distributing "able" children among groups was a second strategy for constructing groups, spontaneously mentioned by six of eleven teachers. Abilities mentioned as important to distribute among groups included leadership and social skills, athletic skills, and artistic ability. Same-sex and mixed-sex groups were both seen. The tenure of the small groups depended on how well children played and carried out tasks together. Teachers planned to maintain the same groups for periods ranging from one term (four months) to two years; most teachers expected to maintain the groups without major changes for at least one year. When teachers made changes in the groups, it was sometimes a de facto recognition that children were not functioning together as a group: "We don't change the groups: the groups change." Children were frequently referred to collectively by group name.

Dismissal and other rewards were sometimes conferred by group, and group murals with the names of each group member were in evidence in many classrooms. Teachers planned activities which required children to elicit and accommodate other children's intentions. For example, in one classroom, the teacher asked each group to make a *kamishibai* (paper theater) by having all children in the group make pictures which fit together in a continuous story. This task required children within the group to agree on a story line and to divide up the story among group members. The teacher in this classroom used an interesting technique for physically orienting group members toward one another. Before starting the activity, all groups were asked to find their members, hold hands in a circle, lie back in a pinwheel, and then sit up. As the groups planned the paper theaters, the teacher circulated through the room, physically orienting toward their groups any children who were turned outward. In addition, the teacher deflected children's questions to their fellow group members, telling children, "Ask the other children in your group what they want to make" and "Remember to make pictures that fit together in a story, not the same picture."

Play Materials and Cooperation. Foreign visitors to Japan are accustomed to seeing familiar objects miniaturized to fit an environment where space is a precious resource. An interesting exception to this was the oversized heavy wooden blocks, of three feet or longer, which were observed in eight of twelve schools. Such blocks are extremely difficult or impossible for one child to manipulate without help. These large blocks would seem to demand cooperative play.

Observation notes suggest also that classroom materials may be distributed in a way that facilitates cooperation. For example, a teacher in one classroom placed paints on each group's table, providing fewer brushes than children and asking the children to consult each other about paint use so the paints would not be spilled. A subsequent interview with the teacher confirmed that the teacher had deliberately chosen to provide fewer brushes than children and to place the paints in a location (the center of each group's table) where they would be spilled if children failed to confer about their use. Other teachers spontaneously mentioned that they withdrew toys as children became older, to help children learn cooperation. In some respects, these findings ran counter to the original hypotheses: teachers viewed scarce, not plentiful, resources as a means for promoting cooperation among five-year-olds.

Minimizing Competition for the Teacher's Attention. With thirty to forty children per classroom and only one adult, teachers could hardly minimize competition by giving close personal attention to all children. During interviews, several teachers commented on the use of aides and parent helpers in American nursery schools and expressed envy of the greater flexibility this would allow classroom teachers. However, these teachers also remarked that the presence of parents in the nursery class could undermine children's formation of friendships with other children.

Neither did teachers choose to minimize competition by interacting with the class as a whole. In only 22 percent of spot observations did teachers interact with the class as a whole. However, hand waving and other forms of competition for the teacher's attention were not in evidence, perhaps because much classroom authority was delegated to children. As we will see below, children were encouraged to consult other children, not the teacher, on matters ranging from what to draw to how to settle a playground fight.

Strategies for Controlling Children's Behavior. How is a transition made from the indulged, undisciplined early child-rearing at home to a nursery school structure which must, at the very least, ensure the safety of thirty to forty children? As noted above, a growing research literature suggests that salient external control—beyond that necessary to elicit compliance with a request—tends to undermine children's internalization of the norm in question. On the other hand, control strategies which elicit compliance using minimal pressure tend to foster internalization of norms. From this point of view, four aspects of teachers' control strategies were particularly interesting: (1) minimizing the impression of teacher control; (2) delegating control to children; (3) providing plentiful opportunities for children to acquire a "good girl" or "good boy" identity; and (4) avoiding the attribution that children intentionally misbehave.

Minimizing the Impression of Teacher Control. One way to minimize the salience of teacher control in the classroom is simply to tolerate a wide latitude of child behavior. The observations suggest that Japanese nursery school teachers may do just that. In view of previous suggestions that the behavior of Japanese children in nursery school is somewhat regimented,[19] the noise and chaos level of the Japanese nursery schools was perhaps the single most astonishing aspect of the observations. Very high levels of spontaneous background noise from children (shouting, laughing, and so forth) partially obscured almost half of the dictations of teaching behavior, even though the tape recorder was held directly to the observer's mouth and the children were rarely within two feet of the observer. One possibility is that Japanese adults positively value children's *genki* (vigor) and that considerable classroom noise does not necessarily reflect negatively on the teacher.[20]

The spot observations also suggest that teachers kept a low profile as classroom authorities. In only 53 percent of the spot observations were all children even within the teacher's sight. In 13 percent of the spot observations, none of the children in the classroom were within the teacher's sight. These percentages do not include situations in which another adult was responsible for watching the children, or all children were in an area, such as the playground, where supervision was not required. (Subsequent questioning confirmed that teachers did not expect the observer to watch the children in the teacher's absence.) Nor was it the case that classrooms had been childproofed to obviate the need for adult presence. In six of ten schools one or more of the following were within reach of the children: sharp scissors, razor blade knives, leather punches, or nails. Teachers recognized that children could hurt themselves with these objects but believed children would only use them under supervision. My questions about whether children would purposely use these objects to hurt other children elicited puzzlement. Perhaps, as we shall see below, the puzzlement centered on differences in attribution about intent. Teachers stated that the children were capable of self-supervision on occasions when the teacher was called out of the room. Beliefs about children's capacities for self-control and self-regulation have received some attention but deserve further research in the future.[21]

A low profile as classroom authorities was suggested, also, by teachers' responses to misbehavior. The dictated descriptions of teacher behavior and the observation notes include numerous incidents, such as the following, in which teachers made requests but did not enforce the requests or did not check to see whether children complied:

> Teacher tries to turn child's attention to building a race track, but he brings more sand to throw. Teacher, "If you fill up the tunnel with snow you can't have a race." Teacher turns to student teacher and says, "It's no use. They want to make it snow no matter what you do."[22]

Interviews with teachers about these incidents and others suggested that their goal was not necessarily to make children comply but, rather, to make them understand what was proper behavior. (Other investigators provide further evidence on this point.)[23] In another incident described in the field notes, boys had been dropping clay "bombs" on the fish in an aquarium. The teacher explained that the clay could hurt the fish but did not specifically tell the boys to stop (nor did they). In her announcements to the whole class at the end of the school day, the teacher explained that some boys in the class thought they were "helping" the fish by throwing in clay "food," but that actually the boys were harming the fish.

Delegating Control to Children. Frequently, children were responsible for calling the class together, overseeing class projects, and even managing disagreements. For example, in one class thirty-eight children initiated preparations to go home on the basis of one quiet remark made by the teacher to a few children playing near her. When interviewed, the teacher indicated that ideally she should not need to mention going home even to a few children since they should keep an eye on the clock and remember it spontaneously. Similarly, when classes assembled for some program (such as a puppet show or singing) it was common for the teacher to make only one quiet statement to a few children. Sometimes children would be asked to check and see if their friends or group members had assembled; frequently teachers themselves did not attempt to find or involve children who did not appear for lunch, dismissal, or other class activities. Children were frequently seen searching for missing classmates, reminding isolated or distracted classmates about class activities, and improvising noisemakers to summon or quiet classmates for an activity.

Examples from the observations and interviews suggest that teachers often encouraged children to manage their own and other children's problems without teacher intervention. For example, when a child reported to the teacher that members of the "tulip" group were throwing stones out of the playhouse window, the teacher did not herself investigate the situation, but said, "Tell the tulips it's dangerous." In another example from the field notes, a teacher asked two girls to encourage a boy to finish his lunch. The girls sat with the boy, helped him assemble scattered grains of rice and exhorted him to eat, and finally reported to the teacher that the boy had eaten. Interview and observational data also suggest that teachers preferred not to intervene directly in classroom aggression but to have the children themselves manage aggression.

In one of the few aggressive episodes recorded in the field notes, two boys had a fight which progressed from sand throwing to hair pulling and hitting. The teacher did not directly attempt to stop the fight; in fact, she cheered on the smaller boy, saying, "Give it your best" and "Look, Taro's gotten strong; now he can fight without crying." When asked by a child why the two boys were fighting, the teacher said, "You'd better ask the fighters." The teacher encouraged two bystanders to question the fighters about the problem and then asked each bystander to report what he had learned. After eliciting the reports, the teacher said, "You're the caretakers, so you should decide what to do" and turned her back. The caretakers tried to get each fighter to apologize but failed. The caretakers then became frustrated and abandoned their mediation efforts. The fighting then resumed, and the teacher asked a girl watching the fight to help the two fighters make up. At the same time, the teacher said, "I am washing my hands of this" and walked away. The girl and a second nearby girl each began to question the fighters, saying, "Are you mad? If not, say 'I'm sorry.' " Meanwhile, the teacher drew a circle around the fighters and children solving the fight and asked the rest of the children to start cleaning up to go home. The two girls succeeded in getting the fighters to apologize to each other. Each girl held hands with one fighter and brushed the sand off him, and then the two girls joined hands, forming a chain with the two fighters. From a distance, the teacher said, "Great! The problem has been solved, due to the two girls." Noticing that one boy was still crying, the teacher said, "Now it's your problem alone, if you've already made up." Although class dismissal time had already been delayed by about fifteen minutes by the fight, the teacher discussed the incident with the whole class, assembled for dismissal. The teacher named the fighters and described in detail how they had thrown sand, pulled hair, and hit. She also named all four mediators and praised them for helping solve the class's problem. Parents picking up their children were kept waiting for about twenty minutes beyond the normal dismissal time.

Providing Opportunities to Develop a Good-child Identity. In addition to children's informal involvement in classroom management, fourteen of fifteen schools had a formal system of daily rotating *toban* (monitors). *Toban* were responsible for such visible leadership roles as leading the class in greetings and distributing tea at lunch.

The *toban*'s authority might include deciding which group to dismiss first, deciding which group was quiet enough to have lunch, giving permission to individual children to go outside after lunch, and finding children who were missing at lunch time or other assembly times. *Toban* were addressed as "san," a higher honorific than that normally used to address kindergarten children.

Some schools had a *toban* from each group, while others had one or two *toban* from the class as a whole. The *toban* changed daily, and picture charts showed when each child's turn would come up. Although all children became *toban* automatically in turn, considerable pomp and circumstance were attached to the position. In most schools, at the beginning of each day, a song or ceremony identified the new *toban* and a badge was conferred. At the end of the day, the *toban* received formal thanks from the whole class. The honor was keenly appreciated by children: teachers reported parents had difficulty keeping ill children home from school if it happened to be their *toban* day. The *toban* system afforded each child an opportunity to develop an identity as a classroom leader and authority figure.

A further incident from the field notes suggests that teachers helped children find peer-based, not teacher-based, methods for dealing with breakdowns in cooperative work. In the course of asking groups to report to the class on their chores, a teacher was told by the bird group that they did not finish their chore because they "began playing in the middle." The teacher solicited suggestions from the whole class about what to do if a group could not get its members together to work. The teacher passed over suggestions that the group members be punished, saying, "It's not a good situation when people work because they are forced to." The teacher appeared satisfied when one child finally suggested that the group members ready to do chores could "get together and shout to call the people who aren't there." This solution focuses not on punishment or reward of behavior but on a pragmatic strategy for eliciting cooperative behavior.

Avoiding the Attribution That Children Intentionally Misbehave. As illustrated in the case of the boys who did not "understand" not to bomb the goldfish, teachers frequently attributed children's misbehavior to something other than malicious intent. For example, children had "forgotten their promises" or did not "understand" what was right. Misbehavior was often described as "strange" behavior. Frequently, discipline by teachers took the form of a simple explanation of appropriate behavior or of a series of questions which assumed that the child would not knowingly commit wrongdoing. For example, a boy who hid the shoes of a boy washing his feet was questioned as follows: "Did Ben ask you to move his shoes?" "What happens when you finish washing your feet and your shoes aren't there?" "Do you know it would be nicer to help Ben?" The teacher's questions concluded with, "This time is over, but remember these things next time." Similarly, a boy with his hand cocked back about to throw a large rock was asked to "lend" the rock to the teacher who demonstrated, by touching the child's head with the rock, how he could be hurt if such a rock hit the back of his head. The teacher then returned the rock to the child, asking him to carry it carefully. The teacher did not ask the child to put down the rock or imply that the child intended to throw it.

When questioned about children's misbehavior, teachers frequently volunteered that enjoyment of school was the key to good behavior for children. An emotional attachment to the teacher and friendships with children were considered critical elements in the child's enjoyment of school. Techniques for building the teacher-child relationship included keeping the same teacher for two or more years (seven of nine schools) and teacher visits to the children's homes (four of eight schools). Some schools offered special preparatory classes for children who had cried during their nursery school interviews; prior to the school year, these children visited the nursery school as frequently as was necessary to adjust to the new setting. Teachers' elaborate efforts to construct children's groups which "successfully" played together were described above. One school even held regular meetings of the mothers' groups corresponding to the children's small groups. These parallel maternal networks were intended to strengthen the children's groups.

Discussion

Interviews with teachers revealed conceptions of child development which deserve systematic comparison with concepts held by Americans. The observations revealed some concepts which are strikingly similar to those described historically for the Japanese: for example, that children younger than age six or seven are incapable of intentional wrongdoing.[24] The child's capacity for self-management, the child's capacity for willful misbehavior, and the child's responsiveness to peer versus adult disciplinary sanctions were all suggested as potential areas of interest. The consequences of these concepts for teacher behavior also represent a key area for future research.

Delegating Authority to Children. Children in Japanese nursery schools appear to receive considerable encouragement to be their brother's keeper. Peers, not teachers, may have authority to manage aspects of classroom life ranging from participation in class events and finishing one's lunch to fights with other children. While interesting evidence exists on peer management of classroom behavior by older students,[25] little is known about consequences of peer management in nursery schools. Research on children's moral judgments suggests that peer justice may be unduly harsh,[26] but little is known about how these moral judgments translate into actual behavior.

What are the likely effects of peer versus adult enforcement of rules on children's internalization of rules and their attitudes toward authority? Several speculations are in order. First, delegating authority to children enables teachers to make few behavioral demands on children. In the Japanese schools observed, peers assume much of the authority for checking that children complete their chores, finish their lunches, behave nicely toward other children, and so forth. This delegation of authority may enable the teacher to remain a benevolent figure to whom children have a strong, unconflicted positive attachment. A second speculation is that delegation of authority allows children to experience negative sanctions as intrinsic consequences of their acts. When the *toban* fails to realize it is time for lunch and is hit on the back by hungry group mates attempting to redirect his attention (to take an actual example from observations), the child may experience this very differently from a teacher's reprimand. Children's sanctions may appear less contrived and external and more like the direct, natural consequences of the child's own acts, thus fostering greater behavioral change. Finally, it may be that peer criticism, in comparison with adult criticism, poses less of a threat to the child's identity as a good child. Research on moral judgment suggests that, in the mind of a five-year-old, morality and adult authority are inextricably linked.[27] Thus, criticism by adults may, to a much greater degree than peer criticism, cause the child to feel like a bad child. The "good child" identity may, in turn, be a critical determinant of the child's subsequent willingness to obey rules.[28] The fragile "good child" identity may fare better in an environment in which peers, not adults, bear messages that the child has misbehaved.

An earlier section of this report poses the question, How is a transition made from the indulged, undisciplined early child rearing at home to a nursery school structure which must, at the very least, ensure the safety of thirty to forty children? The present data suggest several answers. Teachers may tolerate, at least initially, a wide latitude of behavior by children. Compliance, orderliness, and classroom harmony may be viewed as consequences which naturally follow when children understand what is proper behavior, not as behavioral goals which must be quickly achieved. Since it is frequently the peers, not the teacher, who are responsible for eliciting proper behavior, there is reduced need for the teacher to exercise authority. Further, teachers provide plentiful opportunities for children to shape classroom rules and formally to assume positions of authority. The attribution theory discussed above suggests that providing children with opportunities to cooperate and act in accordance with classroom rules, without salient external pressure from the teacher, will promote strong internalization of classroom values. Thus, these Japanese nursery school practices may promote strong internalization and, ultimately, high compliance, while maintaining the role of the teacher as a benevolent, though perhaps not quite indulgent, figure.

Notes

1. *Nihon Kyoiku Nenkan* (Tokyo: Nihon Kyoiku Nenkan Hanko Iinkaihen Gyosei, 1982). Statistics are as of April 1980.

2. W. A. Caudill, "Tiny Dramas: Vocal Communication between Mother and Infant in Japanese and American Families," in *Mental Health Research in Asia and the Pacific,* vol. 2, ed. W. P. Lebra (Honolulu: East-West Center, 1972); William Caudill and Carmi Schooler, "Child Behavior and Child Rearing in Japan and the United States: An Interim Report," *Journal of Nervous and Mental Disease* 157 (1973): 323–38; Nancy Shand, "Cultural Factors in Maternal Behavior: Their Influence on Infant Behavioral Development in Japan and the U.S.," Progress Reports I and II (Meninger Foundation, 1978); William Cummings, *Education and Equality in Japan* (Princeton, N.J.: Princeton University Press, 1980).

3. Robert Hess and Hiroshi Azuma, "Family Effects upon School Readiness and Communication Skills of Preschool Children in Japan and the United States," Data Reports 1–6 (Stanford University Graduate School of Education and University of Tokyo Faculty Education, n.d.), Robert Hess et al., "Maternal Expectations for Early Mastery of Developmental Tasks in Japan and the United States," *International Journal of Psychology* 15 (1980): 259–71; L. Peak, "Training Learning Skills and Attitudes in Japanese Early Educational Settings," in *Early Experience and the De-*

velopment of Competence, ed. William Fowler (*New Directions in Child Development*, No. 32) (San Francisco: Jossey-Bass, 1986).

4. Takeo Doi, *The Anatomy of Dependence* (Tokyo: Kodansha International, 1973); Hiroko Hara and Hiroshi Wagatsuma, *Shitsuke* (Tokyo: Kobundo, 1974); Ezra Vogel, *Japan's New Middle Class* (Berkeley: University of California Press, 1963).

5. Cummings.

6. Figures as of May 1, 1981, from Gakko Kihon Chosa survey, reported in *Japan Statistical Yearbook* (Tokyo: Statistics Bureau, Prime Minister's Office, 1982).

7. Harold Cook and Sandra Stingles, "Cooperative Behavior in Children," *Psychological Bulletin* 81 (December 1974): 918–33.

8. Ezra Vogel, *Japan as Number One: Lessons for America* (Cambridge, Mass.: Harvard University Press, 1979).

9. Chie Nakane, *Japanese Society* (Berkeley: University of California Press, 1972).

10. Robert Cole, *Work, Mobility and Participation: A Comparative Study of American and Japanese Industry* (Berkeley: University of California Press, 1979).

11. Spencer Kagan and Millard Madsen, "Cooperation and Competition of Mexican-American and Anglo-American Children of Two Ages under Four Instructional Sets," *Developmental Psychology* 5 (1971): 32–39; Millard Madsen and Ariella Shapira, "Cooperative and Competitive Behavior of Urban Afro-American, Anglo-American, Mexican-American and Mexican Village Children," *Developmental Psychology* 3 (1970): 16–20; Ariella Shapira and Millard Madsen, "Cooperative and Competitive Behavior of Kibbutz and Urban Children in Israel," *Child Development* 40 (1960): 609–17.

12. J. Aronfreed, "The Socialization of Altruistic and Sympathetic Behavior: Some Theoretical and Experimental Analyses," in *Altruism and Helping Behavior*, ed. J. Macaulay and L. Berkowitz (New York: Academic Press, 1970).

13. Teresa Amabile, William DeJong, and Mark Lepper, "Effects of Externally-imposed Deadlines on Subsequent Intrinsic Motivation," *Journal of Personality and Social Psychology* 34 (1976): 92–98.

14. Moses Goldberg and Eleanor Maccoby, "Children's Acquisition of Skill in Performing a Group Task under Two Conditions of Group Formation," *Journal of Personality and Social Psychology* 2 (1965): 898–902.

15. D. Baumrind, "The Development of Instrumental Competence through Socialization," in *Minnesota Symposia on Child Psychology*, vol. 7, ed. A. D. Pick (Minneapolis: University of Minnesota Press, 1973); Eleanor Maccoby, *Social Development: Psychological Growth and the Parent-Child Relationship* (New York: Harcourt Brace Jovanovich, 1980); Catherine Lewis, "The Effects of Parental Firm Control: A Reinterpretation of Findings," *Psychological Bulletin* 90 (November 1981): 547–63.

16. Hara and Wagatsuma; Vogel, *Japan's New Middle Class*.

17. Vogel, *Japan as Number One: Lessons for America;* Nakane.

18. M. Lepper, "Social Control Processes, Attributions of Motivation and the Internalization of Social Values," in *Social Cognition and Social Behavior: Developmental Perspectives*, ed. E. T. Higgins, D. N. Ruble, and W. W. Hartup (San Francisco: Jossey-Bass, 1981).

19. Leslie C. Bedford, "Rakuto Kindergarten: Observations on Japanese Preschooling," *Harvard Graduate School of Education Association Bulletin* 23 (Spring 1979): 18–20; Ruth Bettelheim and Ruby Takanishi, *Early Schooling in Asia* (New York: McGraw-Hill, 1976).

20. Christena Turner, personal communication, July 1979 (diss. in progress, Stanford University).

21. Robert Hess et al. (note 3, above).

22. All translations are mine.

23. Vogel, *Japan's New Middle Class* (note 4 above); Mary Conroy et al., "Maternal Strategies for Regulating Children's Behavior in American Families," *Journal of Cross-cultural Psychology* 11, no. 2 (1980): 153–72.

24. Hara and Wagatsuma (note 4 above); Hideo Kojima, "Childrearing Concepts as a Belief-Value System of Society and Individual" (paper presented at the Conference on Child Development in Japan and the United States, Center for Advanced Study in the Behavioral Sciences, April 1983).

25. Urie Bronfenbrenner, *Two Worlds of Childhood: U.S. and U.S.S.R.* (New York: Pocket Books, 1973).

26. R. Johnson, "A Study of Children's Moral Judgments," *Child Development* 23 (1962): 327–54.

27. L. Kohlberg, "Morals and Moralization: A Cognitive Development Approach," in *Moral Development and Behavior,* ed. T. Lickona (New York: Holt, Rinehart and Winston, 1976).

28. Lepper (note 18 above).

4

Japanese Preschools: Academic or Nonacademic?

Gary DeCoker

The purpose of this paper is to explore the variation among Japanese preschools by presenting information based on case studies of seven preschools. Through descriptions of the seven schools, I will discuss the differences between Japanese preschools operated according to academic and nonacademic philosophies. I define academically-oriented preschools as those that stress reading, writing, and computational skills and nonacademic schools as those that do not systematically include these "academic" activities. In both types of schools, of course, children develop such things as oral language, fine-motor coordination, and the ability to pay attention and follow the routine. Children in all preschools also spend a great deal of time at play. Nevertheless, the schools that I visited differed distinctly in their approach to the three R's. Another difference, one that is more difficult to document, is the degree of intensity and formality at the academic preschools. This difference will become more clear in the descriptions of my observations which are included in subsequent sections of this paper.

I have based my research on observations and interviews conducted at seven preschools in Kyoto from February through May 1985. Of the seven schools, two fit the category of academically-oriented and four the category of nonacademically-oriented. One school fits best somewhere between the two categories. For that reason it is perhaps more appropriate to view the distinction between the two types as a continuum rather than an either-or dichotomy. For the purpose of this paper, however, I will treat the two categories as distinct in order to set up "ideal types" by which other preschools can be compared.

The differences between the two categories are especially visible in the structured activities that the children do as a group. For that reason I limit myself to a discussion of two aspects of preschool programs: (1) morning assemblies and (2) curriculum and teaching methods. In doing so I am not diminishing the importance of other aspects of preschool education such as play or of other purposes of preschool education such as socialization. My primary concern, however, is in contrasting schools with academic and nonacademic orientations.

Yochien operate under the auspices of the Ministry of Education and admit children from three years of age until entry into first grade. As a rule, they are in session four or five hours a day from Monday through Saturday for 220 days per year, following a schedule similar to first- to twelfth-grade schooling. *Hoikuen* come under the jurisdiction of the Ministry of Health and Welfare and care for children from infancy until entry into first grade. Entry to *hoikuen* is restricted. Parents must lack family care for the child during the hours he will attend school.[1] In most cases this means that both parents work during the day. Because of their day-care function, *hoikujo* operate for about eight hours daily except Sundays and holidays for about 300 days a year. Also *hoikuen* must provide meals and snacks for their children. At *yochien* this is optional.

Both *yochien* and *hoikuen* receive government curriculum guidelines, *yochien* from the Ministry of Education and *hoikuen* from the Ministry of Health and Welfare. The recommended curriculum for the final two years is nearly identical.[2] Due in part to its day-care function and infant and toddler program, however, many Japanese still regard the *hoikuen* as having a lesser educational role than the *yochien*. Another reason for this could be that the government requires *yochien* to group children by age, the same as in elementary school, whereas it does not regulate *hoikuen* in this regard. Yet many *hoikuen* also group their children by age. The government limits the class size in *yochien* to forty, although most schools have a lower student-teacher ratio than one to forty. In *hoikuen* for children three years of age and older the student-teacher ratio is limited to one to thirty.

Preschool teachers are primarily young and female. At *yochien* in 1984 women made up 93.8 percent of the staff and 99.4 percent of the full-time teachers. Over half of the teachers were twenty-six years of age or less, and the average age was only slightly over thirty years.[3] Most teachers hold teaching certificates. In 1980 over 83 percent of the teaching staff of *yochien* had received a certificate.[4] All new teachers must earn a certificate from a junior college or equivalent school of higher education. Over 98 percent of the *hoikujo* teachers held certificates in 1984.[5] They gained these either by passing an examination or by attending a teacher-training institution.

Enrollment at the seven schools that I visited ranges from 60 to 250 students. Four are religious, three Buddhist and one Christian. At the four neighborhood schools most of the children live within walking distance. The three regional schools provide bus transportation for the students who live outside the neighborhood. Some Japanese preschools place special emphasis on one subject area such as English language, computers, or music. One of the schools that I visited specializes in music.

To arrange my observations of the seven preschools I made contact with each school directly by introducing myself as an American researcher of Japanese preschools. I observed each school from two to four times, about four hours per visit. My knowledge of the Japanese language allowed me to understand conversations among teachers and students and to interview principals and teachers. I restricted my formal observations to children three years of age and older, although I viewed some groups of younger children.

Morning Assemblies

The schedules of the seven schools were similar and included a morning meeting, morning and afternoon classroom activities, two or three recess periods, and lunch. Although school day activities began about 9:30 or 10:00, most schools opened their gates much earlier for supervised free play on the playground. Instruction ended at three or four o'clock, but at *hoikuen* some children stayed until six o'clock. Because of their long hours most *hoikuen* also scheduled time for a snack and a nap.

All of the schools began with a morning meeting of about thirty minutes which was either an assembly of the entire school, a group meeting held in individual classrooms or both. At this meeting the children sang songs and often did calisthenics. In the working world, too, the day often begins with a morning assembly and calisthenics. In the preschools these calisthenics are not very vigorous and provide less of a workout than most of the children get during free-play on the playground. But exercise is not the only purpose of the gathering. As it does in the work place, these exercises and songs signal the beginning of the day, turn everyone's attention to the group, and provide those in charge the opportunity for an inspirational speech.

The day at E school, a Christian, nonacademic *yochien,* officially starts at 9:30, but on my second visit parents began leaving their children outside the cement wall that surrounded the playground at 9:00. Each child walked through the open iron gate and directly into the school. There he met the two monitors, who were five-year-old children chosen to assist the teachers that day. These two children helped him put his lunch in a wooden box labeled by class. Then they placed a stamp in the child's attendance book for the appropriate day. Each child was responsible for his attendance book which he received from the school. After returning it to his book bag and hanging the bag on his hook, the student went to the playground.

Children darted this way and that on the dirt playground. Others climbed on the metal and wooden jungle gyms or in the trees that lined the wall. Gymnast rings, wooden balance beams of various heights and lengths, a sandbox, and a twelve-person seesaw completed the playground equipment.

At 9:30 one of the monitors rang a hand bell while the other helped a teacher turn on recorded music. Upon hearing the music from the large speakers, one teacher started calisthenics. She was joined by an increasing number of children in unkempt lines. When all the students assembled, the monitors went to the front, faced the group, and continued the exercises: arm movements, running-in-place, clapping, and hand motions.

Following calisthenics the children sang the "Put Your Hands on Your . . . " song, and finished with the school song. Then they rearranged themselves by class and proceeded one by one to the gymnast rings. Each child held the rings and did a flip, with the help of a teacher if necessary, then hopped on one foot into the school.

The children entered the school and proceeded to the restrooms to wash up before going on to their classrooms. The last child walked into the four-year-old classroom of twenty-six children at 10:05. He finished drying his hands on the hand towel, which every child had hung around his neck, and sat on a chair completing a semi-circle of children. The teacher, who sat at an electric organ facing the children, began a series of songs that lasted twenty minutes. They sang a Japanese version of "Old McDonald," a counting song, and others. Then the teacher chose four children who stood in front with her. The rest followed in a song of prayer asking for protection, a nice morning, a good tomorrow, and an enjoyable lunch in the name of Jesus and the Bible.

Academically-oriented B *yochien* occupies a modern two-story building in a crowded residential section of town. Many of the 200 children ages three to five come from other parts of the city on a one-hour school bus ride to participate in the school's program. On a day when I visited children began arriving at 8:45 and played outside until 10:00 when the teachers signalled them to line up and enter the school.

The teacher of a five-year-old class watched her twenty students change into their indoor shoes and then followed them to the classroom. She immediately sat down at the piano with her back to the children. Without saying a word she began playing marching music. The children followed with skipping, clapping, toe tapping, and walking backwards. Each time she changed the music the children, in unison, changed to the next movement. As the music came to an end, the children spun around a few times and sat down on the floor. Then the teacher asked the day's monitor to step forward. A child came to the front of the room, already having seen his name hanging under the monitor sign. "What is the month and date?" the remaining children chimed. "March-the-twelfth," answered the monitor. After stating the day, weather, his address, and his phone number, the boy picked up a stack of name cards and showed them one-by-one to the children. When a child saw his name, he raised his right hand and shouted "Yes." For those who were absent the children vied to be the first to yell, "Absent today." Once when a child raised her left hand instead of her right, she was met with a chorus of "Wrong hand!"

The singling out of an individual child as part of the morning assembly was unique to B school. The precision of this activity also separated B school from the rest of the preschools, as did the name cards themselves which were written in Chinese characters. In the other preschools each child's books, bags, clothing, and the like were labeled with the child's name in *hiragana,* one of two phonetic alphabets used to write the Japanese language. According to Ministry of Education guidelines, these alphabets, called *kana,* are to be taught in first grade. Although the explicit teaching of reading and writing is not mentioned in guidelines for preschool education, children often know most of the *kana* before they enter elementary school. Along with the phonetic alphabets Japanese children must learn Chinese characters, the third element of the language. By the end of first grade students should know about 76 of the 2,000 Chinese characters taught in the nine years of compulsory schooling. Chinese characters used in names can be especially difficult because names sometimes include characters not taught until junior or even senior high school. The typical name has four Chinese characters, therefore, the children in this class at B school gained the ability to recognize nearly eighty characters.

C *yochien* falls somewhere between the categories of academic and nonacademic. The school occupies a new two-story building on property lent to them by a temple of the Pure Land Buddhist sect. Many of the children come by school bus from outside of the neighborhood, riding up to twenty minutes each way. Upon arrival at the school they play in the playground until school begins. At 10:00 the children enter the school and walk to their classrooms. In the four-year-olds' classroom that I visited, the children entered, changed into their smocks and beanies, and sat down. The light blue and pink smocks identified a child as a boy or girl and the red beanies revealed the class and age group. The teacher sat at the organ and played one chord. Upon hearing that chord, the children stood and sang the "Child-Buddha Song," followed by a silent prayer, the "Good Morning Song," and bows and greetings to the teacher and each other. To take attendance the teacher called the girls' names first. When a child heard her name she raised one hand and said "yes." All the children yelled "absent" when appropriate. After the children read the date in unison, two children flipped through the weather cards. Showing a picture of rain they asked, "Is it this?" The children responded "no" and viewed the next picture card. Finally they chimed, "Today's weather is sunny." The children knew the routine well even after only six weeks.

D school, a small nonacademic *hoikuen* of sixty students, is owned by the school's principal. The children spend their day in either of two classrooms, one for children under three years of age and the other for older children. Most of the children come to school with a parent, either on foot, by car, or on the back of a bicycle. The actual school day is from 10:00 to 3:30, but children come as early as 8:00 and leave as late at 6:00. I visited on a crisp, clear day in early March, so when the children arrived they went straight to the playground. By 9:30 almost all of the older children busily played on the swings and slides or in the sandbox. Tires of various sizes rolled to and fro, as did some children. The one- and two-year-olds clustered near the school building, probably to avoid danger and to be close to the teacher who sat inside watching the children through the open glass doors.

At 9:45 the principal appeared and clapped his hands. The children quickly lined up and followed him out the gate. Each with his hands on the shoulder of the person in front, they bounced happily down the street to the large playground below the school. With the heel of his shoe the principal drew in the dirt a large circle which was soon filled with children jumping up and down and clapping. He continued making lines for their many games before he dismissed them for ten minutes of free play. Then the principal clapped his hands again, signaling the children to line up and follow him as he walked a rambling line all over the playground. The children followed their pied piper, eventually coming to the school.

The major difference between the morning assembly at academic and nonacademic schools was one of degree: the straightness of the lines of children, the attention the students paid to the activity, the children's adherence to the musical or other cues given to the class by the teachers. In some schools the children reacted quickly to every directive. In others they resembled a group of young ducklings, following their leader but easily distracted.

The form of the morning assembly varied little. Academically-oriented B school, however, also used the morning assembly as an opportunity to reinforce language skills and to allow individual children to answer various questions. Teachers at the other schools tended to include only exercise, organized play, and singing in their morning assemblies.

Curriculum and Teaching Methods

Academically-oriented schools tended to develop curriculum guides that included specific skills such as the sight recognition of the two phonetic alphabets (*kana*) or the identification of musical notes played on a piano. Some schools held meetings where the principal, more experienced teachers, or in-service teachers informed the faculty of the subject matter and method of teaching for the following week. At other schools teachers determined class activities individually or together with teachers of the same age group. Some schools provided teachers with instructional devices such as mimeographed activities and other commercial materials. Other schools relied on teacher-made materials.

During one of my visits to academically-oriented B school the teacher passed out a ready-made packet containing a folding pop-up scene of a castle, moat and forest, a detachable ladder, boat, and shining prince. The fair maiden stood locked in the castle. Each child sat on the floor with his set which he fit together without any teacher assistance. In the end most children came up with the correct construction. Some waited until others finished and then copied them. Later the teacher asked individuals to think of a scenario for the maiden's rescue using the available materials. She always encouraged the children regardless of the response and gave each child an opportunity to finish his story. B school's language program also included workbooks and ditto sheets as did the mathematics program. Children learned to recognize the phonetic alphabets and the numerals one through one hundred. They also were exposed to many Chinese characters.

The language program at academically-oriented A school, a large *hoikuen*, was the most advanced. The administration determined the curriculum for each class and wrote detailed plans a month in advance based on the yearly plan of the school. When I requested to visit a language lesson, the assistant principal checked her records and told me the times of future lessons. She suggested I should come two weeks later and told me the exact lesson I would be able to observe. I visited that class and found twenty-seven four-year-olds and one teacher finishing the reading of a Japanese version of *Three Billy Goats Gruff.* The teacher introduced me and took the opportunity to discuss cultural differences between Americans and Japanese. The thirty-minute language lesson began on time at 10:40. The children looked at pictures of various things, named them, and clapped out the syllables in each word. Later the teacher put the pictures and magnetic *kana* letter cards on the chalkboard and asked individual children to spell the words by placing the correct cards below the pictures.

Graduates of the school learned both of the phonetic alphabets and thirty Chinese characters. Roughly equivalent to the middle of the first-grade reading curriculum as determined by the Ministry of Education, this instruction began at A school at four years of age. The children also practiced writing each character using pencils and various purchased and teacher-made materials. I did not observe writing practice at any of the other preschools. And only A and B schools exposed the children to Chinese characters.

As a supplement to language teaching at A school the children memorized fifteen poems from the "Single Poems of One Hundred Poets," an anthology of classical thirty-one-syllable poems from the seventh to the thirteenth century. The principal explained that he hoped the children would eventually learn all one hundred poems and compete in contests in which contestants match pairs from two hundred cards containing either the first or second half of a poem. These poems, written in the classical language, are very complex and are difficult for most adult Japanese.

At C school, which was between the categories of academic and nonacademic, the teachers did not explicitly teach the written Japanese language, but they did use the phonetic alphabet when writing on the chalkboard and to label things. In the same way, arithmetic lessons at C school occasionally involved the writing of numerals by the teacher but not by the children. Rather than having the children write, the teachers used toys and objects from the children's daily life to teach mathematical concepts. For instance, during one activity six children with hand puppets stood and were served bowls of imaginary rice. The teacher altered the number of bowls and had the class discover how many puppets would be fed. Later the children colored and cut out five plates and pasted them on a picture of a table with six people. The teacher pointed out to me that this activity combined mathematics with art and also developed their fine-motor coordination. Another time the teacher divided the children into two groups and while changing the number in each group discussed the concepts of more and less.

Nonacademic schools did not explicitly teach language or math skills as did the academically-oriented schools. At nonacademic E school I watched the children prepare for a game at 10:25 by moving their chairs into a circle. Each child was given a teacher-made headband with a drawing of one of four fruits. The teacher said "strawberry," signaling the children with strawberry headbands to stand and go to an empty chair. Because children outnumbered chairs, one child could not sit down. This child said, "There's a big storm. There's a big storm. Apples." The apple children stood, walked around, and all but one sat down. This person began again repeating the ditty and naming the fruit of his choice.

At 10:50 the teacher chose one child to collect each type of fruit headband and told the children to stack their chairs by color and go to recess. Class reconvened at 11:15 with the students sitting at tables. The teacher read a story from large cards with a picture on one side and the words on the other. The children seldom saw the teacher's face behind the cards, but they heard her voice as she imitated the sounds of various animal characters. The morning ended with religious music played while the children had their heads resting on the tables. Then the teacher chose the quietest group to wash up and get ready for lunch. "Don't forget to push in your chair," she cautioned as the last child left.

The morning activities at G school, a Buddhist, nonacademic *hoikuen*, were a combination of music and art. One of the days on which I visited began with a morning assembly of the entire school. Then the children went to their classrooms for a second morning assembly. The first ten minutes of the class included attendance, the introduction of the monitors, and four songs. Then to the accompaniment of the electric organ they practiced a new song that had been introduced at the morning assembly. Following that the teacher played a glissando signaling the children to sit in their chairs. At 10:43 the teacher led a discussion of the previous day's field day and told the children they were to draw a picture of the event. At 10:48 the children prepared for this by moving chairs and tables to the sides of the room, getting paper and crayons, having the teacher write their names and the date on their papers, and finding a suitable place on the floor to work. At 10:58 the teacher looked up at the children, who all were waiting quietly, and told them to begin. They drew pictures until lunch at 11:30. This ended the day's only formal learning activity. The routine in the other classrooms resembled the four-year-olds. The fourteen two-year-olds with their two teachers strung beads on a thin string. The two classes of three-year-olds, fifteen per class, played with clay. The five-year-old class, thirty-four with one teacher, watched a video tape of the field day.

The activities at nonacademic D school began after the songs of the morning assembly. Following this twenty-minute activity, the children tried to guess what bus the teachers rode to school. The clues from the teachers were so vague that the children resorted to random guessing. This continued for fifteen minutes and seldom did a clue provide an impetus for thinking. Perhaps for this reason a number of children stopped participating and ran around the room for the remainder of this activity and throughout the reading of a story by a teacher.

The morning ended with a game where the children ran, crawled, hopped, and did other movements around the kerosene heater in the middle of the room. Piano music dictated the movement and when it stopped so did the children. Those who continued to move were out of the game and had to sit down and amuse themselves.

Teachers and children crawled and rolled around in a giggling mass of bodies. Through collisions, tears, and laughter, the piano player gradually removed the participants and finally declared the last five children the winners.

At nonacademic schools the teaching of skills occupied a minimal part of the day and those skills focused on physical and social development without including language and mathematics. Academically-oriented schools set aside larger blocks of time for lessons and the lessons included academic as well as physical and social skills. Both types of schools varied their activities and method of instruction. Sometimes the teachers required the children to sit at tables and conducted the class in a style similar to elementary school classes. At other times the structure was less formal. More than the teaching style, however, the content of the lessons distinguished the two types of schools. All of the schools included a great deal of time for free play, which was most often held on the playground. When the children were at play, the schools seemed similar; during activities and assemblies they differed.

Academic and Nonacademic Preschools: Sources and Significance

The major difference in the schools that I visited was the integration of reading, writing, math, and advanced music skills into the academically-oriented schools' curriculum. In addition there was a difference in the degree of formality and intensity between the two types of schools, although I have not attempted to document this conclusively. Academically-oriented A and B schools and partially academic C school were the largest of the schools observed and they had newer and more expensive equipment and facilities. These three schools required student uniforms and provided school bus transportation; however, uniforms also were found in some nonacademic schools. The teacher-student ratio did not follow a pattern. Of the schools with the lowest ratio, one was academic and the other was nonacademic. All of the schools employed a principal, although at E school the principal occupied a nominal position and delegated most of the administrative responsibility to the head teacher.

Principals made decisions regarding the schedule, curriculum, and equipment and also influenced the teaching style of individual teachers, most of whom were young and without many years of experience. Some teachers even said that they chose the profession to learn about children and that they considered the principal their greatest resource. Many principals expressed the feeling that they were responsible for the education of the parents and teachers as well as the children.

My discussions with the principals revealed some of the philosophical differences in academic and nonacademic preschools. Principals differed greatly over the issue of the appropriateness of reading and writing in the preschool curriculum. Two of the principals of nonacademic schools mentioned research which showed that by fourth grade there was no difference in the reading ability of children who were taught reading in preschool and those who were not. These principals followed the Ministry of Education guidelines for language which state that *yochien* should encourage the children to speak about and listen to things that interest them and that arise out of and further their play. One principal said that at her school they try to make the children interested in reading without actually teaching it: instead, speaking and listening are emphasized as the basis for future literacy. These principals stress the child's active use of language and shun such teaching tools as computers and television, which they feel move too quickly and superficially for the children.

In contrast, the principal at academically-oriented A school insisted that students at this age were ready for and could benefit from reading and writing instruction. He looked forward to the day when his teachers could use computer programs to teach their students to read. The principal at B school said that preschool-age children need to be challenged by the curriculum, even if that means doing things usually reserved for first grade.

The increased competition for the shrinking number of preschool-age children caused by the decline in birthrates for this age cohort has influenced some of the principals.[6] The principal at nonacademic G *hoikuen* said that she recently decided to accept two-year-olds in order to keep enrollment at a desired level of 120 children. She added, however, that she would have preferred the image of a *yochien* which only enrolls three- to five-year-olds. The principal at C *yochien,* which is between an academic and nonacademic school, said that she would soon begin an advertising campaign for her school in order to attract a sufficient number of students for the following year. She said that she does not support the use of advertising by preschools but feels compelled to advertise in order to compete with other schools which have begun advertising. Many of the principals whom I met expressed pride in their ability to rely on their reputation rather than advertising to recruit new students.

In order to better compete for students, some schools have begun expanding their curriculum. This appeals to the many parents who enroll their preschool-age children in private lessons in addition to preschool. At present the most popular are musical instruments, drawing and painting, swimming, and English. Preschool principals are well aware of the popularity of these lessons. Academically-oriented B school provides all of these activities as part of its curriculum. All of the schools provide at least one. School A's plan to add computers will meet another area of growing popularity among parents.

Emphasizing "academics," that is, the three R's, as a preparation for elementary school is another way to attract parents. In this sense, there are some parallels between the "cram schools" (juku) of later schooling and the academically-oriented preschools. The "cram schools" have made themselves almost compulsory for the children of success-oriented parents by playing on parental anxiety concerning examinations. The owners of academically-oriented preschools may be able to create the same need for their product by convincing Japanese parents that their children cannot succeed in future schooling without going to an academic preschool.[7]

For the time being, Japanese parents exercise more freedom of choice on the preschool level than they do on any other level of schooling and generally find these kinds of choices very uncomfortable to make. Some parents, thinking that their children will receive the skills necessary for success in future schooling, will choose academically-oriented preschools even though these preschools operate contrary to the government guidelines, which recommend nonacademic education. Other parents will choose nonacademic schools.

For American researchers of Japanese education, numerous areas remain in need of further study. First, we need to develop definitions of academically- and nonacademically-oriented preschools. In addition to looking at achievement levels in basic skill areas, we need to consider the size of the school, the time spent on structured activities and at play, the role of the principal, the educational and economic background of the parents, the future educational success of the students, the tuition and other fees, and the approach to recruitment of students. Most importantly, however, we must realize that in Japan, just as in the United States, education at all levels is diverse. Cross-cultural comparisons must be balanced by studies of the diversity within the educational systems in each country.

Notes

1. Male pronouns are used generically to refer to both sexes.

2. The *yochien* curriculum guide consists of the following six sections: health, society, nature, language, music, and art. The *hoikuen* curriculum guide for ages four to six includes the same six areas of study under slightly different headings.

3. Mombusho Daijin Kambo Chosa Tokeika, *Mombusho Tokei Yoran* (Tokyo: Mombusho, 1985), 41.

4. Zenkoku Hoiku Dantai Renrakukai. *Hoiku Hakusho* (Tokyo: Soto Bunka, 1984), p. 32.

5. Ibid., 33.

6. The population of children before the age of enrollment in first grade was 12,860,000 in 1975, 11,520,000 in 1980, and is predicted to be 8,700,000 by 1990. Zenkoku Hoiku Dantai Renrakukai, *Hoiku Hakusho* (Tokyo: Soto Bunka, 1984), 116.

7. The U.S. Department of Education report *Japanese Education Today* includes a section titled "Pressures on pre-elementary education" which points to a growing minority of parents who "are concerned that the traditional nonacademic focus of the official preschool and daycare curriculum is insufficient." This section also states: "This trend toward introduction of academic instruction in preschools is not regarded in an entirely favorable light by elementary school officials and social commentators. Emphasis on academic training at this stage is seen as interfering with proper development of children's social skills and daily habits." U.S. Department of Education, *Japanese Education Today* (Washington D.C.: U.S. Government Printing Office, 1987), 23.

5

Class Size and Student/Teacher Ratios in the Japanese Preschool

Joseph Jay Tobin, David Y. H. Wu, and Dana H. Davidson

What are we to make of the Japanese preschool's typical ratios of thirty students per teacher and per class for four- and five-year-olds? Japan is a wealthy country, a country that gives great importance to education, a country whose students from first grade on outperform Americans (and indeed, most of the rest of the world) on international academic achievement tests.[1] Yet, Japanese schools function with class sizes and student/teacher ratios that far exceed American prescribed limits on students per teacher and that are wildly out of line with what most American experts on preschool education believe to be ideal. Mombusho, the Japanese Ministry of Education, has set a limit of forty children per class for *yochien,* which are comparable to U.S. nursery schools for three- and four-year-olds and to U.S. kindergartens for 5-year-olds. Koseisho, the Japanese Ministry of Health and Welfare, prescribes upper ratios of 4:1 for infants, 8:1 for toddlers, and 30:1 for three-, four-, and five-year-olds in *hoikuen,* which are analogous to U.S. day-care centers

An earlier version of this essay was published in *Comparative Education Review,* Vol. 31, No. 4 (November 1987). Copyright © 1987 by the Comparative and International Education Society. Reprinted by permission of the University of Chicago Press.

for children four years old and younger and to U.S. kindergarten for five-year-olds.

The Research Method

The key to our method is the use of videotapes. We began with a traditional ethnographic approach, observing a dozen preschools in Tokyo, Hiroshima, Osaka, and Kyoto. We next chose two Japanese preschools on which to focus—one a *yochien* (nursery school), one a *hoikuen* (day-care center)—and filmed a typical day in a classroom of four-year-olds in each school. We edited the more than six hours of videotape shot in each school down to approximately thirty minutes. We then took these edited tapes (which we call "visual ethnographies") back to Kyoto, to the schools where they were made and, using a portable videocassette recorder and television monitor, showed them in separate screenings to groups of parents, children, teachers, and administrators. As these audiences watched our tape of their school, we asked them, first, if these edited thirty-minute videotaped portraits succeeded in reflecting their schools as they saw them (and if not, how not). We asked the teachers who appeared in our tapes to explain the meaning of their actions. We asked administrators to explain their schools' philosophy for caring for and educating young children. Sometimes, when we showed our tapes to audiences of parents, children, teachers, and administrators, reactions and explanations emerged spontaneously. At other times, we had to stimulate discussion by asking questions. We taped these sessions of teachers, administrators, parents, and children watching, discussing, and explaining their actions and thus literally gave them a voice in our study, as their words eventually became the narration for our films and the ultimate source of authority in our papers.[2]

The next step in our method involved showing a tape we made and edited of a preschool in the United States to audiences of Japanese children, parents, and preschool staff members. Once again, we videotaped the discussions that followed the screenings of the tapes, and we also asked our informants to record their reactions on questionnaires.[3]

Rather than assume that Komatsudani Hoikuen and Senzan Yochien (the Japanese preschools where we taped) are representative, we showed our tapes of these two Kyoto preschools to audiences associated with preschools in Hiroshima, Osaka, Tokyo, and Chiba. We recorded the comments of 280 Japanese preschool parents, teachers, administrators, and education students telling us in what ways they found Komatsundani and Senzan to be familiar and unfamiliar, typical and unusual.

In this paper, we present Japanese preschool teachers' and administrators' explanations of the films we made in their schools and their reactions to the film we showed them of an American preschool. The view we get of Japanese preschools from these two kinds of data—Japanese insiders' views of their own schools (autoethnography) and Japanese outsiders' views of another culture's school (ethno-ethnography)—challenges us to rethink the issues of teacher/student ratio and class size.[4]

"Tell Me: Why Do You Have Such Large Classes?"

In 1985, when we returned to Kyoto to show children, parents, and staff of Komatsudani Hoikuen and Senzan Yochien edited versions of the tapes we made of their schools, and of American and Chinese preschools as well, we expected our Japanese informants to tell us why they preferred large classes with high student/teacher ratios to small classes with low student/teacher ratios. We were therefore puzzled and a bit worried by the first responses we received after showing teachers at Senzan a tape of an American preschool with a student/teacher ratio of 8:1. Saito-*sensei* (teacher) began the discussion with a sigh: "Gee, it must be great to teach in a school with such small classes." Tanaka-*sensei* said, "I envy the way the American teacher in the film plays with the children in such an uninhibited, 'barefoot' way." Seeing our hypothesis unraveling before our eyes, we desperately sought clarification: "You're saying you would like to have smaller classes in your school?" "Sure," the teachers all agreed, "it would be much easier to teach a smaller class." Before abandoning our hypothesis, we tried one last question: "We want to make sure we understand this. You're saying it would be better to have a class size of ten students instead of twenty-five or thirty?" Saito-*sensei*, looking a bit puzzled, responded: "No, we didn't say better. Well sure, better for the teacher, but it wouldn't be better for the children, would it? Maybe I'm wrong, but it seems to me that children need to have the experience of being in a large group in order to learn to relate to lots of kinds of children in lots of kinds of situations."

Tanaka-*sensei,* who had commented favorably (or at least her comments had seemed to us to have been favorable) about what she had called the "barefoot" play style of the American teacher in our tape, then explained:

> I envy the way the American teachers, with such small classes, have time to play so affectionately with each child. That's how I like to play with my nieces and nephews. That's a good way for aunts and uncles and parents to play with their children. But I don't think that's necessarily the best way for a teacher to relate to children. Teaching is different from being a parent or aunt or friend to a child. Sometimes I feel like playing very warmly in a down-on-the-floor, barefoot sort of way with my students, and sometimes I feel like hugging some of my students or having an intimate chat with one of the little girls. And sometimes I do these things, of course. I'm a human being, as well as a teacher, and I'm not suggesting that teachers should be cold or formal. What I am trying to say is that I believe a teacher should emphasize relating to the class as a whole, rather than to each student, even if this is a little sad for the teacher sometimes.

Teaching and Mothering

Americans expect consistency between teachers' and parents' approaches to child care and between children's behavior at home and at school. For example, Barbara Culler, a day-care center director in Honolulu, told us:

> We feel it's crucial that children get the same sort of messages at home as at school. If we teach children here at school to use words instead of hitting to deal with disagreements, and then these children go home and get slugged by their parents, it undoes what we are trying to accomplish. When situations like this arise, we ask parents to come in to talk about our different approaches to discipline. If we can't re-

solve our differences, we occasionally have to counsel parents to change schools.

Belsky similarly emphasizes continuity between home and school, concluding that the same factors that make for good parenting make for good day-care.[5] Feeney and Chun point out that American preschool administrators tend to select teachers for their programs "who emphasize the maternal role."[6]

Our discussions with Japanese parents, teachers, and administrators suggest, in contrast, that in Japan, the worlds of preschool and home, of teacher and mother, are viewed as largely discontinuous: little consistency in approach or behavior is expected across the two domains.[7] As Tanaka-*sensei* pointed out to us after watching our American preschool film, "barefoot," intimate, motherlike, one-to-one interaction is good for children and satisfying for adults and children alike, but it is not the role of teachers to provide this kind of play. Teachers are not parents, and, to the degree a Japanese teacher allows herself to slip into a mother-like stance toward a child in her care, Tanaka-*sensei* suggests, she has compromised her role as a teacher.

We can see in these different views of the teacher's role larger cultural differences between Japan and the United States. In the United States, where dyadic relations are emphasized over triadic (group) relations, any relationship between an adult female and a small child (as, for instance, between preschool teacher and student) cannot help but reflect in important ways the mother-child bond. Conversely, in Japan, where group relations are emphasized over dyadic bonds, a preschool teacher is less likely to play a motherlike role vis-à-vis the children in her care.

The typical career path of the Japanese preschool teacher works to provide a steady stream of nonmotherlike employees. Most Japanese preschool teachers are hired directly out of college or junior college at twenty or twenty-two years old, and they generally work only three to five years before retiring to marry and start a family. As young, unmarried women in Japan, teachers' culturally proscribed role demeanor is very unlike the way married women behave. Unmarried young women, including preschool teachers, are expected to be energetic, cheery, cute, and girlish. A Japanese preschool teacher is likely to appear to the children in her class to be more like a (much) older sister than a mother. It is precisely at that point in her career when she begins to tire of her girlish role and to desire a child of her own that a Japanese teacher is most likely to retire (permanently) from preschool teaching. The average age of the Japanese teachers in our study was twenty-four, as compared to twenty-nine in the United States and thirty-four in China.

High student/teacher ratios in Japanese preschools also function to keep teachers from being too motherlike in their interactions with students. Large class sizes and large student/teacher ratios are disliked by Americans because they make intense dyadic relations between teachers and students more difficult. Our interviews suggest that, in Japan, this loss of dyadic intensity, rather than being an undesirable by-product of large ratios, is an anticipated and intended effect. If the ratio were to fall below twenty or so students per teacher, the teacher would become increasingly accessible and her attention increasingly attainable by individual students. Not only would this threaten the group ethos that Japanese value highly and interfere with children's play with peers, but it also would make the teacher more motherlike and thereby encourage children to behave more like dependent sons and daughters, thus blurring the distinction Japanese feel is crucial between school and home, teacher and mother. Dr. Sakuma Toru, a clinical psychologist we spoke with at the Juso Community Center in Osaka, made this point very powerfully when we asked him to speculate on why he thought in the past few years therapists in Japan have begun to see more cases of school phobia as early as the preschool level:

> I would suggest one major factor coming into play might be the decreases in class size that have become so common in Japan in the past ten years or so. As the student/teacher ratio drops from 40:1 to 25:1 and even to as low as 15 children per teacher, this can have a deleterious effect on some children. Japanese teaching theory and practice is based on working with large groups of children. This is what Japanese teachers are trained to do. This is what they do best. Most Japanese teachers are not prepared to teach children in smaller groups, with smaller ratios. I believe that a teacher who doesn't change her approach as the class size drops can have a harmful effect on some of her students. There is safety in numbers, you see. In a larger class, children can hide more easily. But, in a smaller class, the teacher's personality becomes more important, as does the quality of the teacher's relationship to each student. Perhaps a good teacher will do well with any size class. But if the teacher is only ordinary or mediocre, decreasing class size can have the

paradoxical effect of causing more discomfort and anxiety in students struggling with emotional and developmental problems and thus produce more school phobia.

The child's transition from the dyadic world of home to the triadic world of school and society is facilitated not by offering teachers who are mother substitutes but rather by offering a program of large class size and high student/teacher ratios, a program structured to limit face-to-face, emotionally intense interactions between children and teachers.

These points were also borne out in the reactions of Japanese parents and teachers who watched our tapes. Most Japanese mothers and teachers praised the creativity and warmth of the American teachers in our films, but many also wondered if in preschools in the United States there was not, perhaps, too little chance for children to enjoy spontaneous, unsupervised child-child interactions and too much emphasis on the child-teacher relationship. For example, a *yochien* mother in Tokyo said of the American film:

> The teacher is so stimulating and creative! The children look happy and bright. Everything looks so exciting. But, as I was watching, I found myself wondering if it might sometimes not get to be too much. I wonder what it is like for a child to be in a class where the teacher is always so fun and creative and exciting, and so important to the children. Wouldn't the children get to be too dependent on the teacher's always being there to organize their play and show them how to have fun?

Developmentally Appropriate Chaos

We have seen that many Japanese preschool parents and educators believe that it is vitally important for teachers to be unlike mothers and for school to be unlike home. A key distinction between the worlds of home and of school is the level of chaos. The home of a young Japanese child at times may be noisy and disheveled but never as chaotic as a *yochien* or a *hoikuen*. This chaos is a result, to a great extent, of school size, class size, and student/teacher ratios. Americans believe that large class size and large student/teacher ratios create the potential for chaos, which in turn creates the necessity for teachers becoming (undesirably) authoritarian and rigid in their approach to children. For example, Clarke-Stewart and Gruber write: "With a larger group of children, aggressive behavior—chaos—in the day care setting cannot be tolerated. Teachers may more actively discourage children from negative behavior with their playmates when there are more of them around."[8]

Though agreeing with Americans that large class size and large student/teacher ratios tend to lead to chaos, many of the Japanese we spoke with view chaos in preschools as normal and even desirable, an important transitional experience between the sheltered life of the homebound toddler and the tumult of the real world. Japanese teachers who believe that a healthy environment for young children includes periods of chaos can teach large groups of children without feeling compelled to become too authoritarian or rigid in an attempt to maintain tight control of the classroom. When we asked Higashino-*sensei*, the assistant principal of Komatsudani, "Doesn't the noise and chaos ever get to you?" she responded: "Aren't children in America wild and noisy? The purpose of preschool is to give children a place to be children. To be a child is to be wild and noisy. Children growing up in Japan these days too miss a chance to get to be real children. I think preschools should give them a chance."

Teaching Group Mindedness in a Changing Japan

In explaining their philosophies of preschool education, several of the Japanese teachers and administrators we spoke with agreed with Higashino that preschools have an increasingly important role to play in helping children grow up in a Japan they view as rapidly changing. Demographic and cultural changes in postwar Japan have led to profound changes in the Japanese family, and these changes are reflected in the way Japanese think about their preschools and, specifically, in how they think about class size and student/teacher ratios.

In the last 100 years, and particularly since the war, there have been a rapid urbanization and nuclearization of the Japanese family.[9] Numbers of children per family have dropped.[10] Young people have moved from the country to the city and from the city to the suburbs, leaving grandparents and other kin behind.[11] The "salari-man" life-style of commuting white-collar husband and nonworking stay-at-home wife has become the ideal typical family structure in contemporary Japan.[12] In the context of these changes, Japanese preschools have grown and flourished, taking over the child-rearing and child-minding functions traditionally performed less by moth-ers than by the extended family and the community (by the *sekken,* the ever-watching, supportive, and critical community of concerned others).[13] Even the Japanese mothers who work full time that we spoke with viewed the role of preschools less as providing a substi-tute form of mothering than as offering something no mother can provide: a first experience of living out in the world.

Parents in contemporary Japan living in inner city high-rises and in apartments in the newly created "bed towns" that ring the larger cities look to preschools to give their children the chance to enjoy the kind of spontaneous interactions with other children that they recall experiencing as children growing up in families of four and five children surrounded by a friendly sea of cousins, family friends, and neighbors. In this rapidly changing world, Japanese believe that it is in preschools, and, specifically, in preschools with large ratios and large classes, that children are most likely to get the chance to interact with other children and to learn *shakaisei* (social consciousness) and *shudan seikatsu* (group life).[14]

Several of the Japanese preschool administrators we spoke with suggested to us that large classes with high student/teacher ratios are traditionally Japanese and that small classes with low ratios are American. But the system of large classes currently in use throughout Japan actually reflects a relatively recent Japanese borrowing from the West. The contemporary Japanese school sys-tem, with large classes and high student/teacher ratios, was devel-oped a little over one hundred years ago in the early Meiji era; it was based on Western educational models of the time and re-vised, under American direction, in the occupation period. Japanese education before Western influence emphasized small classes, individual turorials, hands-on training, and learning through apprenticeship.[15] The contemporary Japanese education system of large class size and large student/teacher ratios is traditionally Japanese less in the sense of being a legacy of the distant past than in the sense of promoting what Japanese believe to be important traditional values. In an era in which family size has shrunk and extended family and community networks of kin, neighbors, and friends are feared to be unraveling, large class size and large ratios have become increasingly important strategies for promoting the traditional Japanese values of groupism and selflessness and for combating what many Japanese believe to be the dangers of Western-style individualism.

Survey questions we included in the questionnaires we distributed following the screenings of our videotapes suggest that Japanese view the most important function of preschools as teaching and promoting groupism. Sixty-one percent of the 280 Japanese preschool administrators, teachers, and parents who filled out our questionnaires chose "to learn to be a member of a group" as their first answer to the question, "What is the most important reason for a society to have preschools?" In contrast, the top American answer was "to make children more independent and self-reliant."

In a discussion that followed a screening of our Japanese and American tapes, Nagami Kengo, the director of a consortium of *yochien* and *hoikuen* in Hiroshima, suggested that large student/teacher ratios in Japan are necessary to promote groupism: "These days in Japan children are growing up in such small families that they don't have the chance to learn what it means to be a member of a group. It is our job as educators of young children to see that children get this experience before they go on to primary school, where they will be expected to know how to behave properly and to be comfortable in large classes." Okubo Chie, an Osaka *hoikuen* administrator, explained:

> The task of the preschool is to produce *ningen-rashii kodomo* [humanlike children].[16] To be fully human is to be not just an individual but also a member of a group. From what I've seen of American schools I would have to say they do a wonderful job of making children creative and self-reliant and individualistic. But as important as those characteristics are, we believe it is also important that children learn how to live as a member of a group. That's the real trick. To find the right balance between individualism and groupism, isn't it? I guess, seeing your films, my personal, honest reaction is that I would have to say we may go too far in the direction of stressing groupism in our preschools. But you see, this is not just a problem of the preschools; it is a problem of our whole society because groupism is stressed not only in our preschools but also in our primary schools and junior highs, and high schools, and universities, and in business and so forth.

Implications for the United States

What lessons are there here for Americans? Japanese perspectives on class size and student/teacher ratios have implications that go beyond the Japanese preschool: they have implications for American preschool pedagogy, implications for ethnically and culturally appropriate approaches to preschool teaching in a multicultural country such as the United States, and implications for cross-cultural preschool research.

Japanese perspectives on preschool education can lead us to ask if there are not, in addition to the obvious benefits, some hidden costs to the American system of preschools of small class size and small student/teacher ratios. These costs may include an overreliance on the teacher as disciplinarian and keeper of the peace with the undesirable side effect of preventing children from coming on their own to an understanding and acceptance of the need for self-control and internalized rules of conduct. A related cost of small student/teacher ratios is that contact with the teacher may become more attractive to children than playing with or paying attention to their peers, thereby undermining children exploring as fully as they otherwise might ways of relating to their age-mates.[17]

Our discussions with parents and teachers in Japan and, more specifically, the comments of Dr. Sakuma, suggest that in preschools (and perhaps at other levels of education as well), there may be a danger zone of ratios and class size from approximately twelve to approximately twenty children per teacher and per class. Inside this danger zone, children may tend to become frustrated and confused as they try to compete for their teacher's attention and approval, just as they would in a smaller class. A teacher with a "danger zone" class of fifteen or sixteen students may be tempted to relate to the children on a one-to-one, interpersonally intense basis but will find herself thwarted in her attempts by the sheer numbers of students in her care. In classes of this size, a student may be tempted to approach the teacher for some individual attention only to be interrupted by one of the other equally needed and now perhaps jealous students. In a class of twelve to twenty children, the illusion that the teacher is available and in control may tend to preclude children becoming a real group and discourage children from taking on roles of leadership and responsibility in the classroom. In classes with ratios greater than 20:1, teachers and students are more likely intuitively to realize that mutually satisfying dyadic interactions between teacher and student are unlikely. In these larger classes, children may tend to have more realistic expectations and to adjust their modes of interaction accordingly.

Our research in Japan suggests that large student/teacher ratios seem to function effectively when preschools employ methods of instruction and teacher-student interaction specifically suited to a large-group format. Most of us in the United States believe large class size and high student/teacher ratios to be, for various reasons, undesirable. But where high ratios are unavoidable, instead of attempting to use a small-class model of instruction with a large class, we might benefit by rethinking our pedagogical strategies more along Japanese lines of thought. When class size grows too large, rather than employing a watered-down, second-rate version of the American, individual-oriented, small-group teaching style, we might do well to look to Japanese large-group preschool teaching techniques, including (1) delegating authority to children, (2) intervening less quickly in children's fights and arguments, (3) having lower expectations for children's noise level and comportment, (4) using more musical cues and less verbal ones, (5) organizing more highly structured, large-group daily activities such as *taiso* (morning group exercise), (6) using a method of choral recitation for answering teacher's questions rather than calling on individuals, and (7) making more use of peer-group approval and opprobrium and less of the teacher's positive and negative reactions to influence children's behavior. Tanaka-*sensei*'s comments about "barefoot" play suggest that working with large groups of young children may require teachers to give up some of the one-to-one relating to children that we find so natural and enjoyable as friends, aunts and uncles, and parents.

Japanese perspectives on preschool class size and student/teacher ratios also hold implications for ethnically and culturally appropriate preschool education in the United States. One question raised by our research is whether the American small-group, low-ratio preschool education model is not better suited to the strengths and needs of some children than of others. The American preschool model, in emphasizing the importance of children verbally expressing individual feelings, staking claim to individual possessions, respecting individual rights, taking pride in individual accomplishments, and talking out interpersonal disputes, may be promoting a personality style more consistent with the values of white middle-class America than with the cultural traditions of black, Hispanic, Asian, or Native Americans.[18]

Conclusion

Our interviews with Japanese parents, teachers, and administrators following screenings of videotapes of typical days in Japanese and American preschools show that Japanese preschools are not just overpopulated versions of preschools in the United States. Instead, Japanese preschool ratios and class size, when explained by the Japanese, can be seen to reflect larger Japanese social and cultural values. Our research suggests that Japanese believe that their preschools, with their large class sizes and high student/teacher ratios, offer the spoiled and overly individualistic mama's boys and girls of today's increasingly middle-class, urban, nuclear-family-oriented Japan the chance to experience the pleasures and responsibilities of life in a group and thus to become, in Japanese terms, fully human.

Notes

1. T. Husen, *International Study of Achievement in Math: A Comparison of Twelve Countries* (New York: Wiley, 1967); H. Stevenson, J. Stigler, and S. Lee, "Achievement in Mathematics," in *Child Development and Education in Japan* (New York: Freeman, 1986), 201–16.

2. The idea of using film in this way—and specifically for turning ethnographic subjects into authors by recording their reactions as they watch a film about themselves—came from Linda Conner and the compelling series of ethnographic films she made in Bali with Tim and Patsy Asch (see Linda Conner, Timothy Asch, and Patsy Asch, *Jero Tapakan: Balinese Healer* [Boston: Cambridge University Press, 1986]).

3. Questionnaires distributed to parents, teachers, administrators, and education students who watched our twenty-minute tapes of Chinese, Japanese, and American preschools used five-point Likert-scaled items to quantify responses to our tapes. Respondents were asked to make judgments about each culture's preschool on twenty items, including strength of the curriculum, children's activity level, materials, safety, warmth of teachers, and overall quality of the program.

4. Generally, the term "emic analysis" is used to refer to an outsider (usually an anthropologist) explaining a foreign culture using insider's terms and concepts. We introduce the term "autoethnography" (after the term "autobiography") to refer to the more direct presentation of insider's theories about themselves and their institutions. We use the term "ethno-ethnology" to refer to people of one culture's beliefs about another culture's people, customs, and institutions. Thus, the study in this paper of Japanese parents', teachers', and administrators' thoughts about American preschools is an example of an ethno-ethnological approach.

5. J. Belsky, "Two Waves of Day Care Research, Developmental Conditions of Quality," in *The Child and the Day Care Setting* (New York: Praeger, 1984), 26–27.

6. S. Feeney and R. Chun, "Effective Teachers of Young Children," *Young Children* 41 (November 1985): 47–52.

7. Though teachers of three-, four-, and five-year-old children in *yochien* (nursery schools) try to be nonmotherlike, the situation is quite different for *hoikuen* (day-care) teachers caring for infants. In the nursery section of the Japanese day-care center, teachers clearly play motherly roles toward the children in their care.

8. A. Clarke-Stewart and C. Gruber, "Day Care Forms and Features," in *The Child and the Day Care Setting,* ed. R. Ainslie (New York: Praeger, 1984).

9. T. Koyama, "Changing Family Structure in Japan," in *Japanese Culture: Its Development and Characteristics,* ed. R. Smith and R. Beardsley (Chicago: Aldine, 1962).

10. T. Iritani, *The Value of Children: A Cross-national Study,* vol. 6, *Japan* (Honolulu: East-West Center, 1979).

11. S. Linhart, "Changing Family Structure and Problems of Older People in Japan: Present Trends and Future Prospects," in *Social Structures and Economic Dynamics in Japan up to 1980,* vol. 1, ed. G. Fodella and M. Gianna (Milan: Luigi Bocconi University, 1975); I. Taeuber, *The Population of Japan* (Princeton, N.J.: Princeton University Press, 1958).

12. Ezra Vogel, *Japan's New Middle Class* (Berkeley: University of California Press, 1971).

13. M. White and R. LeVine, "What is an *Ii Ko?*" in *Child Development in Japan,* ed. H. Stevenson, H. Azuma, and K. Hakuta (New York: Freeman, 1986).

14. "They Reflect Cultural Values in Young Children?" *Young Children* 38 (1983): 13–24. For *shudan seikatsu,* see Taniuchi, "Inter-Relationships between Home and Early Formal Learning Situations for Japanese Children" (paper presented at the meeting of the Comparative and International Education Society, New York, November 26, 1984).

15. Ronald Dore, *Education in Tokugawa Japan* (Berkeley: University of California Press, 1965); Richard Rubinger, *Academies of Tokugawa Japan* (Princeton, N.J.: Princeton University Press, 1982).

16. Shigaki; White and LeVine.

17. T. Field, "Preschool Play: Effects of Teacher/Child Ratios and Organization of Classroom Space," *Child Study Journal* 10, no. 3 (1983): 191–205; J. Reuter and G. Yunik, "Social Interaction in Nursery Schools," *Developmental Psychology* 9, no. 3 (1973): 319–25.

18. For a discussion of class and ethnic differences in day care, see Vivian Suransky, *The Erosion of Childhood* (Chicago: University of Chicago Press, 1982).

6

Japan's Group Orientation in Secondary Schools

Hiroshi F. Iwama

Japan's school management system is much more group-oriented than that of America. In this type of society, teamwork, cooperation, consensus in a group, harmony, group effectiveness, equal treatment of members, devotion to the organization, and members' participation are expected. The basic motivation in Japanese society seems to be "social needs," or needs for belonging, and for acceptance by fellow members. Each group member tends to avoid being seen with members from different groups. And the value of individualism, uniqueness, and independence seems to be less important than the value of teamwork and cooperation in this society. Japan's school system is not an exception; Japan's school management system as well as Japan's society are deeply group-oriented systems.

Japan's Group-Oriented Society

From the beginning of Japan's history, harmony in society was emphasized. For instance, about 1,400 years ago Shotoku Taishi, who was one of the most important men in Japan's history, as the first crowned prince and regent to his aunt, the Empress Suiko carried out political reforms and established official and cultural relations with the dynasty of China. And he made a profound study of Confucianism and Buddhism, introduced Buddhism more widely to Japan, and stressed respect for harmony in his *Constitution of Seventeen Articles,* which is a statement of fundamental precepts relating to the maintenance of the state and the observance of morality.[1] This *Constitution* has deeply influenced Japanese society throughout history.

Going back as far as two or three centuries before the time of Christ, rice has been growing in Japan. Aside from the plentiful rainfall between June and July, rice cultivation demands enormous amounts of labor. Close cooperation over the sharing of water resources and labor between neighborhoods of small communities is needed, and "such cooperative efforts over the centuries have contributed to the notable Japanese penchant for group identification and group action."[2]

During the Tokugawa, or Edo, Period (1600–1868), when Shoguns governed Japan for over 250 years without war, the group spirit spread over Japan.

> Samurai were organized into bands of retainers (*kashindan*) and further into smaller personnel units (*kumi*), each with its unit head or disciplinary officer. Peasants were organized by village (*mura*) and further into mutually responsible groups (*goningumi*), usually consisting of ten families. Thus they came first under the authority of the group head and then the village headman (*shoya* or *nanushi*). The smallest unit of Tokugawa society was the family (ie), and the individual existed only as a member of the family—as family head, as son and heir, as second son, daughter, wife, and the like. Family status and the preservation of the family unit, to which all property and privileges adhered, became a matter of deep concern at all levels of society.[3]

In order to give a philosophical background to Tokugawa's new legal and political order, neo-Confucian doctrines were introduced into Japan's society. Concepts of loyalty to the political order (*chu*) and to the family (*ko*) universalized the most basic social requisites of the age. Abstract concepts of status-conduct provided its "way" (*do*), such as *bushido* (the way of the samurai) or *chonindo* (the way of the merchant).[4]

In contrast, the spirit of independence and the value of individuals came to be emphasized by new leaders in the transition between the end of Tokugawa Period and Meiji Period (1868–1911).

One of the leaders of that period was Fukuzawa Yukichi who traveled to the West several times, wrote immensely popular books, such as *Seiyo Jijo* (*Conditions in the Occident*), founded Keio University, and took a leading role in the 1860s and 1870s in popularizing knowledge about the West. In particular, he stressed the importance of individual self-reliance as the secret of Western success through two very influential translations, Samuel Smiles' *Self-Help* and John Mill's *On Liberty*.[5] His emphasis on self-reliance or independence challenged the dominant philosophy of his age, neo-Confucism. But in spite of the effort of new leaders in the Meiji Period, and the strong influence of American policy after the Pacific War, Japan's society still retains its original spirit of harmony, cooperation, and team work.

Today Japanese society is still group-oriented. For example, Yoshio Yoshida, who guided the Hanshin Tigers to their first Japan Baseball League title in thirty-five years, in response to the question "What was the main reason for the victory?" answered, "The 3-F philosophy: 'fresh,' 'fighting spirit,' and 'for the team,' and that we play as a team were the main reasons."[6] Usually this kind of answer arouses sympathy and moves people in Japan. In popular cartoons and television dramas and movies emphasis is on team work, not on one superhero or heroine as is the case in America.

A group or team of employees of a Japanese company assumes joint responsibility for a set of tasks. "They know quite clearly that each of them is completely responsible for all tasks, and they share that responsibility jointly."[7] This is typical of Japanese team play. Moreover, compared to the American corporate system, Japanese decision-making and job responsibility is collective, not individual. All through the Japanese company, teamwork, cooperation, consensus, equalization, human relationships, consciousness of belonging, and devotion to the company are observed.

Japan's Group-Oriented School Management

Japan's school management system is not an exception. "Students talk about improving their performance in group sessions of self-reflection. Self-discipline is taught through stories of great men and women and in discussing classroom procedures for the group."[8] The school organization centers on small groups, as do so many Japanese organizations, and this makes morale, leadership, and participation into crucial managerial concerns, for they are critical to the effectiveness of a group-based approach. Shimahara points out that cooperation, participation, and group-centeredness as well as orderliness, precision, and diligence are very important to Japanese school functions as a moral community.[9] Cogan emphasizes that a standardized educational system in Japan helps to keep Japan homogeneous and monocultural, even as it affords learners both equality of educational opportunity and socialization into the kind of consensus-seeking that characterizes adult life in Japan. On the other hand, in America, Cogan says, individual initiative and independent thinking are highly valued, so a decentralized educational system better serves American interests.[10]

In the group-oriented system, usually the full participation of members is characteristic. Cummings indicates that it is of considerable interest to find that Japanese teachers participate extensively in the government of their schools—much more so than is found in the United States. The various schedules, teacher and student class assignments, and a multitude of other matters are all made at teachers' meetings, even though officially the teachers' meeting is not a decision making mechanism, but the organizational arm of the principal. These meetings are held every morning for about five minutes and for an hour or so one afternoon per week, and are chaired on a rotating basis by each of the teachers.[11]

The Iwaizumi Town Public Junior High School in Iwate Prefecture

In the Iwaizumi Junior High School, a short teachers' meeting is held from 8:10 to 8:20 every morning, Monday through Saturday. Another longer meeting is held once a month from 3:00 to 3:55 P.M. on a Thursday. Unlike American schools, each Japanese school has a large teachers' room next to the principal's room where each teacher has a desk and meetings are held. Teachers of music, art, industrial arts, home economics, science, and physical education have their own rooms, but they also have desks in the teachers' room. The teachers' room is used in various ways, such as for meetings, communication between teachers, and between teachers and students, preparation and evaluation work for teaching, individual study, and drinking tea or coffee. This arrangement provides a good example of Japanese group-oriented life.

In addition, Japanese teachers share in various roles beyond teaching, such as heavy student guidance duties.[12] Unlike. the

United States, teachers in Japan have a twelve-month contract, and are prohibited from having another job even during vacation or after school. Many teachers work for a couple of hours in their schools after their official responsibilities are over and sometimes they work at school during the long vacations.

Students also have many opportunities to participate in school management in Japan. They perform a great variety of managerial tasks: they call roll, clean classrooms and buildings, serve their own lunches, run the intercom system, develop and enforce codes of conduct, plan and manage sports days, and take virtually total responsibility for the diverse program of school clubs. Moreover, they organize some student committees, such as the students' Central Committee, and the committees of grades, clubs, special subjects, and cheering party.[13]

Parents participate in school activities through the Parents Teachers Association (PTA) and generally support school management, especially in Japan's elementary and junior high schools. Three mothers and sometimes a father are chosen to participate in the council on the PTA from each homeroom and the most active among these are made officers. The council meets rarely, but the officers frequently telephone council members or send out notices. On the other hand, the officers meet almost weekly with the school principal and thus have abundant opportunity to learn about the school as well as to convey parental concerns.[14]

Daily School Schedule

In a group-oriented society, meetings are regarded as important for maintaining harmony, consensus, and good relationships within the group. Hence, there are various meetings in Japanese schools (see Table 1), such as a morning gathering (*chorei*), short homeroom meetings, long homeroom meetings, teachers' meetings, meetings of various committees, and PTA meetings.

In the case of Iwaizumi Junior High School, the morning gathering is usually held on Monday, when the principal, vice principal, the whole staff, and all students gather together and line up on the school grounds or in the gymnasium. At that time there is a short speech by the principal and various announcements from teachers and reports from students on committees. Other morning gatherings are held for each grade level on other days. Athletic team members and their managers also meet on a regular basis.

Table 1. Daily schedule in 1983,[15] Iwaizumi Town Junior High School

Time	Monday	Tuesday	Wednesday	Thursday	Friday	Saturday
8:10	Staff and Students Arrival					
8:10–8:20	Teachers' Meeting and Students' Self-Study					
8:20–8:35	School Morning Gathering	Short Homeroom Meeting				
8:40–9:30	1 Moral Education	Morning Gathering 7th *	Morning Gathering 9th *	Morning Gathering 8th *	*	*
9:40–10:30	2*	*	*	*	*	*
10:40–11:30	3*	*	*	*	*	*
11:40–12:30	4*	*	*	*	*	11:35–11:50 Cleaning 11:55–12:05 Short Homeroom 12:05 Students Dismissal 12:10 Staff Dismissal
12:35–1:00				Lunch		
1:00–1:45				Break		
1:45–2:00				Cleaning		
2:05–2:55	5*	*	*	*	*	
3:05–3:55	6*		Required Clubs	Short Homeroom	Counseling, Study, or Short Homeroom	
Mon, Tue, Thurs. 3:00–3:20 (Wed: 4:00–4:50)						
3:20–4:50		Club Activities			Long Homeroom or Committees	
4:50–4:55	Students and Staff Dismissal					

* = Various Subjects

Just as Japanese teachers have their common room, Japanese students have common classrooms. Students remain in the same classroom except for special subjects such as music, art, industrial arts, home economics, science, and physical education, when students move to "special rooms" (*tokubetsu kyoshitsu*), usually as a group. The students have about a ten-minute break between study hours when they usually stay in their rooms and talk with classmates. On the other hand, the break between classes in American schools is shorter and students do not have time to talk with their friends because they have to go quickly to other rooms. American secondary schools do have homeroom hours in the morning, but these hours do not seem to be used effectively. Rohlen reports on the Japanese common classroom system as follows:

> Each classroom is a homeroom, the students of the same homeroom stay together in the same classroom for most of the day. For an entire year they take all their courses together, including physical education and electives. American high school homerooms, by contrast, are of little consequence. An American student's locker is typically his or her most permanent physical location, and student groups are continually forming and disbanding from one class period to the next, both within and outside classrooms. Whole grades are rarely together physically even at assemblies in American schools.[16]

The Japanese homeroom system with a single homeroom teacher, the same classmates, and a common room, remains a family system in school. In the classroom, especially in the homeroom, students discuss their problems or plans with each other and with their teacher. The homeroom system was introduced from America after the Pacific War, but it has been Japanized in the group-oriented Japanese society.

Unlike students in American schools, students in Japan take their lunch to their classrooms except for a small number of schools which have a cafeteria system. There is a rotating group of four or five students who serve lunch each day. They wear white aprons and masks and deliver lunch from a kitchen in the school to their classrooms. Classroom teachers also eat with their students, and at that time table manners are taught. The Japanese school lunch system as a reflection of the family system is tightly connected to Japan's classroom management system. Hence, if a Japanese student who is familiar with Japan's lunch system studies in an American school, he or she will be at a loss.

Keiko Ono, who spent one year in an American senior high school in St. Louis, describes her first experience in the American school in her book *American School Life* as follows:

> As soon as I step out of the room, I could not find any place to go or any people to meet. I became sad every lunch time. I wondered where and how I should take lunch. . . . I have no place to stay! Where should I go? Who am I? What am I doing here? Why am I here? What is the meaning of me?— When I lost the identity of a proud "foreign student," I almost lost myself.[17]

After a couple of months, she finally conquered those fears, which are not unusual for many junior and senior high school students who come from Japan to study in the United States. Even American students often report feeling alienated or painfully anonymous amid the mass of students flowing to and from classes in American large high schools.[18]

Cleaning

From elementary school to senior high school, students take turns cleaning their classrooms, rest rooms and hallways by themselves after classes each day. Of course, there are some custodians in Japanese schools, but the number is small, and their main job is repairing or maintaining school buildings. In some schools even teachers share in the cleaning.

Yutaka Okihara, President of Hiroshima University and professor of comparative education in Japan, emphasizes in his book *School Cleaning (Gakko Soji)* that Japan's school cleaning system has a significant background in Japanese culture and tradition. Japanese take off their shoes in the house, they do "general house cleaning" (*ōsoji*) once or twice a year, and Japan's temples and shrines are cleaned frequently. Through the influence of Shintoism and Buddhism, it is felt that cleaning means keeping the mind as well as keeping the body and surrounding places clean. Cleaning has been regarded as one of the significant processes of training in Buddhism.[19]

Student cleaning as well as the lunch service in Japanese schools is a form of moral education. Cummings reports:

> This lunch routine contains several moral messages: no work, not even the dirty work of cleaning, is too low for a student; all should share equally in common tasks; the maintenance of the school is everyone's responsibility. To underline

these messages, on certain days each year the entire school body from the youngest student to the principal put on their dirty clothes and spend a couple of hours in a comprehensive cleaning of the school building and grounds.[20]

The moral meaning of cleaning is related to the group-oriented way of living, because members of a group feel responsibility to their buildings. Rohlen reports:

> Students are responsible for their homerooms and setting things straight after school is everybody's job, at least in principle. Little tasks are parceled out so that everyone has some formal role to play. One student wipes the blackboards after each class, another carries messages to the teachers' room, and others represent the homeroom on committees.[21]

Club Activities

In Japanese junior high schools, there are two kinds of student clubs. One is "required club activities," which are compulsory, and each student must choose one club that meets once a week. In the case of Iwaizumi Town Junior High School, required club activities are held from 3:00 to 3:55 P.M. every Wednesday. The other type of activity is called "after-school club activities." Participation is not compulsory, and most clubs meet every day after school for about an hour, and on Saturday they might meet longer. Moreover, active sport clubs meet even during vacation periods, aiming at local or interscholastic tournaments. It is not unusual for young teachers to devote time to coaching the clubs.

Unlike students in America, Japanese students belong to only one club at a time, and membership is expected to last for the duration of junior or senior high school. Older club members are addressed respectfully as *sempai.* Cummings reports:

> In our own study of several Kyoto middle schools it was found that 80 percent of all first- and second-year middle schools participated in these club activities, and over half participated on a daily basis. The clubs were organized along remarkably democratic lines and clearly reinforced many of the norms for group interaction, instilled during the primary school experience. They encouraged participation, expressiveness, and cooperation, and deemphasized competition. Students viewed these activities as the most rewarding part of their school experience, and indeed of their lives.[22]

Clearly, through school meetings, homeroom meetings, school lunches, the classroom cleaning system and club activities, Japan's daily school schedule has a tightly group-oriented structure.

Annual School Calendar

There are many more days of school in Japan than in America. While the minimum number of school days is 210 in Japan, most schools are in session from 240 to 250 days, in contrast to about 180 days in the United States. In the case of Iwaizumi Town Junior High School, there are 245 school days a year. The students are not always at their desks, but they participate in various events, such as ceremonies, festivals, excursions, and class trips. For example, in Iwaizumi Junior High School, the following meetings or activities were held in 1983: entrance ceremony (April) and graduation ceremony (March), open ceremonies (April, August, January), athletic meetings (May, September), school excursions, seventh, eighth, and ninth grades (May), cultural festival (November), joint athletic meeting of all junior high schools in Shimokita district (June), baseball tournaments for all junior high schools in Shimokita district (July), Shimokita district track and field meets (September), Shimokita district long-distance relays (October), chorus contest (October), eighth grade camp (July), students' general meetings (May, November), election of student associations (November), round-table meeting of districts, students' general meetings (May), teachers-parents-students' meeting (ninth grade, January), teachers meeting for study (June, September, November, February), teachers' visit to students' homes (April), refuge training (November), mid- and end-of-term exams (June, July, October, December, February), summer vacation (July-August), and spring vacation (March).[23]

On the basis of a review of the annual calendar of Igusa Public Junior High School in Suginami-ku, Tokyo, with 775 students in seventh, eighth, and ninth grade, other meetings can be added, such as recreation meeting (May), "moving school" teachers and students of certain grades spend about three days at a public school's associated facility in the country for swimming training and coaching (July, August), "general cleaning" (ōsoji) (September, January), and a joint music festival (November).[24] These various activities are classified as "special activities" in Japan's Course of Studies. According to the *Course of Study for Lower Secondary Schools in Japan,* the overall objectives of special activities are described as follows: "Through desirable group activities, to promote harmonious development of mind and body, to develop the individuality, to enhance the self-awareness of being a member of a group and to cultivate self-reliant, independent and a practical attitude and to enrich the school life in cooperation with others."[25] Thus the *Course of Study* aims at the development of student individuality through cooperation. Following the *Course of Study,* the object of field activities in Iwaizumi Junior High School is described as follows: (1) to promote a sympathetic relationship between teachers and students, and among students, and (2) to help students recognize the importance of cooperation and rules in a group through the class and group activities.[26]

Morri Robertson, a child of an American father and Japanese mother, experienced both American and Japanese schools, and writes of his experience in a Japanese junior high school as follows:

> A sense of togetherness between myself and the school was engraved in my young and soft mind by taking, together with teachers and students, a two-day trip after entering the school, a marathon race, long-distance swimming, summer judo club training camp, athletic meetings in the Spring and Fall, and the school culture festival for several days.[27]

This is a description of typical Japanese school life. In a group-oriented society, members' participation is very important. Except for some contests or competitions, such as track and field and music and others, participation of all students is usually required. In terms of this, Rohlen writes as follows:

> Full participation is an important value taught by school events. This is the cornerstone of the long homeroom discussion. Teachers and students discuss how pleased they are that not one homeroom member missed Sports Day, or that special funds have been found so that no one will miss the class trip. The concern with full participation in Japanese high schools is a concern with maintaining the basis of the community spirit.[28]

In summary, Japan has been a tightly group-oriented society throughout its history as reflected in its culture, way of life, and today in its school management system. Overall, the school management system in Japan operates very effectively in encouraging cooperation and team work and the harmonious development of individual students. Indeed, there could be some very important lessons for America's highly individualized and departmentalized high school system which has been subject to so much criticism in national reports over the last few years.

Notes

1. Taro Sakamoto, *Japanese History* (Tokyo: The International Society for Educational Information Press, Inc., 1971), 19.

2. Edwin O. Reischauer, *The Japanese* (Tokyo: Charles E. Tuttle, 1977), 17.

3. John Whitney Hall, *Japan, from Prehistory to Modern Times* (New York: Dell, 1970), 180–81.

4. Ibid., 184.

5. Reishauer, 128.

6. *The Japan Times* (November 3, 1985), 11.

7. William G. Ouchi, *Theory Z: How American Business Can Meet the Japanese Challenge* (Reading, Mass.: Addison-Wesley, 1981), 46.

8. Diane Profita Schiller and Herbert J. Walberg, "Japan: The Learning Society," *Educational Leadership* 39, no. 6 (March 1982): 412.

9. Nobuo K. Shimahara, "Japanese Education and Its Implications for U.S. Education," *Phi Delta Kappan* 66, no. 6 (February 1985): 420.

10. John J. Cogan, "Should the U.S. Mimic Japanese Education? Let's Look Before We Leap," *Phi Delta Kappan* 65, no. 7 (March 1984): 464.

11. William K. Cummings, *Education for Equality in Japan* (Princeton: Princeton University Press, 1980), 143.

12. Iwaizumi Town Junior High School, *School Handbook of Iwaizumi Town Junior High School* (1983), 7.

13. Ibid., 10.

14. William K. Cummings, 141.

15. Iwaizumi Town Junior High School, 7.

16. Thomas P. Rohlen, *Japan's High Schools* (Berkeley: University of California Press, 1983), 150–51.

17. Keiko Ono, *American High School Life: My Experience as a Foreign Student* (Tokyo: Obunsha, 1984), 68.

18. Rohlen, 179.

19. Yukata Okihara, *School Cleaning (Gakko Soji)* (Tokyo: Gakuji, 1982), 19–123.

20. Cummings, 117.

21. Rohlen, 179.

22. Cummings, 98–99.

23. Iwaizumi Town Junior High School, 9.

24. Igusa Junior High School, Suginami-ku, Tokyo, *School Handbook* (1983), 6.

25. Japan, Ministry of Education, Science and Culture, *Course of Study for Lower Secondary Schools* (Tokyo: The Ministry, 1983), 126.

26. Iwaizumi Town Junior High School, *Plan for Counseling in 1983*.

27. Morri Robertson, *Often Alone (Yoku Hitoribocchi-datta)* (Tokyo: Bungei-shunjyu-sha, 1984), 42.

28. Rohlen, 203.

7

The Asian Advantage: The Case of Mathematics

Harold W. Stevenson

Poor performance of American children compared to their peers in other countries is evident as early as kindergarten. In mathematics, for example, Japanese five-year-olds greatly out-perform their American peers. After kindergarten, the difference becomes even more obvious. Japanese children maintain their superior status throughout elementary school, while American children's scores show a relative decline. The picture is equally distressing when comparing children in the U.S. with Chinese children in Taiwan. Although Chinese five-year-olds perform at about the same level in mathematics as American five-year-olds, they improve in their relative status throughout the elementary school years. The consequence of these disparities is evident in a comparison of the scores of fifth graders attending a representative sample of twenty schools in the Chicago metropolitan area with children attending a total of 31 schools in Taipei (Taiwan), Sendai (Japan), and Beijing (People's Republic of China). Fifth-graders in only one of the Chicago schools produced average scores as high as the *lowest* average score of fifth-grade classrooms in the representative Asian schools.

An earlier version of this essay was published in *American Educator* (the quarterly journal of the American Federation of Teachers). Copyright © 1987 by the American Federation of Teachers.

This data can be viewed in another way. The samples we tested consisted of approximately 3,500 first-graders and 3,500 fifth-graders, equally divided among the schools in the four cities. Among the students in the top fifth percentile at grade one across all four cities, there were only three American children. Over forty would have been expected if children in each city had performed equally well. The top fifth percentile of fifth-graders contained only two American children. Among the worst students in mathematics, those in the bottom fifth percentile, there were 163 American children at grade one and 181 at grade five. It should be pointed out that these conclusions are not restricted to Chicago, for the results parallel those of a previous study in which we compared first-and fifth-graders in the Minneapolis metropolitan area—which has a more middle-class school population than Chicago—with their counterparts in Sendai and Taipei. For example, only one Minneapolis fifth-grader was among the one hundred top scorers from these three cities in a test of mathematics achievement. In both of these studies, care was taken to construct tests based on the textbooks actually used by the children and to obtain representative samples of children in each of the cities visited.

Data such as these raise serious questions about our national priorities. Is it appropriate to give our main emphasis to improving mathematics training at the upper grades? Remediation is an expensive route to improvement. Would not prevention be preferable, by providing better training earlier in the children's schooling? How can parents be drawn into the picture? Poor performance on a test of elementary mathematical concepts given shortly after children enter kindergarten must reflect the effects of both home and school training. What do Japanese and Chinese parents and teachers provide their children that results in such outstanding performance?

We have sought to answer these questions by interviewing children in kindergarten, first grade, and fifth grade, as well as their mothers and their teachers, about their satisfactions, expectations, and beliefs and about the children's lives at home and at school. We have interviewed hundreds of individuals in Chicago, Minneapolis, Sendai, Taipei, and Beijing. The children in each city were given achievement and intelligence tests, and extensive observations were made of the daily conduct of their classrooms. The data cited in this article are based on these studies.

First, the Myths

American conceptions of Asia are often incorrect. There are few comparative studies, and the information they contain is often misinterpreted. It is important, therefore, to begin by clarifying some of these misconceptions.

Are Asians More Intelligent than Americans?

The cover story of a national magazine a few years ago asked whether the Asian advantage in educational achievement and industrial development was not due to the simple fact that Asians are smarter than Americans (and presumably other Westerners). Confusion between tests of achievement and tests of intelligence and the results of a study reported by Irish psychologist Richard Lynn led many persons to reach an affirmative answer. In fact, while Japanese and Chinese children lead American children in academic achievement, there is no evidence that they are brighter. What Lynn found was that when the responses of Japanese children on a commonly used test of intelligence were scored on the basis of American norms, the average IQ of the Japanese children was significantly above the American average. This would have been interesting information if it were not for the fact that the Japanese data were derived from samples of urban children selected without consideration of their socioeconomic status, while the American norms were based on a truly representative sample of urban and rural children of all socioeconomic levels. We can disregard this study and other studies in which insufficient attention has been paid to critical issues in sampling.

Moreover, when comparable samples have been used, no difference in intellectual functioning has been found. In one of our studies, we tested large samples of elementary school children on ten tasks of the types found in intelligence tests. American children actually obtained higher scores than Chinese and Japanese children in kindergarten; by the fifth grade the overall scores of the three groups of children were equivalent.

Do Asian Children Get an Earlier Start?

The assumption is sometimes made that higher achievement among Chinese and Japanese children is due to their receiving formal instruction earlier than American children. This is not the case. Japanese children may learn to play the violin early, but they receive little early instruction in mathematics. In over 300 hours of observation in kindergartens in Taipei, Sendai, and Minneapolis, we found that the greatest percentage of time spent in direct teaching and structured experiences occurred in the American classrooms. American kindergarten teachers spent 90 percent of their classroom time in such activities, while the Chinese teachers spent only 61 percent and the Japanese teachers 65 percent. Most of the rest of the time was spent in free play and informal types of learning. These approaches to kindergarten education fit the goals of the American and Asian mothers. When asked what they expected their children to acquire during kindergarten, 95 percent of the Japanese mothers, and only 55 percent of the American mothers, mentioned social experience. On the other hand, only 3 percent of the Japanese mothers, and 27 percent of the American mothers, mentioned educational and cognitive goals. The expressed expectations of Chinese mothers fell between those of their Japanese and American counterparts.

The kindergarten observations are also in line with what the mothers told us about their efforts to teach their kindergarten children. Among American mothers, 88 percent said they had taught their child the alphabet at home. Only 33 percent of the Chinese mothers said they had taught their children the symbols used to denote the sounds of Chinese characters, and 31 percent of the Japanese mothers said they had taught their children the symbols for Japanese syllables. The percentages of mothers teaching numbers at home were very similar: 90 percent of American mothers, 64 percent of the Chinese mothers, and 36 percent of the Japanese mothers said they had attempted to teach their children numbers.

Thus, the superiority of Asian children in mathematics would not appear to result from early formal instruction. If anything, our data point to the possibility that young children may benefit more from informal learning situations than from more direct forms of teaching.

The Influence of the *Kyoiku Mama*

Another myth is that of the *kyoiku mama,* the Japanese "educational mom." The maternal image often depicted in Western publications is that of a pushy, demanding, homebound tutor. It is more appropriate to describe the Japanese mother as someone who seeks to provide a nurturant and protected atmosphere for learning. She is ready to assist her child in doing homework if she can, but her major goals are to promote the child's interest and involvement in school and to make sure that the child is progressing appropriately.

In Japanese society it is primarily mothers, and in Chinese society it is all members of the family, who strive to motivate and aid children in their academic work. Through daily supervision of homework and expression of concern and support for their children's academic activities, an environment is created in Chinese and Japanese homes that fosters educational achievement. At times, this means that children are relieved of all responsibilities for assisting in family activities. One of the Chinese mothers we interviewed, for example, said it would break her heart to have her assign her child chores. This, she explained, would take her child away from much-needed time for study.

But Is It All Rote Learning?

Many Westerners subscribe to the myth that Asian classrooms are characterized by group recitation and rote learning. Neither of these are valid descriptions of the lively interactions that occur. Teachers in Chinese and Japanese classrooms rarely rely on choral responding and group reading. In our observations, we found that less than 2 percent of the time was spent in choral responding in Japanese and American classrooms, and less than 10 percent in the Chinese classrooms. Group readings occurred less than 1 percent of the time in all three settings.

Rather than emphasizing rote learning in mathematics, Asian teachers utilize a variety of approaches that stress applications, problem solving, and abstract representations of problems. The consequences of these efforts is evident in the children's performance. Not only did we find that Chinese and Japanese children surpassed American children in tests of mathematical operations that have been described, but they also received significantly higher scores than American children in tests involving word problems, number concepts, graphs and tables, spatial relations, geometry, visualization, and estimation.

Does High Achievement Exact a Psychological Toll?

A final common misconception about Asian children is that their high achievement is accomplished at great psychological cost. The high suicide rate of youth in Japan is often pointed out as evidence.

It is true that Japan's youth suicide rate was nearly three times that of the United States during the 1950s, a time when Japanese youth were presumably depressed about their country's future following its defeat in World War II. Since then, however, the suicide rate in Japan has declined, so that the current rate is approximately the same in both Japan and the United States.

Further, we have failed to discover any signs of special tension in the course of our observations and interviews. Chinese, Japanese, and American elementary school children alike appear to be cheerful, enthusiastic, vigorous, and responsive. Although some of these characteristics may be more vividly expressed in American classrooms, they are readily apparent to the observer who follows Chinese and Japanese children through their school day. In fact, when we initiated a discussion of children's tension patterns with our Chinese colleagues, we found that we were describing types of behavior that were unfamiliar to them. Hyperactivity, hair-twisting, lip-biting, and other indices of tension are rarely observed in Chinese and Japanese classrooms. Perhaps the picture changes in junior high school and high school, but the accomplishments of Asian children during elementary school do not seem to be attained at any notable psychic cost.

We must search for other explanations of the Asian advantage in mathematics.

Our Good Opinion of Ourselves

If children believe they are already doing well—and if their parents agree with them—what is the purpose of studying harder? Children who have unrealistically high self-evaluations may see little reason to study hard, and this may well be the case with the American children. When asked to rate such characteristics as ability in mathematics, brightness, and scholastic performance, American students gave themselves the highest ratings, while Japanese students gave themselves the lowest. American children believed their parents and teachers were more satisfied with their performance and worried less about their own performance in school than did Chinese and Japanese children. When asked how well they would do in mathematics in high school, 58 percent of American fifth-graders said they expected to be above average or among the best students. These percentages were much higher than those of their

Chinese and Japanese peers, among whom only 26 percent and 29 percent, respectively, were this optimistic.

Perhaps these answers represent in part a tendency toward wishful thinking by American children and excessive modesty by the Asian children. But the evaluations made by the children's mothers followed a similar pattern.

Mothers were asked to rate their children on seven attributes, such as intelligence, attention, motivation, ability to learn, ability to remember, and ability to express themselves verbally. On only one scale—that of persistence—did American mothers fail to give their children higher average ratings than those given by the Chinese and Japanese mothers.

Not only did American mothers generally have the most favorable evaluations of their children, they also were the most satisfied with their child's current academic performance. More Americans than Japanese and Chinese children believed their mothers were satisfied, and the mothers' ratings were in line with this belief. Many more American mothers than Chinese and Japanese mothers were "very satisfied" with their children's performance. Mothers also were asked to evaluate the effectiveness of the schools in educating their children. American mothers were very positive: 91 percent judged the schools as doing an "excellent" or "good" job. This was more than double the percentage of Chinese mothers (42 percent) and Japanese mothers (39 percent) who chose these categories.

Within each culture, the mothers' ratings were related to their children's actual levels of achievement. In each case, the scores of children whose mothers were "very satisfied" differed from those mothers who were "satisfied," and these in turn differed from those of mothers who were "not satisfied" with their children's achievement. But the levels of performance related to these levels of satisfaction differed greatly among the three cultural groups. On the average, American mothers said they were very satisfied when their children were at around the seventieth percentile in achievement in mathematics and reading. Chinese and Japanese mothers who expressed such satisfaction had children whose average score was around the eighty-fourth percentile. American children whose mothers said they were not satisfied with their child's performance had an average percentile score of 16, while Chinese and Japanese children had only to be in approximately the thirty-fifth percentile for their mothers to be unhappy with their performance.

In summary, American children had to do less well than Chinese and Japanese children for their mothers to be satisfied and much worse before their mothers expressed dissatisfaction with their academic performance. Such high evaluations of ability and achievement by the American children and their mothers cannot be conducive to a child's diligent study.

Difficulty of Curriculum

Why should American children perceive themselves as being good at mathematics, when cross-cultural comparisons show that they perform relatively poorly? One obvious explanation is that the mathematics curriculum in the United States is less difficult than the curricula in Japan and Taiwan. Children's ratings of how difficult they found mathematics support this interpretation. American children thought mathematics was easy: 58 percent at grade one and 40 percent at grade five thought it was "easy" or "very easy." Judgments by Japanese children, on the other hand, were more sober: only 32 percent at grade one and 30 percent at grade five thought mathematics was "easy" or "very easy." The opinions of Chinese children changed greatly between grades one and five; there was a decrease from 64 percent to 22 percent in the percentage who thought it was "easy" or "very easy."

These assessments have some basis in reality. We have analyzed the point at which various concepts and skills are introduced in mathematics textbooks used in Taipei, Sendai, and Minneapolis, and determined that Japanese textbooks are more difficult than Chinese or American textbooks. That is, although the Japanese and the American curricula contained approximately equal numbers of concepts and skills, they were introduced earlier in the Japanese curriculum. Japan was first in introducing (or was tied for first for) 68 percent of the common topics in the textbooks. Taiwan was first, or tied for first, 18 percent of the time, and the United States, 28 percent of the time. The earlier appearance of the materials in the Japanese textbooks gives the Japanese children a greater opportunity during the elementary school years to practice these skills and use these concepts than is possible for the American children.

Two Philosophies on Working Hard

The dedication of students, parents, and teachers to children's schooling depends on the degree to which they believe that this devotion will yield important benefits to the children. Such a belief is closely related to theories of human behavior long espoused in Asian philosophies.

The malleability of human behavior has often been described in Chinese writings. Uniformity of human nature is assumed; differences arising among people are believed to be primarily a result of life experiences rather than an expression of innate differences among individuals. Emphasis is placed, therefore, on the virtue of effort as the avenue for improvement and accomplishment. A similar theme is found in Japanese philosophy, where individual differences in potential are de-emphasized and great importance is placed on the role of effort in modifying the course of human development. Effort and self-discipline are considered by Japanese to be essential bases for accomplishment. Lack of achievement, then, is attributed to the failure to work hard, rather than to a lack of ability or to personal or environmental obstacles.

The data we collected mirror these differences in the Asian and American philosophy about achievement. For example, mothers of kindergartners were asked how far their child would go in school. After they answered this question they were asked what would determine if the child would get that far. Half of the Japanese mothers, 27 percent of the Chinese mothers, but only 5 percent of the American mothers said that it depended upon how hard the child worked in school. American mothers were more likely to stress other factors, such as whether the family would have enough money. In our interviews with the children, we asked whether any student can be good in math if he or she works hard enough. Japanese fifth-graders agreed with this statement; American fifth-graders disagreed. Most Chinese students took a middle-ground position. On the other hand, for a statement about mathematics such as, "The tests you take can show how much or how little natural ability you have," American children showed the greatest degree of agreement.

Parents and children who believe that success depends on ability rather than effort are less likely to emphasize the importance of studying. And, in fact, materials and activities that might aid or support studying are not used with great frequency by American parents. For example, American parents are less likely to purchase extra workbooks for their children. Only 28 percent of the parents of American fifth-graders, but 58 percent of the Japanese and 56 percent of the Chinese parents, bought their children extra workbooks in mathematics. We noted that in front of nearly every bookstore in Japan were colorful racks of the latest workbooks for children, organized by grade, semester, and area of study.

An extreme interpretation of this philosophy leads to the conclusion that children of high ability need not work hard to achieve, and that children of low ability will not achieve regardless of how hard they work. The remarkable success of Japanese and Chinese children in elementary school appears to be due in part to the renunciation of this view.

Classroom Activities

There are stunning differences in the amount of time given to academic activities in Chinese, Japanese, and American classrooms. We can say this with confidence after analyzing the data obtained in over 1,200 hours of observations of classrooms in each of the cultures. The percentage of time devoted to academic activities was much less in the American fifth-grade classrooms: 64 percent, compared to 92 percent in the Chinese classrooms and 87 percent in the Japanese classrooms. Translated into hours, this means that American fifth-graders were averaging twenty hours a week in academic activities, whereas Chinese and Japanese fifth graders spent forty hours and thirty-three hours, respectively.

These statistics can be broken down further according to time spent on various academic subjects. American fifth graders spent only 3.4 hours a week in mathematics classes—much less than the 11.4 hours for Taipei students or the 7.6 hours for Sendai students. These large differences become even more extreme when the incidence of irrelevant activities, absences from school, and absences from the classroom—all of which were highest in the American classrooms—are taken into account.

Many educators have looked at the longer school day and the longer school year in Asian classrooms and have recommended lengthening the time American children spend in school. Such changes are likely to be ineffective in increasing mathematics scores unless there are basic changes in the organization and conduct of mathematics classes. Increasing the percentage of time spent on mathematics, reducing irrelevant activities, and increasing children's opportunities to learn from their teachers would seem more likely to lead to improvement.

The observer of Asian classrooms is impressed by another factor: the zest and enthusiasm of Asian teachers. Lessons are conducted in a spirited fashion and the teachers are successful in engaging the attention of the children in their large classes—often up to fifty children in Taiwan and up to forty children in Japan. It takes a great deal of energy to do this, even with well-disciplined children. Teachers are able to summon this amount of energy for teaching because they spend fewer hours being directly in charge of the classroom than do American teachers. Asian teachers are incredulous, in fact, when told that American teachers are typically responsible for their pupils throughout the school day. Although Chinese and Japanese teachers spend as much time at school as American teachers, they have much more time available during the day for preparing lessons, working with individual children, and conducting other class-related activities outside the classroom.

Conclusions

Information about education in other countries does not yield ready solutions to our own problems, for practices and beliefs are deeply embedded in each culture. Nevertheless, cross-cultural studies offer fresh insights into the American situation. In contrast to our country's good opinion of how its students are doing, our studies demonstrate how early and how markedly American children are falling behind those of other countries in basic knowledge and skills in mathematics. Our research also points to some rather obvious reasons why: dramatic differences in the amount of time spent in mathematics classes, later introduction of mathematical concepts in the American curriculum, complacency resulting from unrealistic appraisals of American children's levels of achievement, differences in the emphasis on the importance of hard work and effort, and the greater time available to Chinese and Japanese teachers for lesson preparation and work with individual students.

Part II

Discontinuities in Moral Education and Educational Quality

Introduction

James J. Shields, Jr.

Many aspects of the early socialization for discipline and the inter-relationship of the family and the school in Japan strike the outside observer as positive. However, there is a darker side to Japanese education characterized by serious discontinuities. These include issues related to school violence and equality of opportunity which are rooted in a brutal examination system.

Going back to the Meiji period, the school in Japan has been a major agent of moral and religious socialization. Schools became the institutional nexus linking the family with the polity around a hierarchical ideology that sanctified the relationship among children, their parents, ancestors, and the emperor. By means of school rituals, courses of study, and extracurricular activities, principles in the Shinto and Confucian moral order, such as loyalty, filial piety, the discipline of group life, industry, cleanliness, physical strength, and perseverance, were reinforced.

The role of the school is defined so comprehensively and broadly that it extends to supervisory rights over student behavior outside the school. Almost all elementary and secondary schools have prescribed codes over such matters as clothing and places students may go by themselves and with adults. The extremely broad custodial role of schools is strengthened by the importance given to *giri-ninjo,* the web of reciprocal obligations in which the social order is enmeshed. In Japan, these obligations are looked upon as the guarantors of rights and duties in much the same way law is in the United States. Officially, strong acceptance continues for the view that schools should keep their broad custodial roles and strong orientation to moral education. But, in fact, the school is becoming increasingly secularized. As University of Tokyo Professor Hidenori Fujita points out, a qualitative change has taken place in the linkages among schools, families, and the polity. As a result, the effectiveness of traditional patterns of moral education have been so undermined that the very legitimacy of schooling in Japan is open to question.

Fellow sociologist and University of Tokyo colleague Ikuo Amano lends support to Fujita's view that troubled relationships exist between the children who are the main actors in the educational process and the system itself, which has led to pathological phenomena. Amano sees the changed orientation of young people and the unchanged values and attitudes of the older generation as the reason for the problem.

These views are given official support in the summary of the Second Provisional Report of the Ad Hoc Committee on Education Reform released by the Japanese Government in 1986. In the report it is stated, "A general diagnosis must be made of the grave social illness now affecting our educational system, the 'desolation' whose symptoms include bullying, school violence, and excessive competition in entrance examinations."

Japanese children appear to enjoy primary school. Foreign observers generally find that pupils look and sound happy in their environment. The dark side of the system becomes more apparent when pupils reach the second year of junior high school. This is the point at which what they have to do to succeed becomes clear and their feelings and attitudes change. Kazuhiro Mochizuki, long-time Tokyo high school principal, reports that the whole weight of Japan's competitive society falls on the junior high school. He identifies the highly charged atmosphere of academic competition as the cause of the growing violence and the extreme dysfunction in many schools on this level.

Specifically, in many schools there has been a buildup of an unhealthy energy which takes the form of what is called *ijime*. Translated, *ijime* means bullying directed at certain individuals, sometimes with the tacit approval or even the complicity of adults. Usually, the victim who is singled out is particularly vulnerable or seems to be different. Some students have died directly from the treatment, while a number of victims have committed suicide.

There seems to be something in the emphasis on conformity in Japan that makes this form of bullying so destructive. Eighty percent of the incidents of *ijime* occur in junior high schools.

In addition to academic competition, other reasons cited for *ijime* are the increasingly materialistic culture, which gives more importance to possessions than to the dignity of individuals, and the overly indulgent child-rearing practices of this generation of parents. Beyond these reasons, it should prove valuable to examine the way pupils are used to enforce discipline among their peers in the early years of schooling as an important contributing factor to the phenomenon. There is some evidence to support the view that youth, given free reign to do so, often impose more stringent and authoritarian values and attitudes upon each other than adults would.

The Diminishing Role of the School in Guaranteeing Equality

Just as discontinuities have surfaced in the historical role of the school in Japan as a socializing agency for moral development, so too have problems arisen around the role of schooling as a vehicle for upward mobility. Today these two dominating purposes of Japanese education, the one moral and the other economic, exist in destructive tension with one another.

Schooling in Japan is a huge sorting machine characterized by meritocracy and competition, a hierarchical and pyramidal structure with elite universities on the top, and prestige differentiation on every level. Individuals are identified and defined by their university credentials, which are absolute yardsticks for measuring the achievement of each individual as well as for determining his position in the social hierarchy. As we read in the First Report of the Ad Hoc Committee for Educational Reform in Japan, released in 1985, "in evaluating an individual more importance is attached to 'When and where did he learn?' than to 'What extent did he learn?' and such criteria are applied to judging even an individual's value, ability, and personality."

Amano tells us that a key element to keep in mind when looking at the relationship between the educational system and credentials and the examination system that joins the two is the matter of equality of educational opportunity. He believes that because the prime requirements for examination success are intellectual ability and individual effort, equality of educational opportunity has been achieved and is no longer an issue. This, he feels, explains why there are so few calls for reform on this issue in Japan.

Support for this position can be found in the work of William Cummings, who concluded, on the basis of his work in the early 1970s on elementary schools, that available data reveals an educational system in Japan that is equitable and democratic in orientation. More recently, however, the prevailing view is actually more differentiated and negative. Thomas Rohlen argues that while up to high school, the system offers a greater basic equality than American reformers have dreamed possible, after that the system is competitive and produces an elaborate hierarchy.

In his research on equality, Fujita has found an unchanging pattern of differences in academic achievement by father's occupation, which has persisted throughout the remarkable expansion in secondary and higher education. In effect, he found that the higher the father's educational level, the higher the student's academic achievement.

Rohlen's studies also reveal a trend toward a greater role for family factors in educational outcomes. By the mid-1970s, for instance, he found fewer and fewer students from poor families were entering the elite universities. He also found the delinquency rates are closely correlated to the academic rank of high schools and that high schools reflect differences in family background. Japan, like the United States, he concludes, has a school system that partially replicates the status and class system of its society. But the distinct, stratified subcultures are attained through an examination system rather than through segregation as is often the case in the United States.

The Impact of Private Schooling on Equality

Privately purchased advantage in the preparation process for the examination system at *juku, yobiko,* and at private high schools seems to be looming larger and larger in significance. Nationally, successful applicants to Tokyo University are now equally divided between free, public schools and fee-based private schools. It is ironic, argues Fujita, "that on the one hand, people expect the school to be a total agency of socialization and on the other hand, the most fundamental role of modern education, that of developing basic skills, has been personalized and left to alternate institutions."

Gail Benjamin and Estelle James provide excellent insight into the impact of private education in Japan on educational opportunity. They found that public education is primarily limited to compulsory, basic schooling up through the ninth grade for the whole population, and beyond that for only a small elite. At the same time, the government, through partial funding, has encouraged private enterprise to respond to demands for schooling that exceed the carefully regulated public supply.

The number of academic track places in public high schools is limited. As a result, they are oversubscribed. This situation tends to favor upper-class children whose families consider expenditures for private education a good investment and can afford the tutoring fees needed to gain a competitive advantage in examinations.

In metropolitan areas such as Kyoto, Osaka, Tokyo, and Kanagawa, which have the largest and wealthiest populations, we find a pattern of small public enrollments, a large private sector, and large academic track populations. This, as Benjamin and James tell us, is because the politically influential upper classes in these areas have opted for quality not quantity. They know they have a good chance either of getting their children into high quality public schools or of paying the fees required by private schools.

Working urban-class families who prefer more public academic high school places do not have the political power in these prefectures to bring this about. One exception is Tokyo, where the metropolitan government reformed the elitist aspects of the system. The result was a massive flight of "better students" to private schools. The public schools, which used to dominate the admissions lists for national public universities, have been replaced by private academic schools in Tokyo. Thus, a reform designed to be egalitarian has had the opposite effect and has helped push private schools to the top of the status hierarchy.

The results of the reforms in Tokyo are similar to those found in most other nations whenever selectivity is ruled out and attempts are made to homogenize student bodies in open-access public schools. For example, in the United States, as public high schools became less selective so did their reputations as quality institutions. In contrast, Japan, for the most part, has been able to maintain selective and elite public education, with the prestige hierarchy dominated by public institutions. The unanticipated and most troubling effect has been that the elite public secondary schools, along with the private ones, are utilized disproportionately by upper income groups.

School Problems Mirror Societal Problems

The problem of equality in Japan is not a school problem alone. Actually, the structural relationships among the examination system, the stratified educational institutions, and credentials have changed little over the years. What is different is that there has been a large increase in the number of people attending school without a commensurate increase in the number of good jobs in the marketplace. With over 90 percent of the high school-age group attending secondary school, the occupational rewards promised by academic credentials are no longer what they once were.

. For the first time in the one hundred years of modernization, as Amano tells us, Japan has ceased to be a land of opportunities and success stories. Japanese youth recognize this and this has affected their attitudes about schooling. The examination system, which once greatly encouraged the aspirations of parents and their children, has begun to play a role in cooling them down.

On the one hand, the young are aware that earning an academic credential will not necessarily gain them a higher rank in the social order. Yet, on the other hand, they are aware that so many people have diplomas, the lack of one constitutes a serious lifelong handicap. Involuntary school attendance by students with diminished ability and interest in academic work has emerged as a serious problem. Along with school violence and bullying discussed earlier, this has resulted in growing numbers of school dropouts.

The school has done surprisingly little to respond to the problems rooted in the larger society. Reforms are needed in the very structure of schooling itself. As Herbert Passin has argued, there is a real question as to whether the existing university system, which was developed in an elitist period, is appropriate to an egalitarian age. He speculates that the university structure and curriculum, developed for elite societies, may not be useful beyond attendance by more than 10 percent of the population. When universities are no longer the places to prepare people for elite positions, as they were when they were developed, they may simply lose their usefulness.

Although the variations in economic level appear smaller and the United States seems to have greater class disparities than Japan, both nations fit Martin Conroy's definition of democratic capitalistic states. As such, they have both egalitarian and inegalitarian features, with equality on the one hand, and an ideology of capital on the other. In both we can witness an historical tension between democratic equality and unequal accumulation of capital.

To the degree Conroy is correct, the demand for social mobility through schooling will continue, even in the face of unequal employment results, and average attendance rates will be pushed even higher. Even though students find schooling oppressive and boring, families will continue to take seriously the democratic promise that school is the route to higher income. As a result, the pressure on school systems to raise both academic standards and graduation rates will increase.

Cross-nationally, this appears to be what is actually happening. In a 1983 study of eleven nations, it was found that academic quality had moved ahead of educational equity as a policy value in many of these nations, and that national productivity attained fresh prominence in their reports on educational reform. These formulations of educational policy promise to continue the primary goal of schooling as the development of basic skills and academic achievement to enhance national productivity for some years to come. This probably explains why Amano and others find that the issue of educational equity in Japan and elsewhere is no longer a very prominent one.

This does not mean the equity issue has died completely. It appears the focus is shifting to the workplace, where we are finding an acceleration in the intensity of demands as more employees become better educated and underutilized. Grassroots reform movements aimed at the labor market in the future should prove to be more insistent than those aimed at the institution of schooling. The unfortunate effect of this probably will be the slowing down of the important work that needs to be done by educational leaders to revitalize the role of the school as an effective agent of moral development and equality of opportunity.

Social Equality and Educational Opportunity for Special Groups

Society is nowhere nearly as homogeneous in Japan as many would have it, nor is there as much harmony as many believe there is. Vast differences function around an aristocratic structure in which every greeting and every contact indicates the kind and degree of social distance among individuals. The effect has been to render the entire system less socially democratic than that of the United States and other Western nations. As Seymour Martin Lipset has written recently, Japan is a society in which deference and status remain strong. In this respect, the dominant value orientations regarding equality in the United States and Japan are very different.

The United States began as a settler community with very egalitarian communities and was the first country to become democratic. Americans stress equality of respect as well as equality of opportunity. While recognizing that inequalities do exist, there is a pervasive belief that, in social relations at least, all people should be treated with equal respect because they are human beings.

By contrast, in Japan, hierarchy remains important in defining the way people deal with each other. Each person has an accepted place in the prestige order. As a result, as Lipset indicates, the great emphasis on status differentiation in social relations remains.

Article 14 of the Japanese constitution states, "All of the people are equal under the law and there shall be no discrimination in political, economic and social relations because of race, creed, social status or family origin." Although official policy as reflected in this constitutional statement prohibits discrimination against any group and although theoretically the system is open to all, statistically we find it is not. School choice ends up being rationed on the basis of gender; physical, mental, and emotional handicap; foreign study; and cultural background as well as on social class position and examination scores.

The social Darwinism which relegates ninth-graders who score low in examinations to second-class economic status for life with virtually no opportunity for another chance through schooling also by definition has shut out other special populations through differentiated treatment which is legitimately organized and financed. These patterns exist in varying degrees elsewhere, of course. But what seems to distinguish Japan from many other developed nations is the relatively limited amount of attention and effort currently being given to finding solutions to these problems.

Kumiko Fujimura-Fanselow has done a very comprehensive study of the way that schooling for women in Japan functions to perpetuate educational inequality through its structure and by the nature of its curriculum. In spite of reforms, which on the surface appear to offer great opportunity to women, sex differences in education persist. Not only does the overall enrollment of Japanese women in higher education continue to lag behind that of men, but there is a significant difference between male and female patterns of participation in various types and levels of schooling.

A large proportion of women pursue higher education through junior colleges rather than in four-year institutions. Those who do manage to attend four-year institutions tend to limit themselves to majoring in literature, home economics, and education. Junior colleges have become in effect the "women's track" in higher education and as such are looked upon as forming the bottom layer of the university pyramid.

This sex-typed education in schools is to a great extent a reflection of the job discrimination linked with certain employment practices that inhibit women's opportunities for occupational mobility and financial independence. Even women with degrees from national prestigious universities find that the employment options open to them are extremely limited. The acquisition of a university degree is a much surer channel for social mobility for men in Japan than it is for women. The choices women make about courses of study, type of institution attended, and years of schooling mirror the narrow roles defined for women in society at large. As such they provide us with classic examples of the extent to which schooling is the dependent variable in the school-society relationship.

Turning to children with special emotional, physical, and mental needs, the so-called handicapped, we find that in Japan equality for them is defined in terms of education in separate schools. Marilyn Goldberg points out that scant attention is given to individual differences in the regular Japanese school. Even though many parents prefer that their children be given the opportunity to attend regular schools with special classes, resource rooms, and mainstreaming into regular classrooms, they mostly are sent to separate schools. This is especially true for adolescents, for whom there is relatively little help on either the junior or senior high school level. As pupils move up through the system, the options tend to become even more separate and restrictive for children with handicapping conditions.

In a good number of industrial nations, considerable attention is given to finding ways to integrate students with special needs into regular schools. However, equality in Japan has not yet been defined in such a way as to bring these pupils into the "least restrictive environment" in regular schools. By and large, special education means "separate but equal," a concept that has been repudiated by national government mandate in the United States. To date, in Japan there is very little mainstreaming into regular classes. Quality integration for those with special needs continues to be a major piece of unfinished business.

Another special class of children who face prejudice are overseas and returning pupils, of whom there has been a great increase in recent years. According to Tetsuya Kobayashi, the returning children often differ in their academic achievement and personal and social behavior from children at home. In classrooms, it is reported that they often irritate teachers and classmates by their inquisitive attitudes, which are interpreted as disruptive.

Returning pupils create a problem because the Japanese school system has been developed to work with children from identical cultural backgrounds. Inevitably, children who attend school abroad for a time come back culturally altered. In order to cope with these "problem children," special classes have been established for readjustment education. It is not uncommon in these classes, Kobayashi reports, for children to be forced to give up what they have learned abroad because it is considered to be an obstruction to good adjustment at home.

Some parents prefer a much different approach, one which would allow international children to enter Japanese schools with the full advantage of their overseas experience. Potentially, this approach holds great promise not only for the returning children but also for teachers and their fellow classmates to become more internationally aware. Also, it fulfills the mandate of recent governmental reports which call for promoting deeper international understanding among pupils.

Fundamental to all this is the conflict that parents of returning children necessarily have between wanting their children to do well in university examinations and the desire they have that their children retain their international characteristics.

What ultimately brands schooling abroad as a negative rather than a positive experience is the narrow focus of the entire Japanese educational system upon academic preparation for entrance examinations for higher levels of schooling. A school system preoccupied with examinations hinders true progress toward the internationalization of the educational experience. Until this changes, those with different national cultural experiences will continue to be discriminated against and restricted from fully participating in the teaching and learning process in Japan.

The Burakumin

The Burakumin, termed Japan's "invisible people," have become a discrete subgroup outside the pale of the majority. Although racially and linguistically part of the Japanese majority, their association with occupations involving blood and death (butchers, cremators, leather workers, and the like) was used as a basis for identifying them as a hereditary, ritually impure outcaste group with virtually no chance for upward mobility. And, as the research of John Hawkins and others indicates, the exploitive and demeaning discrimination against the Burakumin continues to exist in many ways today.

Hawkins has described how the Burakumin had been able to incorporate the Japanese Socialist Party (JSP) and the Japanese Communist Party (JCP) into their struggles to redress the discrimination and isolation from the mainstream. Because of ideological differences, the JSP and the JCP were not able to achieve much unity and were deeply antagonistic toward each other. Their complex theoretical differences centered around the JSP's position that discrimination against the Burakumin was special and different than that practiced against the poor generally. The JCP defined the problem as one of class shared by all poor Japanese. Nonetheless, both parties agreed that there was discrimination against the Burakumin in schools.

Eventually the political organizations and protests of the Burakumin and their supporters forced the government into policy changes under the rubric of "dowa education," which translated means assimilation or liberation education for the Burakumin. As Hawkins's studies reveal, their struggles provide a good model of how a disenfrancheised group can organize politically to bring about the passage of important government legislation on its behalf.

The government put additional funds into schools to pay for compensatory education. In some instances, expenditures for outcaste children were three times as great as those for other children. In the process, dowa education enforced a new definition of educational equality in Japan, one which moved away from the more restrictive definition of equality based on opportunity or input to a broader one based on equality of outcome or results.

As a result of the political activities of the Burakumin and their allies and an improved economy which has increased employment and income nationally, the plight of the Burakumin did improve.

Educational attainment did rise. Yet, as Nobuo Shimahara and others have reported, there is still a gap in school performance between the Burakumin and majority students. In particular, there is still frustration over entrance examination results for preferred high schools. Because of this, some JSP leaders had advocated special admission policies to provide quotas in senior high schools and colleges. More recently, however, they have retreated from this position due to opposition from universities and other interest groups.

Of all the groups that have experienced varying degrees of selective exclusion in Japan, the Burakumin more than any others have demonstrated that schooling can be molded by subordinate groups to achieve authentic gains in equality of educational opportunity and other democratic demands. Even though not fully successful, the Burakumin provide an important example of how a social movement can change the way a large bureaucratic institution functions.

As Martin Conroy has argued, the power of individuals to alter conditions and their lives through social movements is shaped by the development of a social consciousness and the ability to come together in an essentially political way. Meaningful change is less possible when approached individually or in small group factions. The Burakumin have demonstrated that groups can resist social practices. Their recent history has much to teach other restricted groups in Japan—women, the handicapped, and students who have studied abroad—how to gain more choice and a better voice in schooling and society.

The Examination Hell and School Violence

8

The Dilemma of Japanese Education Today

Ikuo Amano

The most immediate reason why reform is necessary now is the troubled relationship between the children who are the main actors in the educational process and the system itself. A reexamination of that relationship, not so much of educational institutions or of education's role in society, is the key issue.

Student dissatisfaction with the education system began to take concrete form around the beginning of the 1970s. As in other industrialized countries, student activism in the universities was vigorous, even violent. Strikes and sit-ins were common, and the fever of protest showed signs of spreading even to the high schools. Eventually the situation returned to normal, but "antischool" attitudes and behavior began to surface among junior and senior high school students. Disillusionment and dislike of school, refusal to attend school, violence, lapses in scholastic performance, and dropouts are manifestations of that protest.

Of course, it is true that the situation still seems to be far less serious than in some other advanced nations, especially the United States. Only 3 percent of Japanese students drop out of high school.

An earlier version of this essay was published in *The Japan Foundation Newsletter*, Vol. 13, No. 5 (March 1986).

The yearly averages for incidences of school vandalism are 0.3 cases per junior high school and 0.15 cases per senior high school. Some have pointed out that increasing numbers of students have difficulty keeping up with the curriculum, but Japanese students continue to score better than their peers from other countries on international scholastic aptitude tests.

Nonetheless, a sense of crisis is widely felt toward education, not only among those directly involved in the system, but among the general public as well. The strong support for reform derives from the totally new perception of the changes occurring in children on the one hand and of the relationship between children and the education system on the other. At first, people regarded the new developments as transient or due to some kind of minor friction. It was when they realized that the situation resulted from structural problems in Japanese society and the educational system itself that the reform movement gained public support.

Initially, examinations began with elementary school. The academic progress of children and their eligibility for higher grades or for graduation were constantly tested in a continuous stream of examinations. The same was true for secondary school and universities. Graduation rolls listed the names in order of achievement, and seating in the classroom was determined by the students' marks. This endless succession of tests was done away with at the elementary school level in the early twentieth century but remained at other levels.

The distinguishing feature of the examination system in Japan, however, is the entrance examination. It has become standard practice for individual secondary schools and universities to prepare their own entrance examinations, a system that is the exception rather than the rule in Europe. The "examination hell," as it is known today, existed in Japan as early as the 1920s, but the cause was not competition to enter higher grades or to graduate, but rather to gain entrance to schools and universities.

Examinations were also introduced for public service and for the professions, including medicine, law, and school teaching. In other words, certification in most of the professions was granted only to people who could demonstrate, through tests, a certain level of knowledge, skill, or competence. Similarly, only those who passed the government examinations were eligible to become senior public servants. These screening tests were closely linked with the education system, moreover, and only students whose school background was sufficiently outstanding were exempted from taking them. Some of the tests were open only to university students.

The graduates of the Imperial universities, founded in 1886 to train the bureaucratic corps for the central government, were a case in point. Graduates from these universities (there were seven in 1945) enjoyed various advantages in finding employment. Special consideration was gradually extended, in varying degrees, to graduates of some other higher and secondary educational institutions.

Educational Credentialism

The custom whereby the state granted various privileges to the graduates of certain prestigious institutions of secondary and higher education eventually gave rise to the phenomenon that is known today as *gakureki shugi,* or what I shall call "educational credentialism." Essentially it refers to the high priority placed on a person's academic background by government organizations, companies, and society in general.

Educational credentialism became entrenched first in the civil service. In 1887, when the Japanese government established its system for hiring public officials, the factors given the greatest weight were the school from which the candidate had graduated and his results in the civil service examinations. While the basic idea was to ensure that middle- and high ranking bureaucrats were selected fairly through open and competitive government-sponsored examinations, certain candidates were exempted from the exams if their educational credentials were sufficiently illustrious. Educational credentials, especially if they included graduation from an Imperial university, also had an important effect on pay and promotion after hiring.

Educational background was crucial for those who sought to enter the medical profession or become secondary school teachers; if the candidates had graduated from certain government-accredited schools, they were exempted from the qualifying exams and automatically granted professional certification. However, educational credentialism did not take root in society simply because it was the norm in hiring public servants or certifying professionals. Only when it became important in the hiring of white-collar workers in the private sector did it become an overwhelming concern.

The new jobs in the bureaucracy, the professions, and private businesses were created in the process of Japan's modernization and industrialization. They carried high prestige and provided access to wealth and power. The fact that educational credentials were the basic qualification for engaging in these occupations goes far to explain why a person's educational background is still considered a major indicator of his social standing even outside officialdom and the corporate world.

The words *gakureki shugi* and *gakureki shakai* ("educational credential society") only came into common use in the 1960s. But the phenomenon had existed since the early part of the 1920s, and had become one of the most important ways of defining a person's status and prestige in Japanese society.

Equality of Opportunity

In examining the relationships between the education system, the examination system, and educational credentialism, a key element to keep in mind is equality of opportunity. Examinations may be decisive in employment and promotion. But without equal access to education, the education system would be incapable of inspiring young people or functioning as a ladder up to the higher rungs of society. Fortunately, the far-reaching changes brought about by the Meiji Restoration of 1868 and later by Japan's defeat in 1945 contributed to making the system more open.

The first change, made in the wake of the Meiji Restoration, was the dismantling of the country's feudal status hierarchy. Schooling was made available to all, regardless of class or lineage. Of course, education at the advanced levels was still very expensive. On the other hand, even the children of the wealthiest families could not enter the higher level schools, particularly the government-run higher schools or universities that promised elite careers, unless they passed the gruelling entrance examinations. It was this rigorous system of entrance examinations which made access to education equitable. After the defeat in World War II, during the period of the Allied Occupation, Japan underwent its second great social transformation. The social structure became more fluid as a result of pervasive land reform and the dismantling of the *zaibatsu* (business combines). Under the slogan of "democratization of education," the authorities introduced the new "6–3–3–4" education system (six years of elementary school, three years of junior high school, another three years of senior high school, and four years of university education). Compulsory education was extended from six to nine years. The prewar secondary schools, which had been organized in a multitrack system, were rationalized and merged into three-year senior high schools. The higher education system, which had consisted of a few universities and many other short-term institutions, was also reformed into a new system of four-year universities and two-year junior colleges. Universities, which had totaled only forty-eight in the year 1945, increased to 201 by 1950. This made the education system even more open and provided more opportunities for access.

Obtaining this passport required some financial wherewithal. But the prime requirement was intellectual ability and individual effort. It was possible for an intelligent child, diligent and strongly motivated but born into a poor family, to eventually acquire distinguished educational credentials. In the early stages of rapid modernization and industrialization, many people did in fact rise to the highest levels of society in just this way. The examination system stimulated their aspirations, and the intensity of their desire to succeed in turn supported the diligence and hard work required for academic achievement.

The school as a competitive arena was regarded by society, and particularly by enterprises and government offices, as a highly effective system for training and selecting able manpower. As long as the children's achievements were gauged impartially and objectively by the schools, there was no need to measure their ability again upon hiring. Educational credentials provided an indicator of an individual's diligence and ability and both industry and the government placed great weight on these credentials in basic personnel policy. This had the effect of intensifying competition within the school system.

The Japanese education system was very effective in meeting the needs of modernization and industrialization and is often portrayed as one of the country's greatest successes. When the competition generated by the examination system for acquisition of academic credentials became overheated, however, the dark side of the system began to reveal itself.

Entrance Examinations and Educational Credentialism

In Japan, competition at all levels of school education was already severe in the 1890s. This was the reason that entrance examinations and examinations for eligibility to higher grades were eliminated in the nation's elementary schools at the beginning of the 1900s. That was as far as the reform went, however. Schools educating students who would occupy the top rungs of the social ladder considered examinations an unavoidable gauntlet that students must run to separate the able from the rest.

The most serious problem involved the entrance examinations. Japan had borrowed the examination system from Europe, but not without changes. In Europe, students who score acceptably on national standardized exams given at the conclusion of one level of education are automatically guaranteed admittance to the next level. The emphasis, in other words, is not on *entrance* examinations. In Japan, however, individual schools began to use examinations to select which students could enter their halls.

In the days when the education system was still not yet well established, some schools found that they were not receiving a sufficient number of students whose ability was above a certain level from the lower levels of education, and they introduced entrance examinations as a "temporary" means of selecting students to meet their standards. This practice continued even after the education system took firm root, eventually becoming one of the key characteristics of the Japanese education system. The importance of entrance examinations was further inflated because the quantitative expansion of the secondary and higher education was not rapid enough to accommodate the sudden large increase of students who sought to proceed to higher levels.

Although education was an important tool for achieving rapid industrialization and modernization, the government could devote only limited human and material resources to the building of the system. Emphasis was placed on achieving universal compulsory elementary education, and this goal was rapidly achieved (by 1902, over 90 percent of eligible children were enrolled). On the other hand, too few secondary schools and universities and colleges were built to respond to the rapidly growing demand for education advancement that was the natural outcome of universal elementary education.

In addition, in an effort to allocate its limited resources effectively, the government supported secondary schools and universities on a selective basis, according to the degree of their importance to the modernization and industrialization effort. This created great disparities in human and material resources among educational institutions which, at least on paper, were at the same level. This, in turn, made people discriminate among schools in accordance with this allocation of resources, and as a consequence a clear hierarchical system based on social prestige came into being. Among universities, for example, the Imperial universities ranked highest, followed by other government-run universities, and then by the private universities.

These two factors—the paucity of institutions of secondary and higher education and their stratification—ensured that an increasingly competitive entrance examination system would remain a permanent feature of Japanese education. The system has produced phenomena that surely exist only in Japan, such as large numbers of students who failed in one try to pass the university entrance exams to the school of their choice and who are studying for another try (known as *ronin,* after the masterless samurai of old), the proliferation of less selective private schools, and the flourishing cram-school industry.

These distortions produced by overcompetition were already apparent in the 1920s. The government, concerned about programs that laid too much importance on preparation for entrance examinations, directed all schools to be more moderate. In 1927, entrance exams for secondary schools were done away with and an attempt was made to introduce basic reforms into the entrance exam system for universities and colleges.

However, the flames of desire for educational credentials and higher social status had been fanned; as long as they remained alight, it would be impossible to eliminate the entrance examinations. The obstacles posed by the heavy reliance on educational credentials in industry and the government became a social problem in the 1920s, and carried over without resolution to the postwar period.

Far from cooling down, the excessive competition grew even more intense after World War II. A series of social reforms implemented by the occupation authorities brought mobility back to Japan's social structure. This mobility, together with the reformed education system emphasizing democracy and equality, provided further motivation for people to seek better educational credentials and aim for the upper rungs of the social ladder.

The recovery and rapid growth of Japan's economy was partly responsible for the sharp increase of the numbers of students going on to senior high school or college. Japan's industrial structure underwent enormous changes during the process of rapid economic growth, and these were accompanied by great strides in technological innovation. Private enterprises, especially in the secondary sector, experienced remarkable growth, and the demand for university graduates increased rapidly. Opportunities to enter the upper strata of society were abundant. Defeated in World War II and in the throes of revolutionary changes in the educational system and other aspects of its society, Japan once again became a "land of opportunity," and there were many success stories, just as there had been after the Meiji Restoration.

This new wave of rising aspirations made the competition in the entrance examinations even more intense than before the war. First of all, the number of competitors tremendously increased. In 1935, 19 percent of those who had completed compulsory education (six years of schooling) went on to secondary school. Only 3 percent of those who had completed compulsory schooling went on to college. The competition then was among a very small elite. After the war, the scale expanded tremendously: the corresponding figures for 1960 were 58 percent and 10 percent respectively, and for 1980, 94 percent and 37 percent.

Even when nearly 95 percent of junior high school graduates go on to senior high school, they must take entrance exams, and this means an unavoidable ordeal for virtually every fifteen-year-old. The same may be said for almost all of the 70 percent of students at general high schools (those schools which emphasize academic subjects, as opposed to commercial and technical ones). The curriculum offered at general high schools, moreover, is designed in such a way that the main emphasis is on preparation for university entrance examinations. Passing the university entrance exams is the chief educational concern of most senior high schools.

Another important reason why the competition has grown more fierce than it was before the war is that the stratified structure of secondary schools and universities has remained basically unchanged. In fact, despite the postwar reform of the educational system, stratification became even more rigid as more and more senior high schools and universities were built to meet the rapidly increasing number of students seeking higher education. The progress of stratification was particularly marked in the case of universities and colleges, their numbers jumping from forty-eight in 1945 to 201 in 1950. In 1980 there were 446 four-year universities and colleges in Japan. Most of these newly founded institutions are private. Often they are insufficiently endowed and possess few sources of income other than the tuition paid by the students. These schools form the bottom strata of higher education.

After the war, all universities, old and new, were officially ranked equally. Corporations, too, abolished the practice of starting-pay differentials determined by the rank of the school or university of the new employee. Nevertheless, the ranking of universities has not disappeared. A small group of prestigious universities with traditions going back to before the war, including the former Imperial universities, continue to occupy the top of the hierarchy. Most of the institutions established after the war, therefore, suffer from very low social regard.

The personnel policy of businesses—the most important employers of university graduates after the war—has contributed largely to maintaining and expanding the stratification of higher education. The starting-pay differentials may have been dropped, but corporations adopted the policy of preferring graduates of certain first-class or prestige universities in hiring new workers. This forged an explicit connection between first-class universities and top-ranking corporations.

In Japan there is a very close correlation between the size of a corporation and the wages its employees receive, as well as their career stability and social prestige. It is natural, then, that people seek employment at large corporations. Moreover, thanks to the connection just mentioned, the competition for jobs at these large companies begins with the race to enter the prestigious universities at the top of the educational hierarchy. The entrance exams of the universities, then, are part, a kind of first phase, of the scramble to secure a stable career.

The End of Rapid Economic Growth

Even after the end of the postwar period of rapid economic growth, the structure of interrelationships between the overheated "examination hell," stratified educational institutions, and educational credentialism has not fundamentally changed. But the attitudes of the children and young people who are being educated and who take part in the examination competition have changed greatly. In particular, it would seem that their aspirations to receive a good education and climb the ladder of success are weakening. Paradoxically, it was the remarkable economic growth that began in the 1960s that is responsible for this change.

Rapid economic growth brought to Japan affluence such as it had never before experienced. Moreover, this prosperity was enjoyed not just by a few but by all the people. It is well known that of the advanced nations Japan is among the top in terms of equality in the areas of income, consumption, and education. Egalitarianism pervades the popular consciousness, so much so that today by far the majority of Japanese people believe they are members of the middle class.

The affluence, needless to say, is a product of the effort and hard work of people who fervently aspired toward more income and higher social status. But, as attitudinal surveys have shown, the signs of declining aspirations became apparent once Japan became affluent in the mid-1970s. The aspirations of parents, teachers, businessmen—those who belong to the older generations—remain as high as before. They prize hard work and diligence as important virtues and expect their children and young people to follow suit. Many young Japanese are still eager to do so, but the statistics show that their numbers are steadily decreasing.

The more affluent and egalitarian a society becomes—one might say the less hungry the people are—the weaker their motivation for success becomes. After the oil crisis of 1973, it became apparent that rapid economic growth was coming to an end and that Japan was in the process of becoming a mature society. This meant that opportunities to move into higher social classes would grow fewer. It gradually became clear that hard work was not always sure to gain the expected reward. For the first time in its one-hundred-year history of modernization, Japan is ceasing to be a land of opportunity and success stories, and young Japanese keenly feel this change.

In the past, a university diploma ensured its holder prestige, power, and much higher wages than the average (although the degree of these benefits differed according to the university in question). Now that nearly 40 percent of young people go on to college, prestige and privilege is no longer at the disposal of every university graduate. Already there is a growing number of very well-educated college graduates who will not receive promotion to managerial positions, or who cannot even find white-collar jobs.

A university education, particularly at a prominent university, is still an effective passport to employment in a large corporation, of course, but having entered such a corporation no longer necessarily ensures a stable career with lifetime employment and promotion and wage increases by seniority. With the economy in a phase of slow growth, competition among corporations has become fierce both domestically and internationally. The struggle for survival is intensifying not only among corporations but also within them. The white-collar employees and engineers of large corporations, who by now are almost all college graduates, face a severe battle for a few managerial posts, and the chances of winning are getting slimmer.

In other words, the rewards promised by academic credentials are no longer certain. As it is becoming clear that higher wages, greater prestige and power do not necessarily follow from academic credentials, young people's aspiration to aim for the upper rungs of society or to undergo the grueling competition for academic credentials are naturally cooling down.

The "Cooling Down" Phenomenon

Despite weakening aspirations, no basic change has occurred in the educational structure so far. With few exceptions, students still have to pass entrance exams to enter senior high schools or universities. Because of the stratification of senior high schools and universities, moreover, the schools cannot revamp their curriculums, which are designed to prepare students for entrance exams and to put as many students into the good senior high schools or universities as possible. Parents will not let the schools do that. But children and young people are of another mind.

Of course, there are still many children who will study very hard to pass the exams to a prestigious school in hopes of gaining a high position in society. And school education takes it for granted that children are strongly oriented to upward mobility. As a whole, however, such children are becoming a minority.

The existence of a pyramid, the top of which is occupied by a handful of first-rate, prestigious universities, is a fact of life. But the number of places at the top is limited, and the race to gain one of them is harsh. Many children enter the competition with alacrity, and many parents encourage them at every step of the way. But as they proceed through each stage, battling their way from elementary school to junior high school, and then to senior high school, the aspirations of many young people and their parents as well may suddenly cool, for the toll they must pay is heavy.

In order to enter a first-rate university, it is most advantageous to enter a six-year privately run secondary school. Such schools are something like prep schools in the United States or public schools in Britain. The competition to enter them is among the most severe. Another option is to attend one of the few high schools, run by the local governments or privately, that are well known for producing graduates who pass the entrance exams to the top universities. The competition to enter these schools is also fierce.

The children who attend such schools not only study very hard exclusively to prepare for entrance exams; they also repeatedly take mock exams prepared by the exam-preparation companies. The results of these tests are scored by computer and sent to the children and their parents. Like it or not, the computer data tell them exactly where the child's level of academic ability stands in comparison with other children. Many students give up the idea of going to a good university if their showing in such exams is poor.

The examination system, which once greatly encouraged the aspirations of children and parents, has begun to play the role of "cooling down" their hopes. Ironically, the more emphasis the teachers and the schools place on examination-centered curriculums and the harder they push children to study to beat the competition for entrance to better schools, the lower the children's aspirations are becoming.

As long as children want to go to a senior high school or college, they cannot avoid taking part in the entrance examination competition. Not only do their teachers and parents expect them to participate, the school education system itself gives top priority to that eventuality. Students who have little desire to gain better marks or acquire higher academic credentials suffer a serious dilemma at school, and this is the source of the problems that are endemic in junior and senior high schools today, especially the former. Well over 90 percent of junior high school graduates go on to senior high school today, which means almost every junior high school graduate is on track to take entrance exams.

One of the reasons, and probably the greatest reason, for the pathological phenomena occurring in the schools today, including violence and "bullying," is the gap between the changed values and attitudes of young people and the unchanged orientation of the older generation. The educational system and institutions, which are maintained and run by the latter, have changed little.

Children's aspirations are no longer directed solely at gaining academic credentials and higher ranks in the social hierarchy. What the schools must do now is to establish new objectives for education that will nurture and encourage other aspirations. Reforms in the basic structure of the school and educational system are clearly needed, for without them, little improvement can be made in the examination system centered around entrance exams or in the problems of academic credentialism.

9

A Crisis of Legitimacy in Japanese Education: Meritocracy and Cohesiveness

Hidenori Fujita

In March 1983, more than 2,000 secondary schools (about 13 percent) had a graduation ceremony under the outlook of police officers. Needless to say, this was for preventing school violence on the day of the graduation ceremony, a most important school event in Japan. Among various pathological phenomena of school education in contemporary Japan, school violence seems to be one of the most symbolic and serious. According to "A Summary Report on Juvenile Delinquency" by the Police Board (1983), 1,244 incidents of school violence were reported for the first half of the year 1983, and about 42 percent of them were violence against teachers.[1] It should be noted that much school violence in Japan is not individual but collective behavior.

According to a 1980 Report of the Prime Minister's Office of Japan, the percentages of parents and children (from 10 to 15 years old) who think that "not to follow teacher's instructions" should not be permissible are 49.8 and 51.7 percent respectively in Japan. The corresponding percentages are 65.5 and 68.5 percent in the United

An earlier version of this essay was published in the *Bulletin of the Faculty of Education, Nagoya University,* Vol. 32, (1986), and is based on a paper presented at the annual conference of the Comparative and International Education Society held in Houston, Texas, March 1984.

States, 67.3 and 69.1 percent in Great Britain, and 82.1 and 82.0 percent in Korea. On the other hand the percentages of parents and of children who think that "to play truant from school" should not be permissible are 84.8 and 79.6 percent respectively in Japan; whereas the corresponding values are 69.1 and 76.6 percent in the United States, 80.3 and 82.3 percent in Great Britain, and 84.5 and 86.2 percent in Korea. The gap between the percentages of the two questions, both for parents and for children is largest in Japan. These statistics suggest that in Japan great importance is attached to schooling, while the teacher's authority is rather weak.[2] These seem to be a reflection of institutional characteristics of Japanese school education, symbolizing the nature of its crisis, which will be examined in this paper.

Establishment of the Modern School System

Although school education eventually drew the broad and strong support of parents and community, it was initially forcefully imposed upon people and various measures were taken for its diffusion. More than anything else, however, its successful imposition and diffusion was made possible by the fact that the government succeeded in establishing its absolute power and the new social order known as the emperor system.

To establish new orders of family, society, economy, and polity, many important reforms were carried out during the first three decades of the Meiji era.[3] For example, the government abolished the old class system of the military, the farmer, the artisan, and the merchant through a series of decrees which allowed the common people to have a family name, interclass marriage, and so forth. The disposition of stipends for the old military class forced many of them down to poverty, except those who entered the government service or the nobility class. On the other hand, the reform of the land tax and the establishment of the conscription system continued to impose extremely heavy burdens upon smaller farmers and peasants. Furthermore, the government suppressed the liberty and civil rights movements as well as peasants' uprisings, promulgated the Imperial Constitution, and carried out various measures for the development of industries such as expansion of government enterprises, promotion of private capital, and priority production. An important point here is that through all of these policies and measures the government solidified the foundation of its absolute power.

The government was also eager to control the family as a basic unit of the social order, and established the patriarchical family system with Confucian morals through the Census Law (1871) and the Civil Law (1898). By these laws, the head of a family was given such patriarchical rights as consent to marriage of a family member and appointing the residential place of a family member. It is important, however, that this patriarchical right was accompanied at the same time by the duty of the family head to notify the village or town master regarding changes in the status of all family members such as marriages, an offense against which was punished according to the Criminal Law. Thus, the head of a family functioned as a terminal organ of the administrative machinery in the emperor system. That is, through the line from a village or town master to a family head, the government made various regulations generally known to the people, collected taxes and enforced the draft, and hence exercised formal control over family life. Of course, the imposition of schooling was also made through a similar line of control.

There was also social control over family in terms of various informal sanctions such as social reputation, sneering, and gossiping. This was very strong especially in traditional Japanese communities, where neighborhood interactions were dense, where most families in a community were more or less homogenized and under similar economic and social pressures through the Civil Law, conscription, and the land tax, and where Confucian morals penetrated neighborhood relations as well as relations in the family.

The above brief review of the early experiences of the Meiji era suggests how family, regional community, polity, and school were linked with each other under the roof of the emperor system. Family and polity were linked with each other; institutionally the family was a terminal organ of the hierarchical ruling machinery; emotionally family and polity were linked by an indoctrination of an ideology that sanctified the relationship between family and emperor, as in the relationship between children, parents, and ancestry. In between, the neighborhood community served to develop the Confucian norm and moral order and exercised a variety of informal sanctions. School education became an institutional nexus between family, community, and polity and in turn served to diffuse various formal doctrines which advocated industry in work and in learning as well as loyalty and filial piety, and strengthened the Confucian moral order and the emperor system.

School Rituals and School Community[4]

Various school rituals reinforced the functioning of school education and developed emotional ties within the school community. There were numerous ceremonial gatherings such as entrance and graduation ceremonies, opening and closing ceremonies in each semester or trimester, and seasonal festivals and commemorations of various kinds. Such events as athletic meets and interschool competitive examinations also contained some ceremonial elements. As cultural anthropologists suggest, all of these ceremonial events as well as entrance and term examinations functioned as rites of passage and contributed to making schooling the center of childhood. Furthermore, his Imperial Majesty's portrait was installed in schools, the order of the worship was prescribed, and the Imperial Rescript on Education (1890) was recited in unison at almost all school events. All of these promoted the transformation and integration of the traditional belief in a tutelary deity into the broader national belief system, the belief in the emperor system. An important point here is that by this integration school became a major agent for moral and religious socialization of children.

Such events as athletic meets, entrance and graduation ceremonies, and interschool competitive examinations were also to some extent events or ceremonies of the regional community, in which many parents and community leaders participated. Elementary schools were supervised by the superintendent who was generally a man of high repute in a regional community and who functioned as a terminal organ of the national supervisory system of school education. These men of high repute offered congratulatory addresses at various school events and ceremonies. Thus, these school events presumably contributed to developing social and emotional ties between school and the regional community.

Not only emotional ties but also discipline, industry, and various social morals were reinforced by school rituals and by school curriculum as a whole. Orderly manners and behavior were encouraged through all ceremonial occasions. Rehearsals were often repeated for major ceremonies. A moral such as the young should always give precedence to their elders was built into the way to form in line at various occasions. An educational trip was a trinity march by which students were expected to develop their knowledge, to discipline themselves, and to develop emotional ties with each other and with teachers. Near to the main gate of many elementary schools there was a statue of a child, Kinjiro Ninomiya, who carried firewood on his back and was walking and reading a book. It was a symbol to encourage the virtue of industry as well as the value of learning.

Thus, there were many reasons for parents to commit their children to school, though schooling was forcefully imposed upon them and many parents resisted it, mainly for economic reasons, in the early Meiji era. To the extent school curriculum emphasized moral education and promoted the prevailing moral order, people had a moralistic reason to send their children to school. To the extent which the society was perceived as being still stratified, unequal, and repressive, and to the extent which school emphasized the meritocratic principle, people had an emotional reason to expect their children to do well in school. And to the extent which schooling provided chances for upward mobility and for a better life, people had a utilitarian reason to send their children to school. In fact, the idea that schooling should benefit one's career and future life became widely accepted among the majority of people as the industrial and occupational structure changed rapidly and manpower demands increased radically through the booms of the Sino-Japanese War and of the Russo-Japanese War.

School education in Japan was established on the principle of meritocracy and competition. Its structure was hierarchical, characterized by the grade system; the pyramidal school system with the imperial universities at the top, numerous elementary schools at the bottom, and in between, middle schools, girls' high schools, and vocational schools; and prestige differentiation among schools within the same education level. It was an extremely centralized system, both in administration and in the curriculum. All of these characteristics combined to make school education a huge sorting mechanism.

Change in the Notion of Equal Educational Opportunity[5]

The meaning of "equality of educational opportunity" has changed along with the expansion of school education. The Decree for Encouragement of Learning (1872) says that "from this time onward, everyone irrespective of class origins such as nobility, military, farmer, artisan or merchant, and irrespective of one's sex, ought to

learn, so that there should be no family without learning throughout the village and no person without learning in the family. . . .
Although higher learning is up to one's talent, parents should be
blamed if a child, irrespective of one's sex, does not engage in rudi-
mentary learning." Equality of educational opportunity meant
equal access to elementary schooling but not to secondary and tertiary schooling. In fact this period witnessed the realization of equal
educational opportunity in terms of compulsory and free elementary schooling, while secondary and tertiary schooling was accessible only for those who had talent and could afford it.

Then the notion of equal opportunity shifted to secondary schooling, given the diffusion of free elementary schooling. But it shifted
not toward a free and compulsory secondary schooling, but toward
diminishing the differences among and unifying three types of
secondary schools: the middle school which was most selective,
academic, and preparatory for higher education; the vocational
school which expanded rapidly in the 1910s and 1920s along with
the progress of industrialization and economic diversification; and
girls' high schools, the curriculum of which emphasized gentle lady-
hood and being a good housewife. The issue of equality in this
period revolved around the argument that differences among various types of secondary schools should be removed and that a common curriculum should be given to all students of secondary
schools. The advancement rate of secondary education was still only
around 20 percent, and the majority of its constituency was upper
and middle class.

A drastic change took place after World War II through the educational reform under the occupation policies of the Supreme Commander for the Allied Powers. This reform replaced the old
educational system, which was rather similar to those of European
countries such as Great Britain and Germany, with the new school
system, which is rather similar to the American system. In relation
to the opportunity structure, two major changes were introduced
by this reform. One was a change toward free and compulsory secondary education. Junior high school education (until ninth grade)
became compulsory and free, while senior high school education
rapidly expanded in the 1960s and 1970s and reached nearly
the level of compulsory attendance or "quasi-compulsory" senior
high school education. The other was a change toward an integrated, common curriculum for all students aimed at preparing
independent citizens for a democratic society. In fact, the system
was transformed from the multitracked to the single-tracked, and

Table 1. Educational attainment by father's occupation (20–69 years old in 1975) (values are percent)

Occupation	Compulsory	Upper Secondary	Higher Education	Total (cases)
Agriculture	61.2	31.1	7.7	100.0 (1007)
Lower-blue collar	52.8	35.2	12.0	100.0 (509)
Upper-blue collar	37.1	45.8	17.1	100.0 (286)
White-collar	24.3	46.1	29.6	100.0 (382)
Professional managerial	10.5	35.0	54.5	100.0 (323)
TOTAL	44.6	36.4	19.0	100.0 (2507)

Cited from Hidenori Fujita "Kyoiku no Kikai (Opportunity of Education)" 1982.
Data: 1975 Social Stratification and Mobility (SSM) National Survey Data.

Table 2. Educational attainment by father's occupation (20–29 years old in 1975) (values are percent)

Occupation	Compulsory	Upper Secondary	Higher Education	Total (cases)
Agriculture	31.6	54.8	13.6	100.0 (177)
Lower blue-collar	27.3	53.9	18.8	100.0 (154)
Upper blue-collar	21.4	53.1	25.5	100.0 (98)
White collar	12.9	46.3	40.7	100.0 (108)
Professional managerial	7.4	33.0	59.6	100.0 (94)
TOTAL	22.2	49.6	28.2	100.0 (631)

Cited from Hidenori Fujita, "Kyoiku no Kikai," 1982. same as Table 1.
Data: 1975 Social Stratification and Mobility (SSM) National Survey Data.

Table 3. Higher education attainment by father's occupation (by birth cohort) (values without parentheses are percent)

Occupation	Year of Birth				
	1906–15	1916–25	1926–35	1936–45	1946–55
Agriculture	9.2 (0.88)	4.2 (0.28)	6.7 (0.45)	6.7 (0.35)	13.6 (0.48)
Lower blue-collar	4.3 (0.41)	16.1 (1.07)	7.4 (0.50)	9.1 (0.47)	18.8 (0.67)
Upper blue-collar	6.3 (0.60)	21.2 (1.40)	5.3 (0.36)	15.8 (0.81)	25.5 (0.90)
White collar	8.6 (0.82)	32.8 (2.17)	19.2 (1.29)	30.9 (1.59)	40.7 (1.44)
Professional/ managerial	40.0 (3.81)	33.3 (2.21)	54.3 (3.64)	61.8 (3.19)	59.6 (2.11)
TOTAL	10.5	15.1	14.9	19.4	28.2

Standardized rate (cell percent value) (corresponding TOTAL percent value).
Cited from Hidenori Fujita, "Kyoiku no Kikai," 1982. same as Table 1.
Data: 1975 Social Stratification and Mobility (SSM) National Survey Data.

the majority of senior high schools became comprehensive and coeducational.

The question arises as to whether or not the remarkable expansion of school education has prompted equality of educational opportunity among social strata. Tables 1 through 3 present educational attainments by father's occupation, based on the data of the Social Stratification and Mobility national sample survey which was conducted in 1975. To begin with, Table 1 shows clear differences in educational attainments among five fathers' occupation categories. For example, 54.5 percent of those whose father's occupation was professional or managerial achieved higher education, while the corresponding values are 29.6 percent for white collar, 17.1 percent for upper blue collar, 12.0 percent for lower blue collar, and only 7.7 percent for agriculture. Because Table 1 is based on the sample aged from twenty to sixty-nine in 1975, the effects of educational expansion and transformation in the occupational structure are ignored. To consider these effects, Table 2 presents the results for the sample aged between twenty and twenty-nine in 1975.

Here again we find clear differences among five categories, and it is striking that the basic structure of opportunities for educational attainment are very similar between the two tables. Furthermore, Table 3 presents the percentages of college graduates (higher education) by father's occupation for five birth cohorts. The values of the bottom row reflect the overall expansion of higher education during the corresponding period of forty years, and all other cell values of percentage show that the expansion of higher education raised the level of educational attainment for all five social strata. Yet it should be noted that the basic pattern of the differences has not been changed. In addition, the standardized ratios in parentheses indicate that the expansion of higher education brought more benefit to the middle strata such as white-collar and upper blue-collar. Thus, as a whole the examination of these tables suggests that the expansion of school education does not necessarily increase equality of educational opportunity, unless certain compensatory policies are introduced. In fact, it did not do so in Japan.

Then, the question that follows would be why educational attainments differ among social strata. To consider this question, Tables 4 through 6 present scholastic achievements of ninth-graders by father's education. Note that ninth grade is critical in the Japanese educational system after World War II, because in most cities senior high schools are clearly ranked according to the selectivity, and which school children can get into has been largely determined by

Table 4. Academic achievement (mathematics) by father's education (ninth grade, 1968; values are percent)

Grade Point	Compulsory	Secondary	Higher Education	Total
		Father's Education		
1 (lowest)	7.2 ⎱ 31.0	2.6 ⎱ 15.1	0.3 ⎱ 6.9	5.5 ⎱ 24.8
2	23.8 ⎰	12.5 ⎰	6.6 ⎰	19.3 ⎰
3	37.6	35.8	29.4	36.3
4	24.0 ⎱ 31.4	35.8 ⎱ 49.2	35.9 ⎱ 63.7	27.9 ⎱ 38.7
5 (highest)	7.4 ⎰	13.4 ⎰	27.8 ⎰	10.8 ⎰
TOTAL	100.0 (57.8)	100.0 (26.5)	100.0 (9.3)	100.0 (others 6.5%)

Cited from Morikazu Ushiogi and Satomi Sato "Shakai-Kaisō to Gakugyo-seiseki nikansuru Jisshokenkyu (An Empirical Study on Social Class and Academic Achievements)" 1979.
Data: National sample data collected by Ministry of Education.

Table 5. Academic achievement (average of five major subjects) by father's education (ninth grade, 1972; values are percent)

Grade Point	Compulsory	Secondary	Higher Education
	Father's Education		
1 (lowest)	7.3 ⎱ 30.6	6.5 ⎱ 22.5	1.0 ⎱ 11.0
2	23.3 ⎰	16.0 ⎰	10.0 ⎰
3	37.5	42.5	28.0
4	20.7 ⎱ 29.8	25.0 ⎱ 33.9	37.7 ⎱ 60.9
5 (highest)	9.1 ⎰	8.9 ⎰	23.2 ⎰
TOTAL	100.0 (63.1)	100.0 (19.0)	100.0 (8.1)

Cited from Morikazu Ushiogi et al. "Kōkō-fushingakusha Hassei no Mekanizumu (A Mechanism through Which Students Do Not Go on to High School)" 1972.
Data: Gifu Prefecture sample data collected by Ushiogi et al.
Unknowns: father's education 9.8% (compulsory, 2.1%; secondary, 1.1%).

Table 6. Academic achievement (average of five major subjects) by father's education (ninth grade, 1977; values are percent)

Grade Point	Compulsory	Secondary	Higher Education	Total
		Father's Education		
1 (lowest)	9.1 ⎱ 33.6	4.6 ⎱ 16.2	3.6 ⎱ 17.9	6.5 ⎱ 24.8
2	24.5 ⎰	11.6 ⎰	14.3 ⎰	18.3 ⎰
3	42.5	44.4	32.1	40.7
4	20.6 ⎱ 23.8	28.2 ⎱ 39.3	31.5 ⎱ 50.0	25.4 ⎱ 34.5
5 (highest)	3.2 ⎰	11.1 ⎰	18.5 ⎰	9.1 ⎰
TOTAL	100.0 (339)	100.0 (216)	100.0 (168)	100.0 (723)

Cited from Hidenori Fujita, "Kyoiku no Kikai," 1982, same as Table 1.
Data: Shizuoka Prefecture sample data collected by Ushiogi and Fujita.

the results of entrance examination and/or their scholastic achievements of the ninth grade. Table 4 is based on the national sample data and on achievement in mathematics alone, while Tables 5 and 6 are based on prefectural samples and on the averages of five major subjects including mathematics. We may assume that these differences do not violate the comparability seriously, since the prefectures concerned are fairly representative in terms of college advancement rate and occupational composition, and several studies show the unidimensionality and high correlations among five major subjects in the junior high school level.[6]

As clearly shown in these tables, there are large differences in scholastic achievements by father's education. The higher a father's education is, the higher scholastic achievements tend to be. For example, for those whose father attained higher education the majority belong to the higher two achievement levels on the five points scale, while for those whose father's education is on the compulsory level less than one third belong to the higher two levels. Moreover, these three tables suggest that the basic pattern of differences in scholastic achievements by father's education has remained unchanged during the period of the remarkable expansion of secondary and higher education.

There are various explanations of the causal relationships among family background, scholastic achievement, and educational attainment. As for educational attainment, the differences may be partially explained by the differences in family's economic capacity to afford the direct and indirect costs of schooling. It may be partially explained by the differences in values which people attach to higher education. Under the severe entrance examination system, educational attainment may be a function of scholastic achievements or academic capacity. On the other hand, the differences in scholastic achievements may be explained by the differences in material, motivational, linguistic, and other cultural conditions of the family. It may be explained structurally by the cultural continuity/discontinuity between family and school, or institutionally by teachers' biased treatments and attitudes toward children of different social strata. Or someone may explain it by genetic differences.

None of these explanations, however, is definitive.[7] This is not surprising, of course, because the observed relationships are statistical and the evidence about causality are not deterministic but probabilistic. Thus, instead of investigating the relevance of those explanations, let us consider the effects of the expansion of school education on the activities in the school.

Custodial Care and Moral Education

Japanese schooling has an extremely strong and comprehensive custodial component. For example, in most secondary schools extracurricular activities, especially athletics, are very popular, and many students stay for training at school until 6 or 7 o'clock in the evening. Even on Sunday or during the summer vacation many students go to school for club activities. Thus, one of the major duties of secondary school teachers in Japan is to undertake guidance of these various extracurricular activities. Through these activities, students are expected to learn the discipline of group life and perseverance, to develop their physical strength, and to identify themselves with the school community. As it is often said, it is quite conceivable that these extracurricular activities and many other programs during the summer vacation keep students busy with school activities and hence serve to prevent delinquency to some extent.

It is also generally believed as normal that elementary and secondary schools should have supervisory rights over students' behavior outside the school. Thus, almost all elementary and secondary schools have prescribed the details of permissible behavior and activities both inside and outside the school; for example, clothes, places where students may go by themselves and where they may go with parents or other adults, and so on. Some secondary schools require the students and parents to report prior to a long trip during the summer or spring vacation. All of these examples suggest the extremely broad custodial role of school education in Japan.

Parents' expectations of school are also very board in Japan. According to our survey data collected in 1977,[8] parents expect school to teach children the following: discipline of group life (98.3 percent), cognitive training (90.5 percent), love of one's local place (75.3 percent), punctuality (75.0 percent), friendship and good peer relations (75.0 percent), and public morality (63.9 percent). These results again suggest how broad and comprehensive is the role school is expected to take in Japan and how little on this point has changed between the prewar and postwar periods. In fact, for example, elementary and secondary school students clean their classroom and school building every day by turns, through which they are expected to develop the discipline of group life, a sense of responsibility, a sense of cleanliness, and public morality. Many of the ceremonial gatherings and events which were described in the first section are still common in almost all elementary and secondary schools, except those related to the prewar emperor system. Thus, various rituals and informal curricula continue to play an important role in Japanese education, most of which are oriented toward moral education rather than developing basic knowledge and skills.

Yet, many *juku*, *yobiko*, and testing companies are still flourishing. Of course, these phenomena are mainly the consequence of the severe entrance examination system and people's concerns about educational attainment. It is ironic that on the one hand people expect the school to be a total agency of socialization, and on the other hand the most fundamental role of modern school education—developing basic knowledge and skills—has been individualized and partially left to these alternative primitive institutions. This orientation, however, is not new in Japanese education. As the statue of Kinjiro Ninomiya had symbolized, being diligent has always meant to work hard even at home and on every occasion, though this orientation had not been as well-organized as it is today.

Thus, it can be said that many structural and institutional characteristics of Japanese school education were established during the first few decades of the Meiji era and since then have not been changed in spite of its remarkable expansion under postwar school reforms.

Conclusion

A broad range of social, cultural, economic, and educational factors can be related to the various pathological phenomena in Japanese schooling today. First, since the 1970s, postwar economic growth has produced fairly high standards of living, provided a variety of job opportunities, and hence have kept the unemployment rate extremely low. Furthermore, according to several national sample surveys, between 80 and 90 percent of the people perceive themselves as belonging to the middle class, whatever "middle class" means to them. Under these circumstances, many students tend to lose the incentive to get ahead and to study hard for the purpose of realizing a better life.

Second, because of its very meritocratic nature, its deep commitment to the entrance examination system, and the clear prestige differentiation among schools, school education in Japan has presumably failed to validate various alternative evaluation scales, to provide ample images and hopes regarding occupations and career perspectives, and hence to develop self-efficacy in students.

Third, because of the perceived unidimensional, meritocratic philosophy and because of their strong custodial orientation and prevailing school rituals, schools in Japan have occupied a very central position in the life of childhood, both emotionally and institutionally. It is thus under these circumstances that dropping out of school presumably tends to be stigmatized.

Fourth, because of the density of the formal curriculum under the pressure of the entrance examinations and because of poor teaching conditions such as large class size (forty students per teacher), a significant number of students do not understand what they are taught in class. Although it seems to be an exaggerated statement, educational critics often say "Shichi-Go-San," which means that students who understand the subjects are 70 percent in elementary school, 50 percent in junior high school, and 30 percent in senior high school. The term "Shichi-Go-San" is the rhyme which means a gala day for children of three, five, and seven years of age.

Fifth, school rituals tend to produce ritualism, formalism, and trivialism among teachers. For example, many secondary schools have specified a school uniform, and these days many teachers in many schools seem to spend much energy in keeping order. Teachers are often seen in the morning at the front gate standing with a yardstick measuring the width of boys' trousers and the length of girls' skirts. Another major point of a similar kind is hairstyle. Although these phenomena should not be criticized unduly, it is presumably the case that formalistic and trivialistic teachers' attitudes tend to bar the development of trustful relations between students and teachers, and hence the development of cohesive school communities.

Sixth, since the 1970s various opposing opinions and attitudes on pedagogy, evaluation, discipline and many other school activities have become increasingly apparent both among teachers and among parents. This is partly because those in the postwar generation who have become teachers tend to have different opinions and attitudes, partly because economic growth and urbanization have diversified modes of living and enabled many parents to become more aware of their own tastes than before, and partly because school itself, in terms both of organization and of curriculum, has been secularized after the postwar school reform, and hence both teachers and parents have become free to express their own opinions and tastes in various ways. Importantly, this indicates that a qualitative change has taken place in the linkages between school, family, and community, and that the effectiveness of indoctrinatory moral education and unconscious moral education has been undermined.

Seventh, until recently, school had been a single, monopolistic agent of cognitive training and teachers had enjoyed a monopoly of knowledge, skills, and even moral authority. However, as higher education reached a mass stage and many parents have teachers' qualifications, teacher authority has been weakened. Also, as *yobiko* and *juku* have prevailed, the school's major role as an agency of cognitive training has become curtailed. Thus, the legitimacy of school education has been undermined in contemporary Japan.

In any social organization, legitimacy is the key to its maintenance and successful functioning. This is particularly the case in an educational organization. In such an organization as school, legitimacy relies on two mutually related factors: self-evidentness and communality. Self-evidentness here means that activities, both their modes and contents, are believed as self-evident and unquestionable, while communality means that activities are supported as necessary and reasonable by the people of a community concerned. For example, for those who see school education of a certain kind as definitely necessary for their future career, school education tends to be perceived as self-evident. Accordingly, school education can fairly easily keep self-evidentness when society is economically poor and school education is perceived as an important mobility channel. Self-evidentness may be also fairly well secured when everybody is doing the same thing and is treated the same way.

On the other hand, communality depends to a great extent on the cohesion of a community and the homogeneity of its members' concerns and interests. It is presumably true that communality is generally well secured in many traditional, low-mobility societies, and that urbanization, secularization, high social mobility, and class differentiation all tend to undermine the foundation of communality more or less. Japanese school education, until very recently, has kept both self-evidentness and communality. In the last ten years or so, however, both self-evidentness and communality seem to have been weakened, and hence the legitimacy of school education has been undermined.

Notes

1. Cited from NHK Shuzaihan (Nihon Hoso Kyokai, a news-gathering team), *Nihon no Joken 11: Kyoiku 2 (The State of Affairs in Japan 11: Education 2)*, Nihon Hoso Shuppan Kyokai 1983, 248–50.

2. Sorifu, Seishonen-Taisaku-Honbu (Youth Remedy Bureau, Prime Minister's Office), *Kokusai-hikaku: Nihon no Kodomo to Hahaoya* (International comparison: child and mother in Japan) (Tokyo: Prime Minister's Office, 1980). For a further discussion, see Hidenori Fujita, "Gakko to Shakai: Jimeisei no Soshitsu" (School and Society: A loss of self-evidentness), in *Sogo-Kyoiku-Gijutsu* (Synthetic education method) (Shogakkan, May 1981), 146–49.

3. Many characteristics established in the early Meiji era, of course, were found in the orders among the military class during the Tokugawa era. This is especially the case for the moral order of family. Some characteristics of school education in the Meiji era were also found in Terakoya, Shijuku, Hanko, and schools of the Shogunate.

4. Tomitaro Karasawa, *Zusetsu Meiji Hyakunen Kodomo no Rekishi* (Explanatory illustrations of a history of children: one hundred years since Meiji Restoration) (Tokyo: Kodansha, 1972).

5. See Hidenori Fujita, "Kyoiku no Kikai (Opportunity of Education)," in *Kyoiku-shakai-gaku* (Sociology of education), ed. Yasumasa Tomoda (Yushindo 1982), 160–82; Hidenori Fujita, "Koko-kyoiku no Genjo to Shorai" (The Present and the Future of Secondary Education: An Analysis of Specialists' Opinions) in *Koko-kyoiku Gimuka no Kanosei ni-kansuru Kisoteki-kenkyu* (Possibilities of compulsory upper secondary education in Japan), ed. Morikazu Ushiogi, *Toyota Foundation Research Report* III–004, (1979): 9–50.

6. Morikazu Ushiogi, Hidenori Fujita, Mitsuru Taki, Satomi Sato, Tatsuo Kawashima, and Kozo Iwata, "Chugakko-bunka no Kozoteki-bunseki" (An analysis of the structure of junior high school culture), in *Research Bulletin of School of Education, Nagoya University* 27 (1980): 171–216.

7. For the detail of empirical examination and theoretical discussion in Japan, see the following: Hidenori Fujita, 1982, op. cit., and 1978; op. cit. Tatsuo Kawashima and Hidenori Fujita, "Gakko no Shakaiteki-kino nikansuru Ichikosatsu (A study on the function of school)," in *Research Bulletin of School of Education, Nagoya University* 28 (1981): 119–33.

8. Hidenori Fujita, "Gendaishakai ni okeru Shitsuke to Gakko-kyoiku (Discipline and school education in contemporary Japan)," in *Research Bulletin of School Education, Nagoya University* 25 (1978): 167–79.

10

The Present Climate in Japanese Junior High Schools

Kazuhiro Mochizuki

I am principal of the Meguro Tenth Junior High School, and I've been involved in junior high school education for some thirty-three years, almost since the beginning of the new educational system instituted after the War. I'd like to speak in rather broad terms about the actual conditions of Japanese schools today.

In technical terms, compulsory education extends only through the primary and lower secondary schools. Actually, however, in Tokyo 94.7 percent of all junior high school graduates go on to high school; nationwide, that figure is 94 percent. If we allow for special circumstances—handicapped children, children who are educated abroad or at home, and so on—we can say that in effect every lower secondary school student in Japan goes on to high school. High schools have in that sense come to be part of the compulsory education system, and the process of getting into high school is perhaps the most significant issue in Japanese education today. In particular, the entrance examination constitutes a special hurdle that makes the process quite different from what it is elsewhere.

An earlier version of this essay was published as "The Present Situation of Japan's Education: A Report from School," Orientation Seminars on Japan Number 11, Tokyo, Office for the Japanese Studies Center, The Japan Foundation, 1982.

Beginning somewhere between eight and ten years ago, a very strong tendency developed for junior high school students to seek admission to the college preparatory courses in high school; before that, it was considered quite acceptable to attend vocational and industrial high schools that led directly to working careers. Today about half the students at the lower secondary level intend to go on to the so-called "ordinary" high schools, and the enormous pressures of competition that now exist on the route to higher education create special problems for the junior high schools; the prevailing attitude is for the student to reach as high as he or she possibly can, and many of the students caught up in this really ought not to be trying to do college preparatory work. One might say that the whole weight of Japan's competitive society falls back on the junior high schools.

Because virtually every junior high school student wants to take the examination for a good high school, which will then open the path to the university, the focus of their efforts has been narrowed to the study of English, mathematics, and the Japanese language—the three primary considerations on the examination; activities such as student clubs, sports, music, and other school subjects are considered of lesser importance. This makes it extremely difficult for the teacher to provide a well-balanced, well-rounded education. Added to this is the sense of rivalry that pervades the school atmosphere: the student who does well on the examination, does so at his or her neighbor's expense.

Recently, I've been looking at some data about the attitudes of junior high school students; paradoxically, it seems that there has been a great increase in the interest expressed in the "non-core" school activities and functions: physical training, athletic meets, summer school programs, music programs, and so on. The results of the survey do not mesh with the emphasis on preparing for examinations, and they seem to suggest that the children are looking for some form of escape from that pressure. Japanese children in the primary schools very clearly enjoy their education; they look and sound happy in their environment. The first year of junior high school seems to evoke the same sorts of feelings, but once they enter the second year, when what lies ahead becomes clear to them—what they are going to have to do to be successful—this forces them to suppress their real interests and focus on the three critical subjects: English, Japanese, and mathematics. As a result, the students in the second or third year of junior high schools come to view their teachers purely as people whose job it is to evaluate them—to give out marks—and not as people who can help them grow and fulfill themselves. Inevitably this damages the relationship between students and teachers.

What we are looking at, then, is a situation in which the system of entrance examinations for high school exerts a pervasive influence over the whole nature of what goes on in the junior high schools. When a student receives a poor grade in a given subject, he or she generally has two reactions, since this is going to have such an impact on the whole future course of life. One is the development of an inferiority complex, a severe sense of depression; in effect, the child is being told to forget about going on to a college prep high school, to settle for a vocational school—that he or she has lost out in the competition. The other reaction is one of violence against the teacher; as you may already have heard, there has been a great deal of attention focused recently on the problem of violence in Japanese schools, and I see this as part of much larger phenomenon arising from the process of academic competition.

Another issue to take into consideration is the change in the structure of Japanese society itself since the end of the War, and the way that has affected the current situation in the schools. One of the most notable changes has taken place in the size of the family unit; some 85 percent of the students in my own school have either one sibling or none at all. Unlike in the prewar period, children are growing up now in home environments where they are overprotected and indulged; when they encounter the competitive pressures in the schools, they are unable to accept a poor grade or a low evaluation, because they are used to being spoiled at home.

Since the War, Japanese society has become one of increasing material well-being, and the children of the present generation have grown up accustomed to comforts and conveniences. This makes them, on the one hand, rather easygoing; they haven't had to suffer the privations of their parents' generation—when people had to cooperate, look out for each other, and work harder. Students now tend to look to their parents for things; in the past, even junior high school students would go out and get part-time jobs to earn what they wanted. Being so accustomed to immediate gratifications, young Japanese now are far less able to endure hardships of any kind; this applies to the hardships of competition in the school system as well.

This whole situation has produced still another problem, which is that the children experience a great deal of difficulty forming friendships with their peers. You have a classroom with forty children in it, and the teacher tries—unsuccessfully—to "legislate" that they will be friends as a group. This also touches on the issue of *juku* cram schools: of course the major reason for sending a child to one of these schools is for the extra instruction he or she needs to prepare for examinations, but if you ask the children themselves why they attend, they will say that the *juku* gives them the chance to form real friendships.

Embarrassing as it is to report, there are cases of children who are chronically absent from school, and when we investigate we find that they are going to the *juku* instead—and actually doing better academically. Again, the reason the children themselves give is that they can form their own friendships there—that it's more fun. More than that, the teachers in the *juku* have a better rapport with these children: in the regular schools, the teacher will often write off the student who is not doing well, but the *juku* teacher is more encouraging, accepting that the student is having difficulties and trying to help him overcome them. In some sense, then, the *juku* provides a more humane kind of environment; it's not, as we have generally been thinking, a hardship on the students.

Still another problem is the rapidly increasing numbers of women teachers and particularly young teachers in the school system. In the junior high schools there is still a balance of sorts between men and women teachers, but on the primary school level—particularly in Tokyo, for example—women teachers are in a large majority. The predominance of young people in the profession makes for teaching staffs with more training than experience. There is a kind of elitism among these younger teachers, because it has become far more difficult to pass the certifying examinations, and the ones who do have graduated from the better universities and tend to think of themselves as rather special. To have pride in the profession is a good thing, of course, but twenty or thirty years ago, a school teacher was someone who might not have been able to find some other career, and so did not have an inflated opinion of himself. Older teachers, who did not come up through the competitive examination system, tend to stress learning for its own sake, and are not so quick to write off the students who seem unlikely to do well on exams; as a result, the students find them much more sympathetic and warm, and prefer them to younger teachers. In addition, the younger women teachers particularly tend to avoid problems at any cost; their educational priorities more or less follow the lines of least resistance.

The younger generation of teachers poses another kind of problem as well, for administrators like myself. I've visited a number of schools around the country and attended a number of symposia on education, and I've found that especially in the big-city schools there is a great deal of friction between administrations and the Nikkyoso—the Japan Federation of Teachers. The union seems to have fostered in the teachers a very strong sense of their "rights" as white-collar workers; they see themselves as having careers in which they put in a certain amount of time for their salaries and then go home. Where this sort of sensibility is very strong, it makes school administration very difficult; there's an atmosphere of resistance that takes attention away from the children themselves and their education. My own school is by no means a bad one in this regard, but the problem exists even there.

Let me then tie together a few strains that have run through my observations. For one, a great deal of mechanization has crept into the whole educational process; the true spirit of education, which depends on the relationship between teacher and student, has been lost. Teachers now see themselves merely as salaried employees of the system, the limits of their responsibilities defined by the seven and a half hours they are actually in school. I try to stress the importance of the traditional idea of a teacher as someone with a full-time commitment to the students, but I think that in the teacher's concern for his or her own rights, the children have lost their rights to an education that will draw them out as human beings. Instead what we find is the force-feeding of more and more information, without any sense of education as a process of growth and development; the natural result is an increasing number of students who get no joy at all out of going to school and who would not attend if they had the choice. The problem is especially acute in the junior high schools, and so far there has been no real consensus among school administrators about how to solve it.

For the teachers actually trying to provide some kind of life guidance to children who are going astray, there is an additional problem: the children themselves have developed a kind of critical attitude about the adult world, and a much weaker critical outlook on themselves. "Maybe what we are doing is wrong," they say, "but we're not the only ones at fault." This problem has especially frightening consequences for the twenty-first century: the adults of the next generation are now growing up unprepared to take responsibility for their own character. I've taken a great many surveys, and done a lot of thinking about what makes students today so different from those of, say, fifteen years ago, and I think one major factor has been that they have grown up with color television: the television gives them plenty of opportunities to see the adult world in a less than admirable light, and it is much harder to convince them that they are doing anything especially wrong themselves.

Another serious problem which comes into the schools is one that arises in the home when the father defaults on his traditional role. The fathers of the students now in junior and senior high school are for the most part in their early or mid-forties, the age at which their jobs and careers make the heaviest demands on them; they tend to come home too late or too tired to have any meaningful interactions with their children. Of course, Japanese fathers have always worked hard; but as householders they are now under different and much greater financial pressures, and most of the day-to-day parental influence is exercised by the mothers. If there is a problem at school that calls for a conference, almost invariably it's the mother who comes in alone; as children in their early teens begin to think about what they want to do with their lives, it's the mother who provides the direction. Not having those important interactions with their fathers, students have a hard time putting their school work and exams into any proper perspective, and this places an additional burden on the teacher.

What, then, can be done to solve these problems? One thing we need to do as educators, is to introduce greater diversity to the value-orientations of Japan: an elite university education ought not to be the goal of so large a segment of the student population. There need to be more realistic approaches to career guidance, that take individual differences into consideration; the whole idea of academic ability needs to be reexamined in a more humane light. Hopefully, this will move us away from measuring academic success by the amount of information a student can absorb and regurgitate on examinations, towards a more comprehensive vision of what learning and growing up is all about.

11

Bullies in the Classroom

Yoshio Murakami

Bullying among children is nothing new. Over sixty years ago Japan's beloved author of juvenile literature, Miyazawa Kenji, movingly depicted bullying in a passage of his *Ginga Tetsudo no Yoru* (Night of the Milky Way Railroad). The young protagonist of this work, Giovanni, lives with his invalid mother, looking forward to the day when his father returns from his fishing job in distant northern waters with the sea-otter jacket he has promised his son.

A vicious rumor, however, has been circulating among Giovanni's classmates that the boy's father has actually been put in prison, and the ringleader Zanelli takes every opportunity to taunt Giovanni with the refrain, "Giovanni, your sea-otter jacket's on its way." Only words, but they send a chill through the young boy's heart.

One day after school Giovanni runs into a group of classmates, Zanelli among them, on his way home. Zanelli starts the chant, and the others take it up. "Giovanni, your sea-otter jacket's on its way." Red-faced with shame, Giovanni starts to walk past the boys when he spots his friend Campanella among the bullies. Campanella stands there mutely with a wan smile, as if to say, "Try not to be angry."

An earlier version of this essay was published in *Japan Quarterly* (The Asahi Shimbun Publishing Company), Vol. 32 (October-December 1985).

As the story unfolds Giovanni joins his friend Campanella on a dreamlike trip on the Milky Way Railroad.

In whatever age or society, rare is the child who does not possess a streak of cruelty, and in almost every group of children you will find the bully and the bully's victim. What has made bullying such a big social problem in the last five years or so is that once it gets started it knows no stopping point and can easily escalate into suicide or murder. What was normal has become abnormal, like a festering sore that will not heal.

In November 1984 a first-year high school student in Osaka was murdered by two of his classmates. The gruesome way the boy was murdered was bad enough, but what shocked the adult world even more was the revelation that the murder had been triggered by the victim's tormenting of the two boys who murdered him. The objects of constant harassment, the boys had ended up by taking revenge on their tormenter. The details of this case are worth going into for what they reveal about the bullying problem.

Kamazawa Yoshiaki, sixteen, was the son of a sushi shop operator in Osaka and attended a private high school in the city. His body was found on the afternoon of November 2 in a river in the Tenma area. His head had been struck dozens of times with a hammer and his eyes had been gouged out. Police suspicions focused almost immediately on two of Yoshiaki's classmates, A and B, both fifteen. After preliminary questioning, they were arrested on November 11 on suspicion of murder.

A Murdered Classmate

A and B were members of a group of which Yoshiaki had been the leader. Yoshiaki, a stocky boy, had belonged to the school's judo club and was considered one of the club's most promising new members when he joined. A and B belonged to the gymnastics club. It was a mutual interest in sports that brought the three together, and at first they evidently got on quite well.

The boys' high school puts a lot of emphasis on sports and is particularly strong in judo. Yoshiaki was told that if he worked hard at his judo he was sure of making the regular team by his third year. When he realized what a long haul he had ahead of him he became discouraged, and in the summer of 1984 he dropped out of the club.

It was just about that time that Yoshiaki began tormenting the other two boys. He would order them to wallop this or that class mate, and if they didn't would beat or kick them. "What number do you like?" he would ask, and then strike them that number of times. Or he would get on his motorbike and order them to follow him on bicycles. If they didn't keep up he would beat them again.

According to the boys' confession, the last straw came when they were forced to perform an indecent act with an adult toy in their classroom in front of classmates. If we let him get away with this, they reasoned, what will he make us do next?

But even so, what a brutal method of murder! The two took Yoshiaki to a park one night, took turns striking him with a hammer, then, using the claw end, gouged out his eyes. Was it fear that Yoshiaki might come back to life that made them give themselves so relentlessly to the task? When they were done battering him, they dragged the body fifty meters to the river and threw it in. That is how terrified the two were of the boy.

The boys say that on a number of occasions they told teachers and friends about what Yoshiaki was doing to them and sought help. The school maintains that it knew nothing about what was going on. Indeed, one of the most disturbing things about this case and others like it is the pat, bureaucratic response on the part of the school. "We weren't aware of a thing. We're as shocked as anyone. We'll investigate and make sure this kind of thing doesn't happen again." Were the teachers really as ignorant of the situation as they claimed?

When I asked if I could interview a few people at the school, a teacher replied in an eerily matter-of-fact way, "We have a lot of wild kids here, and we don't want you setting them off; there's no telling what they might do. And don't interview any teachers; there's no telling what they might do either." In the subtle but very real atmosphere of violence at this school, both teachers and students have become insensitive to violence. They offer threats instead of concern.

Both the victim and the two murderers in this case come from homes where both parents are present and in their prime, homes with no discernible family problems. In recent years there has been a sharp increase in cases of children from such normal homes suddenly engaging in abnormal behavior.

Victims Have No Friends

Take the case of the second-year junior high school boy in Tokyo's Adachi Ward who hanged himself back in January 1979. Before taking his life the boy wrote a message in the class diary, a portion of which I quote: "I decided to kill myself because day after day I go to school and only bad things happen. Nothing good ever happens to me. If the kids in my class could be in my shoes they would understand how I feel. If only they knew how I feel every day. Even in my dreams there are nothing but bad things. The only one I can talk to is the hamster, but the hamster can't speak back. Maybe I'm just not suited to this world. Maybe July 7, 1964—my being born—was a mistake. I can't stop the tears now. There was one, only one, thing that I wanted while I was alive—a friend I could talk to, really talk to, from the heart. Just one friend like that, only one, was all I wanted."

The boy was a sensitive child and not strong physically, and for this he was made the object of almost daily bullying at school. One cannot help but be deeply dismayed at the rapid spread of an inhuman atmosphere among children. When vulnerability is detected in another child, the tendency seems to be to push the weak points until the individual is crushed.

Let me give another specific example. The setting this time is a small town in the bleak Hokuriku district on the Japan Sea side of Honshu. In February 1984 a second-year student at the junior high school in the town was taken by a number of classmates into the athletic equipment room and there beaten up. When he got home, his face bruised and swollen, his shocked father pressed him for an explanation. The boy reluctantly revealed that this was but the latest episode in six months of almost daily bullying.

They would wait for him on the way home from school. They would emerge suddenly from the shadows, block any escape route, then take him down an alley where they would start hitting him. Although the students were allowed to sit anywhere at lunchtime, no one would ever sit near him. When he went to the toilet, somebody would spread the word. His classmates would gather in the lavatory and stand on each other's shoulders to peek in on him. He would return to the classroom only to find his desk and chair had been dragged out in the hall. Trying to keep back the tears, he would take the desk back to its place, not a soul offering to help.

The students were not the only ones who gave the boy a hard time. There seems to have been a feeling of strong dislike for him among the teachers as well. One of the teachers powdered his head with chalk dust from the blackboard eraser. Another teacher would catch him up on the slightest mistake and hit him with a bamboo sword.

What had the boy done to deserve this concerted harassment that even included the violence of his teachers? At this school the boys were supposed to have crew cuts, but this boy had somewhat longer hair. "At least, that's the only thing I can possibly think of," his father says. "My son did something different, so he was persecuted. The length of your hair, the color of the clothes you wear—things like that are not supposed to be left up to the individual. When everybody's got to have a crew cut, everybody's got to wear the same color, the feeling builds up against anyone who is different: We can't let that guy get away with that! It's a very frightening thing. Well, I asked my son how he felt about it, we talked it over with the teacher, and he decided to let his hair grow."

Official Reports

The day after his son was beaten up, the father went to the principal, told him what had happened, and asked his help. Though he did not say so in so many words, the principal made it clear to the father that the boy was in the wrong for having broken the rules. As far as the father is concerned, this just goes to show what kind of school it is. "To put it briefly, this is a violent school. You have the gym teacher pacing the floor with a bamboo sword in his hand. The student slips up and he's going to get a wallop. Inspections are held to check clothes, hair, what the kids have got in their desks. If your hair is the least bit long, the teacher gets after you with scissors and hair clippers. It's the atmosphere of coercion and violence in this school that gave rise to my son's being beaten up. And can you blame the kids for thinking like that? They figure if it's all right for the teachers to hit people it's all right for them to do the same. Are they wrong?"

The father is appealing to the teachers and to other parents to work to change the school. But there is no indication that either teachers or parents intend to do a thing. The boy in Tokyo who liked hamsters was bullied because he was weak. The boy in Hokuriku who stood out because of his long hair was the object of violence because he was different. We see here a buildup in the schools of unhealthy energy directed at isolating certain individuals—with the tacit approval or even complicity of responsible adults.

There are a few statistics that I would like to mention at this point. In April, the National Police Agency issued its first "Survey of Bullying Incidents," which covers the year 1984. The incidence of bullying cases has only recently warranted the collection of separate statistics. The survey reports that the police investigated 531 cases of assault and battery, other violence, blackmail, and acts of juvenile delinquency that were the result of bullying (*ijime*) and took 1,920 boys and girls into protective custody. Seven elementary and junior high school students committed suicide, apparently as a result of bullying, and four children were murdered or were the victims of attempted murder in retaliation for bullying. Of these cases, 80 percent involved junior high school students and one-third of those taken into protective custody were girls.

The violence inflicted was in many cases quite serious. In one case, a child was paralyzed from the waist down and in another a student was left with a serious speech impairment. But not only physical violence was involved—that is, beating up or pushing around the victim. Verbal abuse was very common, and most cases involved ostracism of the victim by fellow students. A set of statistics from the Tokyo Metropolitan Board of Education sheds light on the extent of such noncriminal bullying as well.

The Board of Education surveyed the public schools in Tokyo, 76.9 percent of which reported instances of bullying between April 1984 and March 1985. Here is the breakdown for those 1,789 schools: elementary schools (grades one to six), 5,450 cases; junior high schools (grades seven to nine), 3,519 cases; and high schools (grades ten to twelve), 515 cases. The last three years of school seem to be relatively free of bullying.

Of the bullying activities 70 percent could be categorized as psychological bullying. This includes making threats, calling names, leaving classmates out of games and other activities, and ostracizing them completely. Some typical bullying taunts are *baikin* (germ), *shi ne* (drop dead), and *kusai* (you stink). The recipients of such abuse are usually the weak children and the goody-goodies. While the strong always prey on the weak and bullying may be fun, the popularity of such psychological bullying might be explained by its invisible effects. Those in authority are more likely to detect torn clothing and black eyes than a damaged ego.

Adults Are Responsible

Although my main concern here is violence committed by children, it should be noted that there has been a recent spate of cases in which students have been killed or have committed suicide as a result of corporal punishment inflicted by teachers. On May 9, 1985, a high school boy from Gifu Prefecture on a class trip to the international science exhibition at Tsukuba City died after his teacher severely punished him. He had violated a school rule by taking his hair dryer on the trip. In another case seven weeks earlier a high school girl, also from Gifu Prefecture, hanged herself after enduring corporal punishment by the teacher in charge of the track and field club. "I'm sick and tired of being hit, and I'm sick and tired of crying," she wrote before she killed herself. A junior high school girl from Nagano Prefecture who had continually clashed with a teacher left this note before putting an end to her life: "I hate school. Everybody tries to cut you down. But I hate the teacher most of all, because she gets you when you're down and then tramples all over you." In cases like this, is corporal punishment by teachers really all that different from bullying by fellow students?

The interactions of children reflect society as a whole. If adults say, "It has nothing to do with me," children echo the sentiment. Only recently have adults begun to open their eyes. During the 1960s when everyone was committed to economic growth, victims of pollution and industrial accidents were ignored. An overriding interest in the GNP distorted people's thinking and ultimately created the bullying phenomenon.

Now that an affluent society has been achieved, some adults are opening their eyes to the victims and unfortunate ones around them, confident that their problems can be solved. But we have not made the progress that we think we have. Most of us still think, "It has nothing to do with me." But it is our problem. All of us must learn to care for others.

12

Public and Private Schools and Educational Opportunity in Japan

Gail R. Benjamin and Estelle James

The size of the private educational sector in Japan can be seen as the direct reflection of central government policies which limit the supply of public education beyond the compulsory level. Since the Meiji Restoration, this policy has been to provide, under central government jurisdiction, basic education for the whole population and further education for a small elite. At the same time, private enterprise has been expected and encouraged, as a matter of government policy, to respond to demands for education that exceed the public supply.

Japan's greatest government commitment to education has been in the nine years of compulsory schooling covering primary and junior high school. The government has a near monopoly as the provider of education to young Japanese at this level. Only 1 percent of students in grades one through nine are in private schools. A substantial degree of uniformity is sought for and achieved within the public sector by equal funding throughout the country, by residential patterns that do not segregate students by parental income or occupation as much as in many other industrial countries, by

This essay is based on material contained in the authors' book *Public Policy and Private Education in Japan* (London: Macmillan, 1988).

central government standardization of the curriculum and texts, and by an unusual degree of cultural homogeneity among the Japanese people.

Beyond the compulsory level, a smaller number of high school and university places have been provided by the government. The public secondary and higher educational institutions are selective on the basis of highly competitive examinations, rationing entry to the most desirable lifetime career paths and therefore highly sought after. Both central and local governments hire mainly national university graduates for their highest levels, and the most desirable private employers, the large firms, also hire graduates of only a small number of universities, most of them national universities. An elite group of public secondary schools supply a disproportionate number of students to these national universities.

Increasingly, since the Meiji period, education in Japan has been seen as the major avenue to good jobs, yielding a high private rate of return. Therefore, demand for secondary education exploded during the twentieth century, in particular after World War I. And, with the number of public places relatively inflexible, the private sector has also exploded, a market response to excess demand.

At the higher educational level, the overall growth rate was almost as rapid, as a college degree was perceived as the major route to social mobility and economic well-being, and most growth took place in the private sector.

The period of greatest growth in higher education, however, was yet to come. During the post-World War II period demand for university education was fueled by skyrocketing incomes and high school enrollments which saturated the relevant age group. Between 1960 and 1980 higher education enrollments went up threefold, almost all of it in burgeoning private institutions. By 1980, 38 percent of all eighteen-year-olds were entering junior colleges and universities, 76 percent of them in the private sector. The Japanese experience suggests that neither public funding nor public management is a necessary condition for educational growth, in the face of a strong demand for education stemming from labor market incentives.

The demand for private education in Japan was thus derived from the demand for access to jobs in the face of a limited supply of public school places. What about the supply of private school places? As in many other countries, Japanese private schools are nonprofit organizations, which cannot legally distribute their profits to shareholders. There are no dividends and no capital gains to reward providers of equity capital. Where then do they get their venture capital?

Some of the capital for new schools comes from retained earnings from profitable older schools. For instance, a university with "profits" will found a feeder high school and offer preferential entrance to the graduates of the new affiliated high school. Through this vertical integration, students reduce the uncertainty of their educational careers and the schools reduce the uncertainty of demand for their places. In addition, founders and managers increase their opportunities for disguised profit taking, in the form of above-market salaries and perquisites such as housing, cars, and expense accounts. Branches or chains of private high schools and universities have thus been established, especially in large urban centers such as Tokyo.

In addition, capital has been supplied by loans from the banking system, which regards schools as safe investments, given the strong demand. During the 1960s, a period of great expansion of the private school system, credit was rationed under an implicit agreement worked out between the banking system and the central government. Access to loans for private schools was then in effect a policy decision, preferential treatment of private schools against other contenders for capital. This enabled educational opportunity to expand at little or no cost to the public treasury.

Secondary Schools

High school is not compulsory in Japan, and the Japanese do not think of students as having a "right" to a place in a particular school. The high school one attends is not determined by residence in a given school district. Instead, admission to high school, both public and private, is by examination and at the discretion of the school. The entrance examinations test academic achievement, not "aptitude," and except for those schools (among the oldest and best) which admit only boys or only girls, no other criteria are used. There is no attempt to have a balanced student body, to admit quotas of certain types of students, or to admit everyone in the neighborhood or region.

Despite the lack of compulsion and open access public schools, 96 percent of the relevant age group today go on to secondary schooling, and 90 percent complete it. These are divided (in roughly equal proportions) between public academic, public vocational, and private academic courses. Several factors interact to determine how a given Japanese student will be placed among these alternatives, and the placement is highly correlated with future success.

Individual Differences Among Students and Schools

The oldest high schools, which tend to be urban and public, are at the top of the academic hierarchy, and they have the first pick of students. They are much in demand, their entrance examinations are difficult, scores required are high, and the resulting student bodies are composed of hard workers and good test-takers. The best students go to these schools, many of them from middle- and upper-income brackets. These schools also spend most per student, and their rates of admittance to the best universities, especially Tokyo and Kyoto, are consistently high. This enables them to stay on top of the hierarchy and keep attracting the best students.

Somewhat less successful are the younger public academic high schools, many of them in rural prefectures. These are followed by private academic high schools, then by the low-status vocational schools, almost all of which are public. Relatively few students, most of them coming from low-income families, choose vocational schools, and the quick response of the private market to consumer preferences for academic schools is in part responsible for this.

Ministry of Education rhetoric encourages students to attend vocational school. However, the labor market does not reinforce this rhetoric. Graduates of vocational high schools are not rewarded by high wages for their vocational courses, and these courses limit their options for future schooling and jobs. It is hardly surprising that students respond to the labor market, not the rhetoric, and prefer academic programs. Hence, few private secondary schools have found the demand high enough to offer vocational courses.

Regional Differences

Large regional differences exist in the way students sort themselves out among these schools and courses. These regional variations are particularly striking in a nation whose compulsory education has largely ironed out such differences and whose higher education system is a national one. We have chosen to look at prefectural variations in public and private high school places, academic and vocational places. Prefectures are the level of government most responsible for determining the number and type of high school places, and the market area of schools among which students can choose or be chosen is usually within a given prefecture.

Although as late as the 1950s and 1960s there were important differences among prefectures in the proportion of students continuing from ninth grade into high school, these differences have largely been erased today. However, large differences remain in the proportions that get public versus private and academic versus vocational schooling.

One major pattern of student allocation is found in those prefectures in metropolitan areas with large and wealthy populations, such as Tokyo, Kyoto, Osaka, and Kanegawa. These are the prefectures with the smallest public school enrollments, the largest private sector, and the largest academic track enrollments. The other pattern, a larger public sector, fewer private schools, and many vocational students, is found in rural, agricultural, low-income areas.

As discussed above, public high school academic places are considered highly desirable and are filled to capacity. Therefore the low public enrollments in the wealthy urban prefectures must be due to limited supply, not demand. Why are these high-income areas also the ones with the lowest supply of public high school places?

Public education in Japan is financed through prefectural funds. Prefectures in turn receive their funds from direct taxation of their own population and from taxes transferred from the central government. Poor prefectures receive more funds centrally than rich prefectures, which are net losers. The effect of the shared central government revenues is to equalize the per capita funds available to local governments for spending, regardless of the per capita income within the prefecture. The major metropolitan areas have chosen to spend more on each high school place, that is, their spending per public school student is higher there than in poorer prefectures. At the same time, they have chosen not to raise their own tax rates enough to provide more places, as well. In effect, they have opted for quality rather than quantity.

The choice of high quality in these rich prefectures is not surprising, given the high income elasticity of demand for educational quality; wealthier people generally prefer higher-spending schools. Opting for low quantity, on the other hand, was cheaper for the public treasury than a larger public sector would have been. In addition, it was cheaper overall, since per-student spending in private schools is less than that in public schools. The politically influential upper classes in these prefectures had a good chance of getting their children into the high quality public schools, and, if not, they saved more on public taxes than they had to pay in private tuition, as a result of this policy of limited government spending. The urban working class would have preferred more public access—but they do not have political power in most prefectures.

The metropolitan areas of Japan could choose this option, further, because they had a supply of educational entrepreneurs available for the expansion of the private school system. This is in part because of a long history of private education in these areas, much of it affiliated with religious organizations. Thus, these prefectures already had many private schools at the end of World War II, and these schools could, in turn, provide the "role models," the managerial expertise, and the venture capital needed for opening new schools. Both the demand for higher education and the supply of academic private schools results in a low proportion of students enrolled in vocational courses in these wealthy urban prefectures.

In contrast, more public high school places are provided by the poorer rural prefectures, relative to their population. In fact, the proportion of public high school places is highest in the prefectures with the lowest per capita incomes. These prefectures also spend the least per student; they have chosen quantity over quality. This is the preference of the farmers and small shopkeepers who dominate there. The private demand for education is low in these areas, as evidenced by the fact that they lagged far behind other prefectures in increasing their high school and university attendance rates. We would also expect an absence of private educational entrepreneurship. Therefore, both because of low private demand and supply, high school attendance could be increased in these prefectures only by providing low-tuition public places.

These prefectures, though poor, happen to be politically powerful and are heavily overrepresented in the Japanese Diet (parliament). As a result of this political wealth, they have been the recipients of large amounts of transferred funds from the central government and have been able to use these funds, rather than locally generated funds, to provide these public educational opportunities. Given the low supply of fee-charging private schools, those who cannot get into the public academic courses fill the public vocational schools which are, therefore, more heavily enrolled in these areas.

Thus, the chances of going to a public versus private high school and to an academic versus vocational program, and eventual access to higher education and jobs, vary greatly depending on whether one's family happens to live in a rich urban or poorer rural prefecture.

Higher Education

High school education, in part because of private demand and in part because of private sector response, is now all but universal for Japanese students. Post-high school education is far from universal, though the proportion of eighteen-year-olds who do continue is among the highest in the world, 38 percent. The disparities between the education offered by the government, and that offered by private purveyors of higher education, is much greater than the disparities seen at the secondary level.

Approximately one-quarter of those Japanese young people who enter postsecondary education go on to junior colleges. This is almost entirely a system of private schools. Another 50 percent of those continuing enter private four-year colleges or universities. Finally, about 10 percent of the age cohort, or one-quarter of those in higher education, enter a public university, quite often after one to three years of private post-high school study as *ronin*.

Differences in Public and Private Universities

Most national universities are schools with several faculties, offering training in a variety of technical and liberal arts fields. They are also research schools and have at least small graduate programs. Their facilities, campuses, buildings, libraries, and laboratories are the best in Japan, and their per student spending the highest. Most important for their continued dominance is the fact that they are the schools the government and the most prestigious private employers look to for new employees. Students, then, prefer to attend national universities because they are cheaper, they offer better educational opportunities, and they almost guarantee good employment at the end of four years.

Private universities cover a wide range of quality and prestige, but in spite of a few schools which can compete with the national universities, the great majority are lower in the prestige rankings than the nationals. They typically offer training in only one or two faculties, usually low-cost humanities and social science fields. Little or no research is done at these schools, and there are no graduate programs. The jobs available to graduates are generally less desirable (middle-management at medium-sized firms) than those open to national university graduates.

The last category of postsecondary education is junior colleges. These offer courses primarily in social science and humanities, though a few are vocationally oriented, usually preparing students for such jobs as nursing or nursery school teaching. Junior colleges are almost the exclusive domain of women, and most women in higher education attend junior colleges, which are popularly known as "brides' schools."

Another way to compare these different forms of higher education is to look at what they cost students and society. While the tuition per student is much higher in the private sector, their expenditure per student is much lower. How are the private educational institutions able to offer education at such lower cost than the public universities? One answer lies in the different kinds of education and facilities provided.

The area of greatest cost-saving, however, is in their use of low-salaried teachers. This is true too of low-spending private high schools. Thus they use many professors and teachers who have retired from the national schools, part-timers who are moonlighting and consequently do not require fringe benefits, and women, who still do not have access to remunerative high status careers in Japan. Whether they are inferior teachers or not is not clear; their formal qualifications often match those at public institutions.

Allocation of Students to Public and Private Universities

The education offered by these three types of higher institutions (private junior colleges, private four-year institutions, and public universities) differs, their costs and funding differ, and the prospects of their graduates differ. How then are students allocated to these different tracks?

The easiest and most direct answer is that competitive entrance examinations channel students into these different schools. This is indeed the way that most Japanese think about it, and it is correct in that there is very little use of other criteria by individual schools and very little dishonesty in the administration of the examinations. A well-developed private industry of practice tests and materials helps students judge which of the entrance examinations they will find it worthwhile to attempt, and the first phase of the national entrance examination for national universities does somewhat the same thing.

When we look at the patterns of students who end up at the different institutions, however, we see that other influences must be at work, because of systematic social differences. First of all, males and females have very different patterns; more females than males end their education at high school. Of those who do continue, most of them go to junior colleges, and these schools are almost exclusively female. Remember that these schools are also almost exclusively private and relatively inexpensive. The higher education of females in Japan is apparently considered a consumption good, not a production good, and hence not worthy of public support.

Since one of the most obvious differences in the forms of higher education is the cost to students of public and private schools, it is reasonable to ask if socioeconomic background favors some students over others and thereby helps to perpetuate social stratification. Our analysis of the family income of students in national and private universities suggests that some income bias does exist in Japan, as in most other countries. Perhaps more surprising, this bias is roughly the same in both sectors. Apparently the more rigorous academic barriers to public education are just as exclusionary as the higher financial barriers to private education. Hence, both sectors are used disproportionately by children of the upper-income groups.

We also suspect that the private monetary costs to the family of public and private education are more nearly equal than is shown by a straight comparison of tuition costs. Many of the students who attend national universities are admitted after one or two years of private study at cram schools following high school, during which they work only part-time, if at all. Their extra years of foregone income, as well as the cost of tutoring both during and after high school, must be added to the tuition cost of a public university education. Very few private universities are considered worth spending time as a *ronin*.

International Comparisons and Policy Implications

How does this picture of the public-private division of education in Japan compare with that in other countries? In contrast to the United States, public education is the elite sector and the more expensive one to society, with the prestige hierarchy of both secondary and higher education dominated by public institutions. Moreover, the public sector itself is selective, differentiated, and hierarchical, with a small number of older academic secondary schools supplying many of the students to the apex universities, Tokyo and Kyoto.

We have argued that these two observations are interrelated: selectivity and competition lead to a pecking order among public institutions and also allow the public sector as a whole to remain ahead of the private sector. In contrast, in situations where selectivity is ruled out and attempts are made to homogenize the student bodies in open-access public schools, private schools rise to the top of the status hierarchy, as in the United States. Public schools then acquire a "low quality" reputation.

In 1967 the Tokyo metropolitan government, dissatisfied with the nonegalitarian aspects of the traditional system, decided to reform it by equalizing the incoming student bodies at its academic high schools. Instead of taking entrance examinations for a specific high school, students would take an exam for a set of schools, and if successful they would be placed in one of the high schools of the set in such a way that the student bodies would be the "same" in each of those schools. The result of this "egalitarian" reform has been a massive flight of "better" students to private high schools, and a change in the public-private hierarchy, as families sought to place their children in schools which had the best students, hence the highest success rates in university admissions. Public high schools in Tokyo used to be widely acclaimed and desired, dominating the lists of high schools sending many students to national universities, especially to Tokyo University. Now not a single such school is found on these lists. Instead, both because of their superior student input and their superior output (as measured by examination success), private academic high schools in Tokyo now head the rankings. And these private high schools are available mainly to the rich. The outcome of the Tokyo reforms was so disastrous for public education that it seems to have killed any desires of other prefectures to reform.

The Tokyo reform, as well as experience from the U.S. and other countries, poses the following paradox. A system which is essentially motivated by egalitarian ideals, equal access to equal public schools, gives private schools, which can retain their selectivity, an advantage relative to the public sector as a whole—a decidedly non-egalitarian outcome. And where the elite schools are private, the upper classes have strongly preferred access because they can more easily pass through the price and academic barriers which are both concentrated there.

On the other hand, where the elite schools are public, the rich still have an advantage in passing entrance examinations, but many working-class children also attend because they are not kept out by high tuition. Society may thus have to choose between two mutually inconsistent kinds of equity, greater access to and equality among the public schools and greater equality in access to elite opportunities. The former often leads to elite private schools and public schools that are popularly regarded as "low quality"; the latter stems from selective, unequal, hence highly regarded, elite public schools. Japan as a whole has clearly chosen the latter in its secondary and higher educational systems.

We have seen that this system provides very different opportunities to men and women, to people coming from urban versus rural areas, and to those with greater and lesser academic propensities. All these distinctions seem to be socially and politically acceptable in Japan. It is not clear, however, that a public educational system which offers such differentiated opportunities would be acceptable in a society that is more divided along religious, racial, or class lines. In such a situation, differentiated public education may accentuate differences that society wishes to blunt. Thus this kind of differentiation and the public-private relationship it implies may not be a realistic option in more heterogeneous societies. It has, however, produced widespread and high-quality education, together with an esteemed public educational sector, in Japan.

Educational Opportunity for Special Groups

13

Women's Participation in Higher Education in Japan

Kumiko Fujimura-Fanselow

In pre-World War II Japanese society, restrictions placed on women's access to higher education were a significant source of constraint on women's participation and achievement in various spheres of social life. Following the postwar reforms, access to education at all levels was legally granted to women, and female participation at higher institutions of learning has indeed shown a tremendous growth over the past twenty-five years.

The fact remains, however, that sex differences in educational opportunities persist in spite of reforms that on the surface seem to offer greater opportunities. Thus, not only does overall enrollment of Japanese women in higher institutions continue to lag behind that of men, but there are also significant differences between male and female patterns of participation in various types and levels of higher institutions. Foremost among these is that a large proportion of women pursue higher education through junior college rather than four-year universities. Even among those women who en-

An earlier version of this essay was published in *Comparative Education Review*, Vol. 29, No. 4 (November 1985). Copyright © 1985 by the Comparative and International Education Society. Reprinted by permission of The University of Chicago Press.

ter four-year universities, there is a tendency to converge on the literature, home economics, and education departments.

An important consequence of these tendencies is that opportunities, particularly occupational options, available to women upon graduation are very limited. Smock proposes that "education is a force capable of generating new life opportunities for women."[1] At a time when Japanese women, like women in so many societies throughout the world, are experiencing profound changes in their lives and confronting new options and opportunities, it is critical that we try to understand the factors hindering women's fuller access to and participation in higher education.

The purpose of this study is to explore the significant determining factors behind existing sex differentials in educational opportunities in Japan. One set of factors underlying such sex disparities is, of course, cultural and attitudinal. Equally important, as emphasized by researchers engaged in the study of women and education in different societies in recent years, is the role played by the institutional structures of society that provide differential opportunities to women and men.[2]

Until very recently there has been a noticeable lack of concern with the issue of sex inequalities in education within Japanese society. Most analyses and critiques of higher education in Japan have failed to take sufficient note of the special situation of women; in fact, women have been ignored.[3] This may derive in part from a widely held assumption that once women had been granted the legal right to pursue their education as far as their abilities would permit at the institutions of their choice, a problem no longer existed. The neglect may also be traced to the fundamental fact, noted by many Japanese scholars in the field of women's education, that society has not really thought it important or desirable to have women participate in society in the same capacities as men and therefore has not been concerned with the question of how women are educated.[4] Whatever the reasons, little effort has been made either to investigate the root causes of sex inequalities or to attempt to redress sex imbalances in educational participation. In this respect Japan is certainly not unique; as Kelly and Elliott note, "Research has shown that few, if any, nations have done more than attempt to provide more access to schools for girls. No country has dealt adequately with the quality of education girls receive, the content of that education, or the structural barriers to women's full participation in social and economic life."[5]

Persisting Sex Differences in Patterns of College Enrollment

Despite the inflation in college enrollment, considerable sex differences have persisted. A close examination of the figures reveals that this expansion has taken very different forms for the two sexes; in the case of women, a substantial part of the enrollment increase has occurred at the junior college level, whereas in the case of males it has taken place almost entirely at the four-year university level. In 1983, roughly 340,000 males and 270,000 females, or 39 percent and 32 percent of young men and women who graduated from lower-secondary school three years earlier, entered college. However, fewer than four out of ten of these women went into four-year universities; the remainder entered junior colleges. In contrast, the overwhelming majority of males—95 percent—entered universities. The relative proportion of women entering universities as opposed to junior colleges is in fact less today than it was in the late 1950s and early 1960s, and the figure has been under 40 percent since 1966. Although women overwhelmingly dominate the student population in junior colleges—90 percent in 1981—they constitute a minority at four-year universities—22 percent; the latter figure has remained almost unchanged since 1975. The proportion of women in universities falls behind that in most industrialized societies as well as many of the less developed countries.[6]

Another significant difference between women and men is that at the university level roughly 30 percent of women are enrolled at institutions with exclusively female student populations, which numbered 88 out of a total of 446 in 1980.[7] Women constitute a very small percentage at the most prestigious coeducational universities.[8] Finally, the comparatively lower rate of female attendance at four-year universities is reflected in their low representation at the graduate level.[9]

Sex differentiation is evident not only within various levels and types of higher institutions but also within various programs of study. In 1981, more than six out of ten women enrolled in universities were clustered in the traditionally female fields of literature, education, and home economics; the figure was 80 percent at the junior colleges. On the other hand, fewer than 4 percent of university women were majoring in science and engineering, compared with about 28 percent among males. At the junior colleges, fewer than 1 percent of all women were studying engineering, compared with over 40 percent in the case of male students.[10]

Cultural and Attitudinal Factors

The fact that women's college attendance continues to take a very different form from that of men points to the persistence of the view that educating daughters is less important than educating sons and that daughters' education has different goals and purposes. These attitudes in turn reflect differing expectations of future roles in Japanese society based on traditional conceptions of sex roles.

Various national public opinion surveys conducted over the past several years demonstrate an overall rise in the levels of education that the Japanese desire for children of both sexes.[11] Nevertheless, people have continued to hold differing aspirations for sons than for daughters. In a 1978 poll by NHK (Japan Broadcasting Corporation), for example, 34 percent of the respondents said that they felt an upper-secondary school education was sufficient for daughters, 39 percent chose a junior college for them, and 24 percent said they should have a university education. When it came to sons, the corresponding figures were 15, 9, and 68 percent with an additional 6 percent desiring a graduate-level education for their sons.[12] As is the case in other societies, those at higher socioeconomic levels, with more education, and in large cities are more likely to want a university education or higher for daughters. Nevertheless, at every level, respondents exhibit lower aspirations for daughters compared with sons.

As has been the case in many societies, women's education has been seen as serving primarily to prepare them to be better wives and mothers. To that end, general cultural enrichment, rather than specialized or vocational training, is what most parents have sought for their daughters. This, of course, harks back to the pre-war concept of *ryosai kembo no kyoiku,* or "education for good wives and wise mothers."[13] Junior colleges are ideally tailored for those parents who share these goals of educating daughters but at the same time are unable or unwilling to finance a four-year university education. The curriculum at the majority of these schools is oriented toward preparing women for marriage and homemaking.

Preference for sending daughters to junior colleges rather than four-year universities also derives from the view, still held by many

Japanese, that a husband ought to be better educated than his wife. The same reasoning seems to underlie the preference shown by many parents who are willing and able to send their daughters to universities for having them attend a women's university rather than one of the most prestigious and competitive coeducational universities, such as Tokyo and Kyoto Universities.[14]

To a large extent, young women themselves have tended to share this view of college attendance. Surveys conducted by the Japan Recruit Center of high school seniors over the past ten years or so have shown females to be more likely than males to look on college as a place to "acquire general education" and "broaden their horizons," whereas males tend to regard college in more instrumental or utilitarian terms as being directly tied to future occupational goals and future security.[15]

That is not to say that young women today have no interest in working after college graduation. On the contrary, in recent years the great majority of college women—80 to 90 percent—have exhibited a desire to work for at least some time following graduation.[16] Working between college graduation and marriage has, indeed, become a socially accepted norm. Some women look on work as broadening their horizons and enabling them to gain some experience in the larger society; others look on it as a time filler until they get married; still others are prompted by the desire to be independent and to have income to spend on travel abroad, clothes, and so forth.

Young women on the whole demonstrate a desire to work after finishing college, but most have tended to view work as a temporary pursuit to be taken up until they get married or perhaps until they have children; few have thought in terms of a long-term commitment. This attitude reflects the fact that young women have been socialized to hold traditional goals for their future—a life centered primarily on home and family—and serious long-range career planning has not been a component of their family socialization, a message conveyed to them through the mass media, or the guidance given to them in schools.

The Dominance of Junior Colleges as the Women's Track

The fact that junior colleges have enrolled a major proportion of women pursuing higher education over the past twenty-five years is to be explained by the fact that in the absence of a concerted government effort to expand opportunities for women to pursue higher education at universities, it is the private junior colleges that have been by far the most aggressive in establishing facilities catering almost exclusively to female clientele. Between 1960 and 1970, as many as 200 new junior colleges were established, nearly all of them through private effort. Although the pace slackened after the mid-1970s, by 1981 there were 523 junior colleges, and fully 83 percent of them were privately run. The increase in enrollment at these institutions has been accounted for primarily by women: in 1950, women constituted slightly under 40 percent of all students, but this figure rose to 68 percent in 1960, 83 percent in 1970, and nearly 90 percent in 1981. An overwhelming proportion of these women—94 percent in 1981—are found in private junior colleges; in fact, over 40 percent of all women studying at junior colleges and universities in 1981 were found in privately operated junior colleges.

Various structural features of junior colleges have made them attractive to young women and their families. The first is the cost factor; tuition at private junior colleges is about comparable to that at private four-year universities, but payments need to be made for just two years instead of four, so the cost comes to one-half of that required to send a daughter to a four-year university. Another characteristic is that junior colleges are somewhat more widely distributed throughout the country and less concentrated in a handful of large metropolitan centers than four-year universities, so they are more likely to be within commuting distance of their students. This is important not only in terms of costs but also in view of the reluctance that many parents feel about allowing their daughters to attend school away from home and parental supervision, especially if they are not able to reside in a college dormitory or the home of a close relative.

Junior colleges, which had originally been established on a provisional basis back in 1950, have become in effect the "women's track" in higher education. The fact is that although these institutions enjoy the title of "university" (they are actually called "short-term universities" in Japan), they are looked on as forming the bottom layer of the university pyramid. Although it is theoretically possible for graduates from junior colleges to transfer to universities, few in fact do so.

Limitations in Curriculum and Program Options

The tendency for women students to be overrepresented in the humanities, home economics, and education and underrepresented in fields such as science, engineering, law, and economics is also attributable to the educational system. The fact is that the range of study options offered at most private junior colleges and women's universities, where so many women are enrolled, is extremely limited. What is offered reflects sex stereotypes about what constitutes appropriate areas of study for women. Women are not given the opportunity to choose nontraditional study options. In this way, instead of preparing women to assume the same roles as men, the institutions serving women tend to reinforce differential expectations concerning the uses of education.

Private colleges in Japan have, in general, placed major emphasis on developing their humanities and social science programs because establishing and maintaining science, engineering, and medical departments is so costly. In the case of women's universities—except at such institutions as Seishin, Tsuda, and Tokyo Joshidaigaku—the faculties of literature and home economics are the only ones available. Traditionally male professional subjects such as engineering, accounting, economics, and law are almost totally absent from their curriculum. This bias in terms of curriculum is even more pronounced at private junior colleges. The national junior colleges (which numbered just 35 out of a total of 523 junior colleges in 1981) offer courses predominantly in the technical and vocational fields, but they enroll fewer than 2 percent of all female junior college students.

Impact of Differential Opportunities in Employment

In considering the Japanese case, it is worthwhile to examine the hypothesis that an important reason why women are less motivated than men to enter universities—especially the most competitive ones—is that they perceive employment opportunities for university-educated women to be very limited, so the economic returns on investment in a university education are likely to be much less than for men. Considerable limitations do, in fact, exist, and they derive from various discriminatory practices against women in the labor market, which in turn are related to certain important features of the Japanese employment system.

Two factors that have played a major part in promoting college attendance among males—the high status of a university education and market demand for university graduates—have not operated in the case of women. Prior to World War II and continuing to this day, the acquisition of a university diploma has been viewed as the most effective channel for social mobility. For the salaried, white-collar male worker, his workplace, work responsibilities, income, and promotion all are heavily influenced by the level of schooling he has attained as well as the prestige of the particular university he has attended.[17] It is for this reason that parents are willing to undergo considerable financial sacrifices to send sons to universities, and young men themselves are willing to undergo rigorous preparation for the university entrance exams, in some cases two or more times, in order to gain admission to the top universities in Japan.[18]

Leaving aside the question of whether many or most women with university degrees wish to work, the fact is that in Japan they simply do not have access to jobs of similar status as those available to university-educated males, except in a few professions where women have long been visible. Once hired, moreover, their prospects for mobility and advancement as well as high remuneration are similarly restricted.

Another critical factor involved here has to do with the traditional patterns of occupational mobility characteristic of Japanese companies (primarily the large ones)—*shushin koyo* (lifetime employment) and *nenko joretsu* (a promotion and wage system based on length of consecutive service within a particular company). It is obvious that women are at a distinct disadvantage under such a system since, given the existing sex-role division of labor, women are often forced to discontinue employment at various points in their lives. Irrespective of whether women can conform to this pattern, however, the fact is that women are excluded from it from the start.

Women are regarded by industry primarily as a source of cheap, short-term, rotating labor. Young women straight out of school are hired for jobs based on the assumption that they will work up until they get married or, at most, until they have a child. As the number of women entering the labor market after graduation from high school has declined, companies have increasingly taken on junior college graduates as "O.L.," or "office ladies," to perform routine clerical work. Women graduates from four-year universities, who are already twenty-two or twenty-three, and thus presumably have fewer years remaining until they leave their jobs, are generally not in demand for such positions, nor are they hired to perform tasks comparable to those assigned to male university graduates.

Many companies, as a matter of policy, do not recruit female university graduates, which partly accounts for the fact that employment rates among these women have been lower than those found among female junior college graduates and male graduates. In a recent survey by the Ministry of Labor of a sample of 5,000 enterprises, of those that said they had hired university graduates in the spring of 1981, only 29 percent said they had hired women graduates. Moreover, of this number, fewer than two-thirds said that the conditions of employment were the same for both sexes; the other third explained that women university graduates are assigned the same work as women junior college graduates.[19] The same study, as well as others, also reveals differential treatment in terms of on-the-job training, remuneration, and opportunities for promotion to managerial positions.

What has been said above helps explain why many young women choose to forego the rigorous preparation, competition, and financial costs involved in gaining admission to the nation's top coeducational universities and instead opt for one of the women's universities or junior colleges (where admission is usually based on interviews and recommendations rather than entrance exams). It also helps account for the fact that few women prepare themselves for business fields by majoring in areas such as engineering, economics, and commerce, from which male students are generally recruited by private industry. Discrimination is less apparent in fields such as teaching (at least at the lower levels), social welfare, and health-related occupations. Women have long established themselves in these occupations, which frequently involve working in the public rather than the private sector.

Conclusion: Emerging Changes in Attitudes and Opportunities

Evidence seems to indicate that more women are beginning to look beyond occupations traditionally favored for and by women and to branch out into such diverse areas as advertising, banking and finance, retail sales, architecture, broadcasting, real estate, and computers.[20] These changes have been reflected in a gradual increase at the university level in the proportion of women majoring in fields such as law, politics, economics, engineering, and agriculture, which have traditionally attracted few women, and a concomitant decline in those majoring in literature, home economics, and education. Correspondingly, there has been a gradual increase in the number of women entering coeducational rather than women's universities. As already noted, programs of study offered at most women's universities are limited to the traditionally female ones, so those desiring to choose nontraditional study options must look to coed universities. At the junior colleges, too, there has been a considerable decrease in the proportion of women majoring in home economics, accompanied by increases in those majoring in education and health-related fields. A further development that is of interest is that many women, following graduation from a junior college or university where they have acquired a more or less general education, are going on to study at a *senshugakko* or *kakushugakko* for the purpose of acquiring specific, job-related skills.[21]

It is important to note that such changes in values and attitudes on the part of young women are a consequence in part of the rise in the levels of education attained by women over the postwar years. Many of those now reaching college age have been brought up by mothers who attended college under the restructured postwar educational system. Women with college backgrounds are apt to hold more liberal attitudes toward sex roles and less traditional aspirations for their own daughters compared with those with less education or with males. In view of this, it is not surprising to find today's young women exhibiting less traditional goals for their own futures.

The rise in interest in pursuing careers and in venturing into less traditional fields of study and work has been stimulated to an important degree by changes in the job market. Although most private enterprises continue to shy away from hiring university-educated women, opportunities are slowly beginning to widen as more companies, in their eagerness to attract talent, seem to be displaying greater willingness to hire women graduates who possess the desired abilities, talents, and skills. This is especially the case among small- and medium-size companies: they are often unable to attract male graduates from the top ranking universities (who opt for the larger, most prestigious companies) so they are turning to women graduates from those same universities who are equally qualified.

A noteworthy development within the last four to five years has been that a number of businesses for which women compose an increasingly important clientele—department stores, supermarkets, retail specialty stores, manufacturers of office and home electrical and electronic equipment, real estate businesses, and financial institutions (banks, securities companies, and consumer credit companies)—have begun to hire female university graduates for positions formerly reserved exclusively for male graduates. An important motivation seems to be the perception that a staff of well-educated women is necessary for dealing effectively with a consumer market made up increasingly of college-educated women.

Thus, despite the many obstacles that remain, career opportunities for women holding university degrees are undeniably beginning to open. This is evidenced by the recent rise in employment rates among female university graduates, from around 60 percent in the latter part of the 1970s to 68 percent in 1981. The continuation of these trends should serve as an incentive to women to seek higher education on an equal basis with men and to prepare for a more diversified range of careers.

Looking at the educational system in Japan, it is evident that sex-typed education has been generally accepted. Most educators and educational institutions serving young women have perceived their task to be primarily that of preparing women for marriage and motherhood. However, as is happening in so many countries throughout the world, women today are confronting new options and opportunities in various spheres of life and at the same time exhibiting new aspirations. In view of this, a critical challenge for junior colleges and women's universities in Japan, which can be expected to continue to attract a large share of college-bound women, is to restructure and expand their curricula and programs to prepare women for new realities and opportunities in their lives.

Notes

1. Audrey Chapman Smock, *Women's Education in Developing Countries: Opportunities and Outcomes* (New York: Praeger, 1981), 1.

2. See, for example, Isabelle Deblé, *The School Education of Girls* (Paris: UNESCO, 1980); Gail P. Kelly and Carolyn M. Elliott, eds., *Women's Education in the Third World: Comparative Perspectives* (Albany: State University of New York Press, 1982);

Janet Zollinger Giele and Audrey Chapman Smock, eds., *Women: Roles and Status in Eight Countries* (New York: Wiley, 1977); Smock.

3. See, for example, Central Council on Education, *Basic Guidelines for the Reform of Education* (Tokyo: Ministry of Education, 1972); OECD, *Review of National Policies for Education: Japan* (Paris: OECD, 1971); Nagai Michio, *Higher Education in Japan: Its Take-off and Crash*, trans. Jerry Dusenbury (Tokyo: University of Tokyo Press, 1971).

4. Hara Kimi, "Joshi koto kyoiku no shakaigakuteki ikkosatsu," *Kyoiku shakaigaku kenkyu* 26 (October 1971): 90–101; Yoshida Noboru, "Josei to koto kyoiku," *Jurisuto* 3 (June 1976): 60.

5. Kelly and Elliott, 4.

6. The proportion of women eighteen to twenty-three years old enrolled in school in 1975 was much lower in Japan (15 percent) than in North America (45 percent), South America (21 to 24 percent), Europe (19 to 23 percent), and the USSR (25 percent) (Deblé, 37, table 3). Figures taken from UNESCO Office of Statistics, *Trends and Projections of Enrollment by Level of Education and by Age* (Paris: UNESCO, 1978), 47–50.

7. Sumikata Masayoshi, "Joshi daigaku no genjo," *IDE* no. 225 (November 1981), cited in Tachi Kaoru, "Nihon no joshi daigaku no gaikyo to joseigaku kanren koza," *Ochanomizu joshidaigaku josei bunka shiryokanho* 4 (1982): 87.

8. In 1980, for example, less than 7 percent of all students admitted to Tokyo University were women; this figure was about 8 percent at Kyoto University and also at Keio University. "Sokuho '80 daigaku gokakusha shusshin kokobetsu ichiran," *Shukan Asahi* (April 4, 1980), 22–29, 179, 189.

9. In 1981, there were roughly 5,000 women enrolled in master's degree programs out of a total of 37,000 students and 1,800 women in doctor's degree programs out of a total of 18,000. Mombusho, *Mombu tokei yoran*, 86.

10. Ibid., 84–85.

11. Sorifu, *Kyoiku ni kansuru yoron chosa* (1968), reported in Central Council for Education, *An Interim Report on Policies for the Future Expansion and Development of Education in Japan* (Tokyo: Ministry of Education, June 1969), 66, fig. I.C.1; Sorifu, *Fujin ni kansuru ishiki chosa hokokusho* (1973), 126–27, table 51, and 128–29, table 52; NHK (Nihon Hoso Kyokai), *Nihonjin no ishiki chosa* (1973 and 1978), reported in *NHK Hoso Yoron Chosajo-hen, Gendai Nihonjin no ishiki kozo* (Tokyo: Nihon Hoso Shuppan Kyokai, 1979), 17, appendix questions 23 and 24; Sorifu, *Kyoiku ni kansuru yoron chosa hokokusho* (1976), 60–61, table 13, and 62–63, table 14.

12. NHK, *Nihonjin no ishiki chosa* (1978), reported in *NHK Hoso Yoron Chosajo-hen*.

13. For discussion of *ryosai kembo no kyoiku*, see Fukaya Masashi, *Ryosai kemboshugi no kyoiku* (Tokyo: Reimei Shobo, 1966); Murakami Nobuhiko, *Meiji josei-shi*, Vol. 1 (Tokyo: Kodansha, 1977), 50–55. Also see the autobiography of Sumie Seo Mishima, *My Narrow Isle: The Story of a Modern Woman in Japan* (New York: Day, 1941).

14. Pharr found this to be the case among women students whom she interviewed at Tokyo University. Susan J. Pharr, *The Status of Women in Japan: Historical and Contemporary Perspectives*, Report for the Ford Foundation Task Force on Women, photocopied (October 1973), 47–48. Vogel found similar attitudes among the Japanese he studied. Ezra F. Vogel, *Japan's New Middle Class* (Berkeley: University of California Press, 1965), 44.

15. Nihon Rikuruto Senta, *Shingaku doki chosa* (1972), 22, table 21; (1978), 46–47, table 12; (1982), 54, tables 9–1 and 9–2.

16. Nihon Rikuruto Senta, *Joshigakusei no shushoku doki chosa* (1976), 3; (1978), 5; (1982), 5.

17. See, for example, Herbert Passin, *Society and Education in Japan* (New York: Teachers College Press 1965), chap. 6; Ronald P. Dore, "The Future of Japan's Meritocracy," in *Social Structures and Economic Dynamics in Japan Up to 1980*, ed. Gianni Fodella (Treviso: Longo & Zoppelli, 1975), 169–86; Koya Azumi, *Higher Education and Business Recruitment in Japan* (New York: Teachers College Press, 1968).

18. The relationship between decisions regarding college attendance and perceptions of the economic advantages of college education is explored in Mary Jean Bowman, *Educational Choice and Labor Markets in Japan* (Chicago: University of Chicago Press, 1981). The focus, however, is exclusively on male high school students.

19. Rodosho Fujin Shonen Kyoku (Ministry of Labor, Women, and Minors' Bureau), *Joshi rodosha no koyo kanri ni kansuru chosa* (Tokyo, 1981), 28–29, appendix table 2, and 30–31, table 3.

20. Between 1975 and 1980 the number of women employed in the following types of work (among others) increased by 50 percent or more: architecture, real estate, advertising, information processing, reporters and editors, administrative civil servants, company officers, and technicians in scientific fields. Nihon Seisansei Hombu Rodobu, ed., *Korekara no Joshi Rodo* (Tokyo: Nihon Seisansei Hombu, Rodo Shiryo Senta, 1982), 34–35, table 2–1, taken from Sorifu, *Kokusei chosa*.

21. These institutions, which are largely private, offer short-term vocational and technical training in a variety of fields. The *senshugakko* in particular, which numbered 2,745 in 1981, are becoming an increasingly popular alternative form of postsecondary education. These institutions do not have university status, but an official academic qualification is granted to their graduates.

14

Recent Trends in Special Education in Tokyo

Marilyn P. Goldberg

In Japan, where the goal is to provide an equal education for all, scant attention is given to individual differences in ability or development in regular schools. Japanese schools provide the same education regardless of variation in pupil ability or interest, and educational leaders generally feel the schools have produced a well-trained population. However, there is increasing displeasure with the inflexibility of a system which mitigates against the slow learner, late bloomer, or creative personality.

Even though tutors and *juku* are utilized, by the time students reach high school many have become "reluctant learners" as their learning needs are not met in lower grades. Also, school violence has resulted which in part is due to the unmet needs of students.

Awareness of the child who is different, the student who needs assistance, is beginning to emerge more and more in Japan. By focusing on those who "make it" through the system, many who are not among the ranks of the successful as defined by Japanese society are neglected and lost.

Since 1979 schooling has been mandated for all students of compulsory education age (six to fifteen years of age). As a result, prefectures were directed by the Ministry of Education to provide special schools for all students with handicapping conditions. There has been some controversy regarding the separatism implied in the special school, especially from parents who would prefer to have their children attend regular schools with special help. Nonetheless, most boards of education have interpreted the Ministry of Education directive to mean that all students who are seriously handicapped should go to special schools. Thus, there is an ongoing debate concerning separate special schools versus integrating special students into regular school programs. Integration can readily take place in a regular school, but it is important to note that simply having a child in a regular school does not lead to quality integrated education. Attempts must be made to truly integrate all students into the academic, social, and emotional fabric of the school.

The Japan Teachers Union had supported the development of special schools because they felt students with handicapping conditions were not being educated properly in regular schools, or were not attending school at all. Today they support the development of quality integrated programs as well.

Each prefecture and the cities of Osaka, Kyoto, and Tokyo have boards of education with certain decision-making powers regarding the kinds of special education programs which will be provided. These boards have the option to interpret compulsory special education to mean only special schools or as special classes, resource rooms, and mainstreaming special students in regular schools.

Tokyo, for example, has over eleven and a half million people with a million and a half public school students, and a total of 2.3 million students of school age. About 7,281 students are in special schools for children with handicapping conditions, and 7,202 are in special education classes in regular schools. Included within the Tokyo Metropolitan Government Office of Education is a Handicapped Pupils Educational Guidance Section which provides special education guidance in regular schools as well as the direct supervision of special schools.

Tokyo, like New York City, has a continuum of special education programs and services to meet the special needs of students in special classes in elementary and junior high schools, special preschool programs and at special schools on the elementary, junior high, and senior high school levels. In addition, there are programs where children attend integrated preschools and kindergartens.

In elementary schools some children with special needs attend a resource center for special education and then attend regular classes for most of the school week. In some junior high school special classes there are a few students who attend regular classes as well. However, most students are in the special classes all the time.

Setagaya-ku Ward in Tokyo

I visited several schools in Setagaya-ku, one of the twenty-three wards of Tokyo, to observe integrated programs for children with special needs. There were some students who were truly participating in the life of their school. However, there were instances where students could have been more fully integrated academically and socially as well as emotionally.

It should be noted here that one of the ideas involved in the continuum of special education services is the prevention of handicapping conditions in students by meeting their special needs early on in their school careers. Some students' special needs are met in Tokyo schools, but the needs of many are not. Very often parents will send their children to a private study center (juku) after school to help their children academically where often their emotional and social needs may be overlooked. All this results in the development of a handicapping condition which could have been prevented by more supportive school programs.

Setagaya Ward Board of Education has decided to provide resource rooms as well as special classes in regular schools on the elementary level. In some junior high schools special classes are available in neighborhood schools as well as some resource room-type arrangement for students with special needs who are in regular classes.

Setagaya is one of the largest wards in Tokyo with 90,000 school age children. In this ward children with handicapping conditions go to the six available resource rooms; thirteen special classes, regular classes, and special schools. A small number of students are on home instruction or in hospital schools. Resource room arrangements are locally determined options since legislation and the Education Ministry do not deal with the issue of integration.

The guidance committee of Setagaya screens students to determine placements before elementary school entrance and middle school entrance. The screening consists of medical and intelligence tests as well as observation. Intelligence, social ability, motor skills, and emotional behavior as well as speech and language are discussed. Teachers', parents', and guidance committee recommendations are considered. Many parents favor regular school placements rather than special schools. Within the regular school, the parents prefer the resource room rather than special classes. In addition to placement, the guidance committee operates a counseling program for parents and children from preschool through middle school. Also, the committee refers extremely difficult cases to the Tokyo Metropolitan Guidance Committee. Unfortunately, all these services fall short of meeting the special education needs of the ward.

Adachi Ward

A particularly famous case regarding this issue of placement options occurred in Adachi Ward. Although neighborhoods in Tokyo tend not to be as economically homogeneous as those in large American cities, Adachi is more working-class than Setagaya. The case centered on a child named Koji with a serious handicapping condition who now attends a regular class in his neighborhood junior high school with special help provided by the local board of education. However, he was only able to do so after a long political struggle which lasted several years. His story is documented in a book entitled *Koji's Aspirations*, published in 1981. On the second page of this book a poem in English translation indicates how emotional this issue was.

> I am Koji Kanai
> In June I will be twelve.
> I don't want to go to the school for handicapped
>   children.
> I hate the physical training that I was forced to do.
> At home I could take off my shoes; sit on a chair; go
>   to the bathroom; take off my trousers, because I
>   wanted to do so.
> By watching what my brothers did, I could learn to do
>   things too.
> When I studied in front of the closed school gates,
> I enjoyed seeing the friends who come
> Somebody brought me a rabbit. . . .
> Even among these are bullies.
> I want to go to school with Hiroshi and Ryo;
> I want to make friends and eat school dinner and
>   play and study and have close friends.

> I am a human being even though I cry a lot.
> I want to become strong and walk.
>
> Koji Kanai

Koji is also one of the children discussed in the book *12 Aspects of Children in Japan* published in 1980. The book discusses children with special problems and barriers to overcome within the context of Japanese society. I visited with Koji and his family and friends to gain some insight into the intense struggle for integration in this case. Something Koji's mother said has stayed with me because I feel it points to a dimension of educational decision-making we so often forget. She said it was Koji's life, not hers, and he had the right to decide what he wanted.

The Problems of Adolescents

A negative and rather infamous response to the needs of students with special problems was illustrated by the Totsuka Junior Yacht School incident. A student died as a result of "training" received there. Adolescent boys and young adults were sent to this private school for training and to "cure" them of an assortment of ailments such as autism, family violence syndrome, school phobia, emotional disturbance, juvenile delinquency, and/or to provide stamina for college entrance examinations.

Professor Hiroshi Inamura, a psychiatrist at the University of Tsukuba Medical School with whom I discussed this incident, indicated that even though there are many similar private "treating places" which are highly disciplined if not as violent as Totsuka, there continues to be a lack of appropriate places and personnel to treat emotionally disturbed adolescents.

Family violence syndrome is thought to be an important reason why parents turn in desperation to "treating places" such as Totsuka. The syndrome often results from pressure parents (especially the mother) exert on a child (particularly a boy) to do well in school. Very often the parent becomes subject to the whims of the child. The parent will do anything to have the child be like all the others in school including giving the child a television with a video recorder or a motorcycle. But often this is not enough, for the indulged teenager may use physical force to be given more. Thus the family is terrorized by the tyranny of this overindulged youngster.

Mainstreaming, Special Classes, and Resource Rooms

In Setagaya Ward I witnessed mainstreaming in several schools. The first school I visited was Sassahara Elementary School where I observed a resource room program for students with visual limitations. I was able to visit two of the students while they were in regular classes. One of the students traveled to the resource room from his home several times a week, which is the usual arrangement. The other student happened to be in her home school.

There were two teachers and eleven students in this program. The number of lessons per week varied for each child. Some students came every day; others came two or three times a week. Some students had eight lessons a week and others five lessons, which appeared to be the minimum. The students were taught individually and in groups of two.

The program appeared to be excellent. The resource room teachers' expertise and the use of the available equipment helped these students to perform well in their regular classes. The resource room teacher used the texts and other materials from the regular classes and communicated with the regular class teacher on a regular basis. The teacher wrote a report every day, and each month the reports were given to the regular school principal. In addition, the resource teacher visited with the regular class teacher and observed the child in class three times a year.

At Sakura Elementary School I observed a resource room for emotionally handicapped students, most of whom it appeared were autistic. Four teachers served the thirty-two students, twenty-nine of whom were boys, who came to the resource room three times a week for an hour and a half each time. The Japanese are quite concerned about the number of male children being identified as autistic. Much research is now being done in this area. Cultural factors such as the fact that babies are carried on mothers' backs thereby limiting face to face communication are being explored as one of the possible causes. Also the propensity for not displaying feelings, particularly by verbalization, is thought to be another possible causative factor.

The program was conducted in a separate area of the school in several rooms, including: a parents' room where the mothers stayed while their children attended the resource room; a room for the opening exercise; a physical activity room; and a bathroom. In addition, children were taken out on the street for roller-skating.

All of the students attend regular classes in nearby elementary schools. I visited one child in his regular class, a second-grade class of forty-three students. Although the child did not really work, his inappropriate behavior was handled well both by the teacher and the students in his class. The mother was also with me during this visit. Although the guidance committee recommended a special class, she informed me she wanted her son in a resource room program.

I visited a special class for emotionally handicapped students at Yamazaki Junior High School. This special class was really an amalgam of situations including a blind student who will be one of the first blind students of Tokyo to enter a regular high school, and who attended only when she took an examination in braille. There was a boy who came to the special class in uniform who attended regular classes as well and who will be attending a special high school for the mentally handicapped. In addition, there were several students who were identified as school phobia cases, but who seemed to be having learning problems as well. Their school phobia appeared to be directly related to the failure of the school to meet their special learning needs. Of a total of eight students in the class, only three or four were there on any given day, even though teachers make home visits to encourage attendance.

Students from outside schools who attend special class or a resource room are not considered part of the host school, and therefore do not receive school lunch. Also, they are not required to wear uniforms. These situations tend to emphasize the differences and mitigate against their acceptance in the society of the school. Particularly in cases of school phobia, integration into the community of the school is especially important.

One of the difficulties presented by the resource room program is coordination of services with regular school programs so that time is not lost from regular classes. This was discussed as a concern during a meeting of the Ward Guidance Committee on placement. Another area of concern is the lack of resource rooms in the middle schools and the almost complete lack of any supportive help in regular high schools where the options became more and more restricted, and separation rather than quality integration is the result.

Conclusion

The emphasis on equality of education in Japan has meant little in terms of helping students with special needs to remain successfully in the least restrictive environment. The goal, for instance, of the Tokyo Metropolitan Board of Education is to provide special facilities for those who need them.

The view is that mainstreaming may violate the rights of handicapped students because there are no special services for them in the regular school environment. Individualizing education means separate but equal facilities in Tokyo for the special student.

A serious concern in Tokyo seems to be that the guidance and screening process (that is, assessment) must be more sophisticated so that students who need special education can be identified earlier. It was felt that many students with learning problems were not being identified or helped. With early identification and training in special facilities it is hoped that special education students will achieve educational equity.

In summary, the Tokyo Metropolitan Board of Education is struggling with an approach that stresses special classes and special schools. Meanwhile, parents are pressuring for more assistance through mainstreamed programs such as resource rooms. The tradition in Japan has been to work for educational equality through rigid standards of instruction, and if students cannot meet these standards, individualized attention in separate facilities is prescribed. To date, therefore, there is no movement towards support of mainstreaming in the regular education program.

Many parents, however, want more individualized and flexible special education programs. In many cases, parents and interested groups have been able to develop such programs with considerable success. For example, there is an integrated program for autistic children at the private but government-supported Musashino Higashi Elementary School in the Tama area of Tokyo and at Midori-No-I (Green House) in Adachi Ward, where there is an after-school program for forty-eight first-through third-graders, many of whom have special needs and come from homes where both parents work. This latter program resulted from a cooperative effort between Adachi Ward and Japan Women's University. Also, the Japan School for the Deaf, a private school, has an integrated program and functions in cooperation with the public schools in the Machida area.

As this review of special education in Japan indicates, there is a great need for a more varied response in public schools to children with special needs. Public schools in Japan must increasingly recognize that all children have a fundamental right to be educated. Nurturing, quality integration for all children in the total public school system remains a major piece of unfinished business in Japan. Clearly, the day has yet to arrive when all children with special needs can enjoy the benefits of schooling in a more fully integrated way in the mainstream.

References

Inamura, H. "Who saves troubled children?" *Asahi Journal* (July 22, 1983): 16–19. (Japanese)

Kusuyama, T. *Koji's Aspirations* (Tokyo: Soju Sa Publishing Co., 1981). (Japanese)

Kusuyama, T., A. Sumida, and T. Asada. *Twelve Aspects of Children in Japan* (Tokyo: Akishubo, 1980).

Public Education in Tokyo (Tokyo: Board of Education, 1982).

Tokyo Metropolitan Board of Education. *A Brief Outline of Special Education in Tokyo* (Tokyo: Board of Education, 1985).

15

Educational Problems of "Returning Children"

Tetsuya Kobayashi

During the past twenty years, education for *kikokushijo*, or return-ing children from abroad, has become an issue in Japan.[1] This problem has been the direct result of the rapid expansion of the Japanese economy and the corresponding extension of overseas ac-tivities of the Japanese since the 1960s. According to the govern-mental statistics,[2] the number of the Japanese nationals temp-orarily residing abroad increased from 83,989 in 1966 to 150,068 in 1976 and to 223,601 in 1983, and their activities have extended not only to trade and industry but also to cultural and educa-tional spheres. The accompanying children of school age also in-creased in number from 4,159 in 1966 to 18,092 in 1976 and to 36,223 in 1984. As their number increased, the number of return-ing children also increased from 1,543 in 1971 to 4,959 in 1976 and to 9,786 in 1983.

This increase in numbers in a fairly short span of time is one of the reasons why education for the overseas and returning children has become so problematic in Japan. To be sure, there had been such children in the period prior to Japan's reentry into the inter-

A version of this essay was published in *Education and Social Concern: An Ap-proach to Social Foundations*, Ann Arbor, Praaken Publications, 1987.

national community in 1951, not to mention the pre-World War II period when there were over 1,400,000 overseas Japanese in the 1930s.

As to education for returning children, special classes were set up in Oizumi Middle School attached to the National Tokyo Gakugei University in 1965, and in 1967 the Ministry of Education designated ten public and private elementary and middle schools as cooperative schools for receiving returning children with governmental assistance. The number of these schools has increased since then. In 1985, among schools attached to national universities, six elementary and five middle schools and one high school provide special classes, and additional schools (one elementary and five middle schools and one high school) admit returning children in regular classes. As to public and private schools, thirty-six elementary, twenty-four middle and twenty-seven high schools are designated as cooperative schools. In addition, at least thirty-five public and private middle and high schools accept returning students through special admission procedures.

These schools are located mostly in large metropolitan regions, because returning children are highly concentrated in Tokyo, Kanagawa, and Chiba, which received 70 percent of all returning children, and Osaka and Kobe, which received 11 percent in 1983. The remaining returning children are scattered throughout almost all prefectures. In 1983 the Ministry of Education designated eleven cities as the Areas for Promoting Education for Returning Children, in which the local education authorities were expected to coordinate educational activities for returning children in schools in their areas.

As to higher education, some private universities such as International Christian University and Sophia University had been long accepting students who have completed their high school education abroad, and by the middle of the 1980s a newly founded national Tsukuba University also began to accept these students through special admission procedures. Their example was followed by other universities, and by 1985 measures had been taken to admit graduates of foreign high schools in twenty-two national, five prefectural and municipal, and thirty-four private universities.

There also exist nongovernmental activities for promoting education for returning children. The Japan Overseas Education Services was established in 1971 by various business groups in order to assist educational activities for overseas Japanese children. Their services include guidance and consultant services for returning children and parents in three guidance centers in Tokyo, Osaka, and Nagoya. There are also a few private or voluntary groups which are concerned with the readjustment of returning children and with the maintenance of foreign language skills which they have acquired abroad.

As mentioned earlier, the rapid increase of returning children has attracted public attention. It was, however, not only the number but also their quality which posed a problem in Japanese society. These returning children have characteristics which seem to be so different from those of other Japanese children that those in the receiving Japanese schools are perplexed. To be sure, those returning children also differ greatly among themselves in their experiences abroad. For example in 1984, some 40 percent of those overseas Japanese children lived in North America, 24 percent in Asia, 22 percent in Europe, and the rest in Latin America, Oceania, the Middle East and Africa, each with different living conditions.

As to their educational experiences, 42 percent of them attend full-time Japanese schools, while the rest go either to local public or private schools or to international schools. The latter group of children includes those who attend part-time supplementary schools in conjunction with their local schooling. In these Japanese schools, children are taught by qualified Japanese teachers who are sent by the Japanese government and through a curriculum which is the same as the one at home. Thus those children who have attended Japanese schools and others who have gone to local schools have quite different experiences. However, even those who have attended Japanese schools may not have come through the same experiences as their counterparts at home. In addition to the different physical and cultural conditions surrounding schools, these Japanese schools themselves are not exactly the same as the schools at home. While some schools are comparable in size and facilities with those at home, a large number of them are small and ill-equipped (nearly 40 percent of Japanese schools have less than fifty students).

Taking an example from the Japanese language skills of these children, many of them are considered to be at a lower level of achievement, though that level may vary according to age and length of their overseas experiences, the amount of Japanese used within and outside family, and other conditions.[3] In the early days, it was not uncommon to see returning children treated as subnormal children because of their Japanese language deficiency. Some were put in special classes with mentally handicapped children or in classes one or two grades lower than those appropriate for their ages. Nowadays, such cases may no longer exist, but the necessity for providing them supplementary or remedial Japanese instruction still remains. In the special classes or cooperative schools mentioned earlier, an attempt has been made to develop Japanese language programs specifically designed for these children. For other school subjects, which may differ in content and degree of difficulty between Japan and other countries, remedial programs may be needed in order for them to catch up to the achievement level of their classmates. Even those returning children from English-speaking countries, who may seem to be in a favorable position in English classes in secondary schools at home, are often in need of special attention, because the teaching of English here emphasizes translation from English to Japanese, thus making their deficiency in Japanese language a liability even in this area.

In addition to the problem of academic achievement, the returning children often encounter behavioral difficulties due to their different cultural backgrounds. In classrooms, it is reported that they often irritate teachers and classmates by their inquisitive attitudes which may be interpreted as disturbance rather than constructive participation in the orderly processes of teacher-directed instruction commonly seen in Japanese classrooms. Often they also have trouble outside the classroom setting with teachers and classmates in personal relations. Thus, special guidance programs may be necessary for them.[4]

Advancement to high school and university is another problem. Since the advancement from elementary school to middle school is automatic, no problem exists at this stage. However, the advancement from middle school to high school, which is not automatic but selective, is a considerable headache to those concerned. The same applies to the advancement from high schools to universities. Although the responsibility here rests fundamentally on the individual children and their parents, teachers are expected to provide students with proper guidance and preparation. It is not an easy task for teachers to help children who have come through different cultural experiences except in those schools mentioned earlier with special admissions programs for returning children.

In the past, the solutions to the problems were left largely in the hands of individual schools and teachers, but of late the government, both central and local, has been taking a more active role in providing for the education of returning children. What, then, are the problems which still remain unsolved?

Looking back over the past twenty years of development in education for overseas and returning children, one may notice significant changes. This change may be phrased, "from adjustment of 'problem children' to nourishment of international children."[5]

In order to cope with these "problem children," a variety of measures were taken in the name of education for returning children, including the establishment of special classes. The term "readjustment education" was popularly used, to represent the approach seen in the early days. This term is still in use nowadays and generally implies the kind of education that aims at facilitating the adjustment of returning children to the social and educational environment in their home country. The schools receiving returning children have developed programs for "adjustment education" and have instituted "adjustment classes," in which efforts are made to cover deficiencies in Japanese language and other academic and nonacademic abilities and behaviors. As long as the returning children have to live in their home country, they have to be educated for adjusting themselves to Japanese society and culture, and in this respect "adjustment education" for returning children has its function to fulfill.

However, it is not uncommon in the process of adjustment education to see children forced to relinquish what they have learned abroad in order to adapt them to their new environment at home. In other words, the knowledge and values which children have acquired in other cultures are looked upon not positively but rather negatively, as an obstruction to adjustment at home. Neither society nor school is expected to adjust itself to the new situations which have arisen from the influx of returning children. It is only the children who are expected to change.

This reality does not disturb many parents living abroad, whose major concern is to compensate for whatever handicaps their children might have as a result of having been outside the Japanese educational system, especially those disadvantages related to entrance examinations to high schools and universities, and employment opportunities. The prime purpose as seen by these parents is to bring their children back into their proper places at home which they would have been occupying had they not been abroad.

Since children at home work hard in order to climb up the ladder in which better and higher levels of schooling are expected to guarantee a good career, it is very natural for parents overseas to desire that their children be given the same opportunities to climb that ladder both while abroad and after their return home.[6] Therefore, it is often in accordance with such parental wishes that adjustment education is being carried out in receiving schools at home, just as classes in overseas Japanese schools use the same curriculum as schools at home.

It should be noted, however, that from the beginning there has been an opposite approach. Many overseas parents have been sending their children to local or international schools in the belief that their children should continue to be educated so as to enhance their international outlooks and attitudes by mixing with other local or international children. In this way, they are able to take full advantage of having been abroad. They have not forgotten the difficulties which their children would face on their return home, but they have been content to provide their children with minimum training in Japanese language in supplementary schools or through correspondence education programs offered by the Japan Overseas Educational Service and other organizations. On their return home, they rely on special programs in receiving schools for the reentry of their children to Japanese society and culture.

Such an idea gained importance in the latter 1970s as the training of Japanese for international activities became an educational issue, and the problem of education for overseas and returning children was explored. In 1974, the Central Council for Education of the Ministry of Education submitted its report *On International Exchange in Education, Science and Culture.*[7] This report held that one of the major policy objectives was "to nurture the Japanese for international society" and recommended in this context that promotion of education for overseas and returning children be implemented with the aim of raising internationally minded children and improving their international understanding. In 1976, a special committee was set up within the Ministry of Education for the purpose of creating policy guidelines for education for overseas and returning children. Its report emphasized this aspect of international education as one of its fundamental objectives, stating that education for overseas and returning children should "aim at making a positive contribution by taking advantage of the overseas experiences of children, to nurture Japanese with a rich international perspective. This is one of the basic goals of our education."[8]

If one accepts this policy, then top priority should be given to developing such international qualities as tolerance and a cooperative attitude toward other cultures and peoples, which these children may have acquired while living abroad, instead of forcing them to adjust to the Japanese career society at the expense of what they have gained abroad. Of course, it would be erroneous to assume that all children residing abroad automatically become internationally minded. In fact, the lifestyle of many Japanese overseas has been criticized precisely because they often form communities which isolate them from the local people and the culture. The role of overseas Japanese schools should be to broaden the experiences of overseas children, so that their international qualities are able to develop. This can be best achieved by providing these children with opportunities for reflecting upon and understanding more fully their overseas experiences.

If such is to be the case, an important factor is the attitudes of teachers and classmates in the receiving schools. The returning children naturally enter these schools with hopes of being accepted. If those on the receiving side expect the returning children to behave exactly in the same way as they do, the latter has only two alternatives: either trying to assimilate fully with others, abandoning much of what they have acquired abroad, or rejecting totally the idea of conforming with the group, resulting in difficulties in their interpersonal relations. Neither of these alternatives is desirable for returning children, who should be allowed to reenter Japanese society and schools with the full advantage of their overseas experiences. Also it would be unfortunate for receiving schools to lose the opportunity for the other children in the schools to profit from the presence of returning children to develop their own international qualities.

In order to facilitate the process whereby the returning children acquire knowledge, skills, and attitudes which are needed for adjusting themselves to a new situation, while maintaining their international qualities, it is important for the receiving teachers and children to respect what they have brought home with them and to cooperate with them in the effort to make the most of their overseas experiences in their new life in Japan. In doing so the receiving teachers and children would, in turn, learn much about international understanding through direct contact and interaction with the returning children.

In summary, it is not only the returning children but also the receiving teachers and children who learn from the education of returning children. The latter will no longer be mere objects to be adjusted one-sidedly to the existing order of schools and society but rather will be subjects bringing changes into the classroom for receiving teachers and children alike. It is only through these mutual learning experiences that effective education for returning children will become a workable possibility. The essence of these reciprocal relations is mutual respect among learners and between learners and teachers, the importance of which lies not only in education for returning children per se, but also in all kinds of education. The success or failure of educational experiments for returning children will thus have much broader implications for the education for all children in Japan.[9]

Notes

1. *Kaigaishijo* or children living abroad, is also being used, and the term *kaigaishijo kyoiku*, or education for overseas children, often has broader implication, including the one for returning children. It is also possible for the term *kikokushijo kyouiku*, or education for returning children, to imply education both for returnng and overseas children, placing the main focus on the former as is done in this paper, although in the general usage this term literally means education for returning children.

2. Mombusho, Kaigaishijo Kyouiku Shitsu, (Section for Overseas Children), *Kaigaishijo Kyouiku no Genjo* (Present status of education for overseas children) (Tokyo: Mombusho, 1985).

3. This point was expressed by many teachers in the receiving schools in a survey conducted by the Ministry of Education in 1976. See Mombusho, Chosa-tokeika, *Kaigaikinmushashijo Kyouiku ni Kansuru Sogoteki Jittaichosa* (Comprehensive survey on the status of education for children of those working abroad) (Tokyo: Mombusho, Section for Research and Statistics, 1976).

4. For behavioral problems of returning children, see Kobayashi Tetsuya, "Adaptation of Overseas and Returning Children in Japan," a paper presented in the Fourth World Congress of Comparative Education Society held in Saitama, Japan, 1980; John I. Kitsuse, Anne E. Murase, and Yoshiaki Yamamura, *Kikokushijo: The Emergence and Institutionalization of an Educational Problem in Japan*, in *Studies in the Sociology of Social Problems*, ed. Joseph W. Schneider and John I. Kitsuse (New Jersey: Ablex, 1984), 162–79; Anne E. Murase, "Higher Education and Life Style Aspirations of Japanese Returnee and Nonreturnee Students", in *Jochi Daigaku Gaikokugogakubu Kiyo* (Tokyo: Sophia University Faculty of Foreign Languages Bulletin, March 1985), 195–229. Among a number of Japanese articles and books on this topic, see Akira Hoshino, ed. *Karucha Shokku* (Culture shock) (Tokyo: Shibundo, 1980).

5. See the paper by Kitsuse and Yamamura quoted above. Also note *Asahi Evening News*, ed. *Chiisana Kokusaijin* (Little international persons) (Tokyo: Asahi Shinbunsha, 1978).

6. Ronald Dore, *The Diploma Disease—Education, Qualification and Development* (London: George Allen & Unwin, 1975).

7. Mombusho, *Kyoiku Gakujutsu Bunka ni okeru Kokusai Kouryu, Chuo Kyouiku Shingikai Toushin* (Tokyo: Mombusho, 1975).

8. Kaigaishijo Kyoiku no Suishin no Kihonteki Shisaku ni kansuru kenkyukaigi, in *Kaigaishijo Kyoiku no Suishin ni kansuru Kihonteki Shisaku ni tsuite*, Mombusho: 1976; Kaigaishijo Kyouiku Shitu, op. cit., 85–103.

9. For further reading in English, see the following: Anne E. Murase, "The problems of Japanese Returning Students," *International Educational and Cultural Ex-*

change 13 (Spring 1978): 10–14; Tetsuya Kobayashi, "Japan's Policy on Returning Students", ibid., 15–16, 47. In Japanese, see Kobayashi Tetsuya, *Kaigaishijo Kyouiku, Kikokushijo Kyouiku* (Education for overseas and returning children) (Tokyo: Yuhikaku, 1982); Tetsuya Kobayashi, ed., *Ibunka ni Sodatsu Kodomotachi* (Children grown up in different cultures) (Tokyo: Yuhikaku, 1983); Katsuo Nakabayashi, *Sekai no Nihonjin Gakkou* (Japanese schools in the world) (Tokyo: Sanshusha, 1978); and Hirotake Sato, *Kaigaishijo no Kyouiku Mondai* (Educational problems of overseas children) (Tokyo: Gakuensha, 1978).

16

Educational Demands and Institutional Response: *Dowa* Education in Japan

John N. Hawkins

Access to education and especially certain selected sectors and institutions in Japan's educational structure is a sought-after goal of most Japanese families regardless of social class, geographic origin, and, as we shall see, caste status. The study that follows was conducted in Japan and concentrated on the political organizations and educational demands of a persistently isolated and discriminated-against group, the *burakumin*. Termed "Japan's invisible race" by Wagatsuma and DeVos, this group remains today, in many respects, a discrete subgroup in Japanese society, outside the pale of the majority and as such lacking the social and institutional connections so vital to individual mobility.[1] Although official policy prohibits discrimination against this group or any other, and although the educational system is theoretically open to all, statistically, the *burakumin* have not participated and been represented in the upper levels of Japanese education and have consistently been the underachievers at the lower levels (as well as problem students, dropouts, and so forth, at least as identified by Japanese educa-

An earlier version of this essay was published in *Comparative and International Education Review*, Vol. 27, No. 2 (June 1983). Copyright © 1983 by the Comparative and International Education Society. Reprinted by permission of The University of Chicago Press.

tional authorities). For this and a variety of other reasons, there is a fairly long history of active political organization and mobilization of *burakumin* to gain access to preferred institutions in Japanese society and to seek an end to official and unofficial discrimination. In this paper we will direct attention to recent political struggles carried out by *burakumin* and their representative organizations under the general rubric, "*dowa* education" (also called *Kaiho* education), which directly translated would mean assimilation education (or liberation education).[2] In an effort to redress what is perceived as educational discrimination and lack of equal opportunity, *burakumin* organizations have generated a series of specific and general demands that they have directed to the appropriate educational and governmental authorities. There have been a variety of policy responses on the part of the educational system, and *burakumin* have reacted accordingly. Here, we focus on ideological characteristics of *burakumin* organizations and *dowa* education, the nature of selected educational demands, the access channels utilized to transmit the demands to the authorities, and the resulting educational policy responses and feedback from *burakumin* organizations. This is an initial effort to clarify some political and educational relations between a subordinate (and in many other respects, marginal) group and the dominant, superordinate majority in Japan.

General Background of "Outcastes" in Japan

Although the history of the origin of outcaste groups in Japan is not well documented, some basic features are clear. For over 1,000 years, long association with certain ritual impurities usually associated with occupation was believed to have changed the very nature of a person so that he became defiled and polluted and that, moreover, this pollution was hereditary and communicable. In fact, as noted by Wagatsuma and DeVos, it was a complex of "economic, social, political and ideological conditions" that led to the development of a status and attitude associated with untouchability[3] in the ninth and tenth centuries. Japanese culture, influenced by Buddhism imported from China and Korea, and merging this system of thought with local Shinto beliefs, generated occupational stratification patterns whereby certain occupations associated with blood and death were considered polluting (for example, skinners, butchers, leather workers, cremators, tomb watchers [*shuku*], and so forth). The rise of outcaste groups was directly related to the development of Japanese guild-protection arrangements (*be*), slavery (*yakko*), and the rise of a "labor market" that operated in closed corporate communities.[4] The fusion of Buddhism (with its strictures against the taking of life in any form) with Shinto (with its notion of ritual impurity) contributed to the development of a hereditary, occupational, ritually impure outcaste group termed at the time (Nara period, 710–784) *eta*. Individuals engaging in certain defiled occupations and, of course, slaves conquered in battle were often forced outside Japanese society. From that time on, they were historically not of the majority and had a monopoly on their particular occupation, which was inherited. Racially and linguistically part of the Japanese majority, they were identified by official papers, residence patterns, occupation, and other identifiable symbols on their clothing and person. During the Edo period (1603–1867), these relationships became even more solidified and formalized, thus resulting in a virtual cessation of upward mobility of the groups in question. From this early period up to the end of the Word War II, a variety of organizational efforts were pursued by members of this group to pressure the Japanese government to enact legislation and other official edicts aimed at ending official and unofficial discrimination toward the outcaste group. In August 1871, the pariah-caste status of this group was officially abolished by the Meiji government, and they were henceforth designated as "new commoners" (*shin heimin*).[5] While their former official outcaste status was removed by legislation, long-standing culturally imbedded negative attitudes toward this group remained among the general Japanese population. They remained in segregated communities, engaged in their historical occupations (without, however, the monopoly protection guaranteed previously), and continued to remain tied to traditional, social, and financial networks. The net effect of such legislation was that although officially liberated, *burakumin* as a group remained poor, impoverished, and isolated from the mainstream of Japanese life. In 1903, the Greater Japan Fraternal Conciliation Society was established to form the core of a more organized political body constituting a "reconciliation movement" (*yuwa undo*). This movement represented an effort at "self-improvement" and shifted responsibility for removing discrimination to the *burakumin* themselves. Poverty and continued discrimination led in 1922 to the "race riots" and the subsequent formation of a more militant liberation movement called the

National Levellers Association (Suiheisha). Heavily influenced by socialist and Marxist ideology, this movement abandoned the notion that discrimination existed because of the deprivation and disadvantagement of *burakumin*, who thus required "self-improvement," but rather that the locus of the problem lay with the majority society and that any acts of discrimination should be met with immediate retaliation. Internal factionalism split this movement during the 1920 international and 1930 international, and with the rise of Japanese militarism, it, along with other left-wing associations, dispersed or went underground, not to emerge again until the end of the war.

The postwar organizational history of the *burakumin* is complex, and only a brief summary will be presented here. In 1946, a special committee was formed to carry on the prewar political struggle, and officially took the name Kaiho Domei, or Buraku Liberation League. Associated with a variety of left-wing groups, the league engaged in both local struggles (accusations of individuals practicing discriminatory activities) and national administrative struggles (aimed at both local and national government). These activities proceeded unevenly, but with significant success, until 1961, when it was decided that a major national demonstration culminating with a petition to the government would be launched. The demonstration, called "The Grand March of Liberation," had three major goals: (1) improvement of social and economic conditions in *buraku* communities; (2) an increase in coordination and cooperation among the diverse political groups supporting *burakumin* (for example, the Socialist Party, Communist Party, and so forth); and (3) to increase the solidarity among those *burakumin* not previously drawn into the struggle. The petitions were accepted by the Japanese Diet and resulted in formal governmental action in the form of a special council at the ministry level (Deliberative Council for *Buraku* Integration [*Dowa Taisaku Shingi Kai*]) to investigate *burakumin* conditions and subsequent submission of a report to the prime minister proposing a plan of action to bring about the end of discrimination against *burakumin* and the effective integration of the group into Japanese society. A sort of Japanese "affirmative action" program developed that stated that the following activities be carried out "systematically and swiftly":[6] (1) improvement of housing and other living conditions through the construction of public facilities; (2) enactment of social welfare and public health facilities; (3) promotion of agriculture, forestry, and fishing; (4) promotion of small-scale industry; (5) improvements of working conditions and employment security through vocational training and guidance; (6) improvement of education and encouragement of higher education; (7) promotion of activities to protect people's fundamental rights; and (8) actualization of any means that are effective for attaining all the objectives stated above.

It was clear that the *Kaiho Domei* had succeeded in successfully involving the Japanese government both financially and politically in the campaign to eliminate discrimination toward the *burakumin*. The ten-year plan (1969–79) that finally emerged had as an underlying theoretical assumption that discrimination would only disappear as a result of economic and social improvement, and that education should be utilized as a major force for such change. Upwards of $80 million (U.S.) was apportioned for this program. Almost immediately, the various political factions within the *burakumin* movement disagreed over the intent and implementation of the report and subsequent legislation. The primary split occurred between the Japanese Socialist Party (JSP) and the Japanese Communist Party (JCP) factions, eventually resulting in the creation of two separate organizations.[7] The reasons for the split and the complex theoretical and practical differences between the two groups are detailed elsewhere.[8] For our purposes, the differences related specifically to education can be summarized as follows. The JSP faction maintains that continued discrimination against *burakumin* is based primarily on a lack of civil rights and access to education and employment—in short, a lack of opportunity. The JCP essentially contends that discrimination is a carryover from the old feudal society, continues under modern capitalism, and is essentially a "class" question. The JCP promotes a more standard Marxist analysis of social class discrimination and has suggested that all poor Japanese are discriminated against, not just *burakumin*. To the JCP the JSP faction is unjust in its accusation of the majority of Japanese and too sectarian in their support of *burakumin*. For its part, the JSP faction accuses the JCP of being divisive and dishonest with the bulk of *burakumin*, who still feel specifically discriminated against. The discrimination practiced against the *burakumin* is of a special kind and over and above that practiced on poor Japanese in general. Therefore, they argue, special programs should be generated to assist *burakumin* specifically and educate both *burakumin* and the overall Japanese population in general. Both groups, however, agree on the need for greater educational opportunities and an end to discrimination in the schools. It is this essentially educational issue that will be explored below. The study will also focus on the overriding political questions involved as both groups have utilized political strategies and tactics to obtain desired goals and objectives.

A brief overview of educational conditions among *burakumin* and within *buraku* districts reveals that, as of 1963, compared to their parents, less than 10 percent of whom went to senior high school, about 30 percent of *burakumin* children were attending senior high school in some districts. This compared with 60 to 70 percent attendance among Japanese in general at the senior high level. In 1973, the situation had improved significantly for *burakumin*, with 64 percent attending the compulsory level overall, but still lagging behind the Japanese cohort in general with close to 95 percent.[9] Although attendance figures demonstrate some improvement over the period under discussion, other factors must also be considered. Absenteeism and wastage are high, and school performance overall is low for *burakumin* children. University attendance is virtually nonexistent (4.2 percent graduating).[10] Due to effective political organization and political struggles in recent years, a variety of additional reforms have resulted in *burakumin* children receiving increased financial subsidies from the government.

It has been suggested that educational conditions have improved in the 1980s, but precise figures remain elusive. It is quite likely that it is precisely in the arena of education that *burakumin* have made significant advances and have gained increased access to Japanese society, and they have done so, it is suggested here, largely because of an effective program of generating, transmitting, articulating, and converting educational demands into public policy. It is this demand process, the supportive political organization structure, and the public policy output that will be examined below.

The Supporting Ideology

Both of the major *burakumin* organizations espouse an ideological position to explain the persistence of continued discrimination against the group and to offer a general critique of Japanese society. Although it is in this area that the most critical differences between the JCP and JSP factions exist, both organizations employ a variant of a basically Marxist interpretation of society and culture. The JSP concentrates their critique on what they describe as a "lagging feudal culture" that has continued to influence social relations, while the economic base has changed and assumed the basic relations of capitalism. This argument holds that while urban capitalism developed during the Meiji and post-Meiji period, feudal social relations continued in rural and semirural regions. As capitalism continued to develop, eventually absorbing other sectors of Japanese society, feudal relations adapted to the new situation without disappearing. However, continued discrimination against *burakumin* is not simply a problem of lagging social consciousness, but rather serves, at this time, a specific political and economic function. Japanese society and economy require a labor pool of exploited workers, so the system of discrimination is consciously maintained to provide a reference point justifying further exploitation of lower-class people.[11]

The JCP organization argues that exploitation of poor people in general has been a characteristic of Japanese society generally, but especially since the development of feudalism. To ease the suffering of poor peasants during the Tokugawa period, a scapegoat was institutionalized by providing still lower classes (*burakumin* and *hinin*) for the mass of poor peasants to discriminate against and look down upon. Yet, they all suffered, as did the newly rising urban working class. It is the position of the JCP, then, that there was nothing unusually special about the exploitation of *burakumin* other than, perhaps, its intensity. Along this line of reasoning, there is nothing to prevent a general union of the *burakumin* liberation movement with other more general struggles for human rights, namely, those of the urban working class, peasants in general, struggles against the military, and so on. The discrimination practiced against the *burakumin* is only one area in a total system of discrimination in Japanese society that includes discrimination against the poor in general, against outsiders of all types (Koreans, Chinese, and any foreigner), and even against the physically handicapped. Thus, any movement to end discrimination must unite with other antidiscriminatory movements to form a general struggle against Japanese capitalism and the supporting social structure.[12]

Each group, of course, finds great fault with the other's theory and practice. For its part, the JSP accuses the JCP of promoting a false "unity" that will only work to the disadvantage of *burakumin* and turn leadership and control over to non *burakumin*, as before. *Dowa* education and *dowa* struggles cannot be formulated collectively in the sense that the JCP promotes. Such a policy will only further isolate *burakumin*, and simply reflects a form of deprivation theory. Correspondingly, to argue that the problems of the *buraku-min* are not special but simply the problems of poor Japanese ignores the extra oppression that the group has suffered for hundreds of years and the social and psychological effects of institutionalized discrimination. To argue further that the educational problems of *burakumin* can be solved within the general framework of education inhibits the development of theories to cope with the historical effects of oppression resulting in low academic achievement and retardation of physical and mental development. In short, the educational and social problems of the *burakumin* are special and not to be categorized or lumped together with those of other oppressed groups in Japanese society.[13]

The JCP criticism is directed more at what is considered to be the lack of political theory on the part of the JSP faction. They maintain that the JSP does not look at all the facts and tends to overexaggerate the problems of the *burakumin*. Conditions among *burakumin* have improved over the years to the point that there is little difference between their political, social, and economic conditions and that of other working-class Japanese. Although the JCP concedes that the lower rungs of the socioeconomic scale are disproportionately occupied by *burakumin*, there are other Japanese at that level as well, and it should, therefore, be the program of any social change-oriented group to improve the conditions of all individuals at this level, not just *burakumin*. Furthermore, within the *burakumin* group there are wide differences between some very wealthy and exploitative *burakumin* in control of major economic enterprises and the mass of extremely poor *burakumin*. Again, it is naive to lump all *burakumin* in one category without distinguishing politically and economically within the group and between the group and the majority society. To maintain that discrimination against *burakumin* is total and complete and a conscious policy on the part of the "ruling bourgeois ideology" is contradictory because it implies that all non*burakumin* belong to the bourgeoisie and ordinary working people are as much to blame for continued discrimination as the ruling class. The net effect of such a policy is to create a new discrimination against non*burakumin*. A characteristic tendency in the JSP's approach to discrimination (again, from the perspective of the JCP) is that they lack objectivity and are unable theoretically to distinguish between specific discriminatory practices against *burakumin* and the discriminatory practices promoted in Japanese society in general. There is no such thing as "discrimination" in the abstract—only certain kinds of discrimination with specific historical and economic backgrounds. In short, the JSP position is slightly metaphysical and ignores the class-analysis strategy so basic to Marxism.[14]

While the ideological dispute is a real one and forms the basis for the lack of unity and the antagonism that characterize JSP and JCP *dowa* relations, the fundamental differences in their respective positions do not appear to be irreconcilable. Both provide a critique of Japanese society that recognizes continued discrimination that is at once exploitative and demeaning. Both assert that *burakumin* have historically been on the receiving end of unusual discrimination, and while the JCP argues that conditions have improved, they do not go so far as to suggest that great progress has been made. In essence, the difference between the two positions is that one distinguishes between the special nature of discrimination against *burakumin* calling for a separate and independent organization and the consequent political control over the resources that have been successfully obtained from the Japanese majority, and the other suggests a broad united front by all oppressed Japanese. These differences become more apparent if we look at some of the specific criticisms made by each group regarding the Japanese educational system and its relation to the needs of *burakumin* in particular.

In keeping with their basic position that the educational problems of *burakumin* are of a special nature, the JSP group has focused their criticism of education in several areas (specific educational struggles and issues will be detailed below; this section is meant to provide a brief overview of some basic critiques of Japanese education). First and foremost, the JSP group maintains that it is the responsibility of each school at both the collegiate and precollegiate levels to provide for a curricular program aimed at improving the self-image of *burakumin*. The study of history, politics, and economics is to provide the base from which an understanding will emerge as to the reasons for discrimination in the past and present. Thus, *dowa* education courses have been designed, texts compiled, and teachers trained to offer courses of this nature. The long-range goal, however, is to move in the direction of permeating the curriculum with *dowa* content rather than to have separate courses. A related goal is to provide *dowa* courses for the general population to make them aware of the causes of discrimination, promote a more healthy image of *burakumin*, and generally raise the consciousness of the Japanese population. *Dowa* education should generally promote educational programs in the area of human rights and specifically focus on the human rights of *burakumin*. A second major issue is that of providing adequate financial support for *burakumin* to attend quality senior high schools and colleges and universities. The financial support would be in the nature of tuition, clothing, educational materials, and a variety of other educational expenses. It is argued that one reason for low attendance rates at the senior high and college level is the poor economic position of most *burakumin* and the necessity, therefore, of children to begin work at an early age. Financial support alone, however, is insufficient, as *burakumin* historically have been unable to compete equally with the majority of Japanese on the rigorous and highly competitive entrance examinations required at both the senior high and college levels. Therefore, some leaders within the JSP group are now arguing for special admissions policies to provide quotas to assure an equitable percentage of *burakumin* at each of these levels. This policy is not to be considered a solution, but a temporary measure until *burakumin* are able to raise their overall educational level to compete with other Japanese. A parallel tutoring program is another aspect of this policy, and the lack of such facilities in the Japanese educational system (although progress has been made) is another source of discontent.[15]

The JCP critique again reflects its position that educational problems in Japanese society are of a social class nature and are not specific to any particular subgroup. The educational system overall is discriminatory because if reflects the interests and needs of the middle and upper classes. It discriminates against all poor Japanese. The educational system serves to reproduce existing social relations in Japanese society, including that held by *burakumin*, by an intense system of intergroup competition. In general, then, the entire educational system is in need of restructuring to provide for a more cooperative school environment. All students should be allowed to work together on problems and develop self-initiative and democratic attitudes. Parents and teachers should also unite in their efforts to provide for a more cooperative and collective school environment, and the medium for such an action program should be the *dowa* educational programs already existing in many schools. Any program designed to foster collectivism should also realize that significant curricular reform is also necessary. The JCP states that current texts and supporting curricular materials contain only the point of view of the ruling-class ideology and, furthermore, are not relevant to the daily needs and experiences of the majority of Japanese. They are especially unrelated to the experiences of *burakumin* and poor Japanese in general. Thus, a complete curricular reconstruction should occur and should be a major component of any *dowa* educational program. Finally, and somewhat contradictory to their previous position on social class, the JCP has argued generally for universal preschool education, high school education, free textbooks, educational allowances, scholarships, tuition exemptions, lower student-teacher ratios (less than fifty to one), fewer teaching hours for teachers, better pay for teachers, and improvement of educational facilities and social education (adult education.)[16] These suggestions are not specific to any social class but are considered to be general priorities for educational reform in Japan.

One general educational issue raised during the past ten years by both *dowa* organizations concerns the cost of education. Although there is no direct tuition, there are a number of indirect educational costs that *burakumin* find difficult to meet (for example, uniforms, textbooks, auxiliary study materials, donations to the school, lunch, expenses for school trips, and other extracurricular activities). Both organizations have stressed the need for governmental agencies to provide subsidies for *burakumin* to meet these expenses (and, of course, the JCP argues that all poor people should receive such subsidies). Also, both organizations agree that *dowa* education should basically seek to improve the overall educating environment through financial subsidies, introduce educational programs to increase the social consciousness of both *burakumin* and the general population, and improve the occupational opportunities for *burakumin* in general (although one informant stressed the fact that somebody must continue to engage in traditional *burakumin* occupations, and that they should not be considered "dirty").

At the precollegiate level, a series of discrimination incidents resulted in specific educational demands in the Osaka area. Often, incidents were reported by students to their parents and then to the local *dowa* office. Usually the discrimination took the form of a remark made by a teacher regarding the low position of *burakumin* and attributing it to some racial or other defect in the character of *burakumin* in general. Occasionally, the incident took place outside the school, but more often during the course of instruction (for example, one instructor made a discriminatory remark about *burakumin* during a lecture on the origin of samurai). Such incidents had the effect of turning the attention of the *dowa* office to the individual school, where first the accused party was denounced (*kyudan*) and pressure applied to have him removed from his position, and second (and more important) the general educational conditions of *burakumin* in that specific school would be analyzed and more specific demands made upon the school and city educational administration.[17] In some cases, the new demands were relatively uncomplicated, for example, identifying priority areas for improvement, such as providing free lunch money (failure to bring lunch money in some schools results in punishment in the form of running laps; *burakumin* children, it was charged, were always punished more severely), free books, and other financial subsidies.[18] In other cases, such as the "Sayama incident,[19] demands included the charge that the entire curriculum for the school district be changed to require that a specific set of texts (the *Ningen* series written jointly by *buraku* children and adults and compiled and edited by Kaiho Domei) be adopted district wide. Educational demands were not limited by the pedagogical needs of *buraku* children only, but included their parents as well. It was felt that parents' educational levels were too low and resulted in their setting a bad example for their children. Thus, at least in one case, demands were generated to stress the importance of formal alliances between *buraku* parents and teachers in *buraku* districts designed to raise the general educational level of parents, especially in such areas as reading and mathematics. The reasoning has been that if parents are better able to augment their children's formal study, the 30 percent variance between achievement levels of *buraku* and non*buraku* children will disappear. Finally, once achievement levels have risen or are on the rise, special admissions policies could be provided for *buraku* children to enter the better public high schools.[20]

Educational demands for higher education are directly related to those identified for the precollegiate. It is recognized that it is absolutely essential to raise educational levels and reduce discrimination at the precollegiate level as a precondition to achieving success for *burakumin* in higher education. For the present, however, there is a feeling that until *buraku* children as a whole are achieving at levels closer to the national norm, it is necessary to provide special tutoring to prepare students for the entrance examinations. Moreover, special admissions policies must be pursued to assure equal representation in Japan's colleges and universities. A second problem is again associated with parents of *buraku* children. Despite the overwhelming importance of higher education in Japan and the direct correlation between university degrees and occupation, many *buraku* parents do not see the necessity for higher education, and for this reason they need to be educated. Third, universities must begin to provide meaningful *dowa* education for all students and assure that it remain an integral part of the curriculum. Finally, one of the first collegiate-level demands (1959) was for a provision to allocate special funds for university scholarships for *buraku* youth. This demand was not met for ten years. There is now some feeling that little progress has been made in this area and that university reform will be one of the most difficult educational levels to penetrate and create new programs for. An increased sense of frustration has been felt, and some have suggested that the entire higher educational system in Japan might have to be dismantled.[21]

The more complicated and complex the educational issue, the higher up the educational decision-making ladder the *dowa* struggle would focus. For example, the effort to have the entire student scholarship system revised for Osaka prefecture resulted in a broad alliance among various *buraku* organizations (the "Osaka prefectural council for duties of *dowa* education" and the "Osaka city council for studies of *dowa* education" formed an alliance with the Kaiho Domei chapter in Osaka to seek support from local PTA and teacher union groups). Eventually, an executive committee was formed (October 1973) and twenty-three additional organizations joined the struggle. The coalition then campaigned for signatures requesting specific revisions in the scholarship system and presented their demands to the prefectural board of education. A series of meetings were held with the staff of the prefectural section for educational institutions (*shigaku-ka*), and the revision was eventually obtained.

Although the specific organizational network employed to gain access to the educating system at the city level varies, a survey of the system in Kobe, Osaka, Ashiya, and Toyonaka reveals a general pattern. Representatives from *buraku* districts, scholars, experts on *dowa* problems, and city personnel form an overall committee for administering *dowa* policies. A more complicated managerial council is formed that may consist of subsections focused on specific problems (for example, environment, welfare, human rights, education) and/or subsections to represent various city departments (for example, finance, health, environment, agriculture, public works, and education). As demands are received and processed into policy they pass through committees composed of city representatives, *buraku* representatives and scholars, and experts who make revisions and finalize the first draft of a program. The program is then sent to the local *buraku* district offices for discussion by *burakumin* and then back to the managerial council (*dowa taisaku renraku chosei kaigi*) for final implementation. If the issue is educational in nature, the composition of the subcommittee under the council is composed of educational personnel (for example, PTA, teacher's union, scholars, and experts, *burakumin*, and city council members). It should be stressed that this is not an ideal channel and does not always operate smoothly. There appears to be continuous jockeying for power in terms of appointments to committees for the purpose of gaining voting blocs. Yet, for many minor educating issues this access channel appears to function well.

The style of demand articulation also varies according to the issue and can range from individual denunciation (*kyudan*) of someone who has obstructed *burakumin* demands or made discriminatory remarks to formal petitions to the appropriate educational authorities. The manner of presenting educational demands also depends on the degree of receptive attitude displayed by the educational body or authority approached. In a case where educational authorities at either the prefectural or municipal level are cooperative and appear to be making positive moves to address the issue, the demand will be presented and stressed in a consistent but nonantagonistic manner. However, where educating authorities and other officials on the prefectural or municipal level do not receive the demands with a sympathetic ear, denunciation and other more drastic steps are taken. A case in point is a struggle that occurred in 1970 in Ashiya city, where five demands were presented by the local Kaiho Domei office (regarding classroom size, student-teacher ratio, scholarships, and admissions requirements) to the mayor and superintendent's office. The superintendent refused to accept the demands and stated that education was really the parents' responsibility. Several denunciation meetings were held, where educational officials were confronted by parents and teachers of the *buraku* districts, and eventually promises were made to redress the grievances and initiate policy for the five areas under question. Although promises were made, the failure to follow through on the part of the superintendent's office resulted in his being kidnapped by the Kaiho office and forced to see the conditions in the *buraku* district and the schools in the area. Such action caught the attention of the city board of education and, of course, the media and contributed to the pressure already on the district to enact reforms. After one month, the prefectural board intervened and forced the Ashiya city board to come to an agreement with the Kaiho office.

The pattern discussed above relates primarily to JSP activities in the Kinki area during the past seven years. The JCP has also engaged in mass meetings and pressure tactics to achieve educating goals, but has criticized the JSP group for excessive use of violence and terrorist tactics. In any case, such practices in the Osaka area have resulted in recent years in several important educational decisions on the part of the prefectural and municipal governments. It is this conversion of educational demands into policy that will be examined next to highlight the scope and degree of educational change that has occurred.

Educational Policy and Feedback

The organizational activities of the *burakumin*, the demands presented to the educational authorities in the Kinki area, and the administrative structure established by both the prefectural and municipal governments in response to the demands have resulted in several important responses in the field of education. Although these responses vary according to prefecture and city, there have been some common areas of emphasis, as revealed by the policies generated in Osaka, Itami, and Ashiya. The policies can be categorized in three major areas: (1) policies for school districts; (2) policies for individual schools; and (3) policies in the broad area of social education (*Shyukai kyoiku*).

District-level policies have generally reflected the belief that the entire child must be assessed in developmental terms—not just the intellectual level of achievement. *Buraku* children must be assured a complete educational cycle from preschool through to guaranteed employment. Policies in most cities have focused on building nursery schools (*dowa hoiku*) and staffing them, thus providing a sort of head-start program for *buraku* children. For older children and adults, policies have been generated that are to provide special *dowa* classes to foster positive attitudes toward *burakumin* and their history. At the general school level, policies have focused on the need to provide adequate nutritional and health care for *buraku* children. District-wide study groups and centers for studies in *dowa* education have been another response in certain cities and have resulted in special communities composed of representatives from the community, labor unions, the business community, and, of course, *burakumin*. While there has been general satisfaction with the policy response at the district level, the Kaiho Domei has criticized these programs for taking too long to implement, being too little too late, and in some cases not well suited to the needs of *burakumin* in general.

At the individual school level, educational policy has rested on the assumption that in each school the role of education is to provide absolute equal opportunity to all children and special measures for *burakumin* because of previous discrimination and deprivation. Programs have focused on special in-service teacher training in *dowa* education, study sessions for parents and teachers, and research groups to study the history of *burakumin* and compile new teaching materials. Additional programs have concentrated on implementing programs to "guarantee scholastic achievement," especially for *burakumin*. Guaranteed achievement is to be assured through a systematic study of the nature of achievement and the relationship between scholastic ability and class size, teacher-student relations, community environment, and so forth. In the area of curriculum, policies have suggested that the entire curriculum be reviewed to assure proper compliance with *burakumin* demands and to remove any remaining discriminatory statements or suggestions that might remain. A review of entrance-examination procedures has also begun, and a program to construct more public high schools closer to *buraku* districts has also been one policy response. While *buraku* organizations have recognized that significant advances have been made with respect to positive policy responses on the part of individual schools and districts, there is frustration that, especially in the area of entrance examinations to preferred high schools, there has been little advance. It appears that in the future educational demands at the school level will focus on the achievement issue and the national examination system.

In addition, a series of policy responses have appeared related to the concept of social education (*shyukai kyoiku*). Policies in this area rest on the assumption that the social and educational problems of *burakumin* are interrelated with the entire fabric of Japanese society and affect everyone. Thus, efforts have been made to foster leaders of *dowa* education courses in the workplace and other social institutions. To support such a program, teaching materials have been compiled (or policy decisions to begin such compilation have occurred) to provide adequate reference materials for the study of *dowa* education in a variety of settings. Special newspaper and newsletter publications have been proposed and implemented in at least one city (Itami). Steps have also been taken to make "social educational facilities" such as libraries, public halls, and museums more accessible to *burakumin* and to encourage such institutions to provide *dowa* education classes for the general public. According to *buraku* leaders in the Osaka area, it is this program

that has advanced the least. While educational officials and governmental authorities seem willing to enact policies that focus specifically at the school level and even generate some overall district-level
policies, the response in terms of the overall community has not
been encouraging.

The continuing involvement of the Japanese government with respect to the *burakumin* testifies to the long-term nature of the issue. This study is clearly exploratory, and, I hope, has revealed a
general pattern of effective political organization to achieve specific
and general educational goals. Clearly, both *burakumin* organizations have been successful in wresting from a reluctant Japanese
educational system a variety of educational reforms and, at the
same time, have succeeded in directing national attention to their
plight. The experience of the *burakumin* is a revealing and fasci-
nating study in the politics of educational reform and the process of
intergroup relations and in the future will continue to be a focus
for research by Japanese and non-Japanese scholars alike.

Notes

1. George DeVos and Hiroshi Wagatsuma, eds., *Japan's Invisible Race* (Berkeley:
University of California Press, 1972).

2. It should be noted that although *dowa* is the commonly used term for educational programs and policies toward the *burakumin*, the term *kaiho* ("liberation") is
preferred by both *burakumin* organizations, reflecting more accurately the conflict-
oriented nature of intergroup relations in this case.

3. DeVos and Wagatsuma, 6–20.

4. Ibid., 19–20.

5. A complete detailed analysis of pre- and postwar political militance and the
organizational strategy of the *burakumin* can be found in DeVos and Wagatsuma,
68–88. This summary draws heavily from Hiroshi Wagatsuma, "Political Problems of
a Minority Group in Japan: Recent Conflicts in *Buraku* Liberation Movements," in
Cast Studies on Human Rights and Fundamental Freedoms (The Hague: Foundation
for the Study of Plural Societies, 1976).

6. Wagatsuma.

7. The faction associated with the JSP continues under the name Buraku Kaiho
Domei, and that associated with the JCP in 1969 formed a group called Buraku
Koiho Domei Seijoka Renraku Kaigi. In this study, when referring to these two
groups, I will simply refer to them in terms of their affiliation with either the JSP or
the JCP.

8. Wagatsuma.

9. Ibid., Kazuhiko K. Kitamura, "Organization of Education in Japan, 1971–1973"
(report presented at the twenty-fourth International Conference on Education,
Geneva, 1973).

10. *Buraku kaiho*, no. 45 (September 1973).

11. "Views on Discrimination," *Asahi Newspaper* (March 1975).

12. T. Ogawa, *Dowa kyoiji no riron to hoho* (Kyoto: Buraku mondai kenkyushko, 1975).

13. *Buraku kaiho*, no. 51 (February 1974).

14. "Views on Discrimination," *Asahi Newspaper* (March 1975).

15. Interviews with representatives of Kaiho Domei, Osaka, July 18, 1976: February 3, 1981.

16. Ogawa.

17. *Buraku kaiho*, no. 57 (July 1974).

18. Interviews with Asuka city educational representatives, July 20, 1976; February 4, 1981.

19. "Kyoiku wo mamoru fubo no kai," *Buraku kaiho domei*, Hojyo chapter, Osaka-fu, 1976.

20. *Buraku kaiho*, no. 56 (June 1974).

21. Interview with Kaiho Domei youth organizer, Osaka, July 26, 1977.

Part III

The Politics of Education: Issues of Centralization and National Identity

Introduction

James J. Shields, Jr.

After the examination system, no issue is more complex in its implications for educational reform in Japan than the highly centralized nature of schooling. While many foreign observers come away with the view that the high levels of academic achievement are due to the tight control of the national Ministry of Education, many Japanese critics trace the deep fractures in the system to this control. Along with early socialization for discipline and effort and the role of the competitive examination system in stimulating school violence and decreasing educational equality, the centralization of political control has emerged as a critical crosspoint among comparative education scholars for assessing the strengths and weaknesses of Japanese education.

Unfortunately, the scholarly exploration of the politics of education in Japan is still in a very early stage of development. Descriptions and explanations of how individuals and groups formulate and articulate change in public educational policy are sparse. An inordinate amount of rhetoric has been poured into this vacuum, of which rarely what is said is meant, little is what it appears to be, words replace action, and not much is to be taken literally. As a result, a good deal of what can be stated about the politics of education in Japan is tentative and exploratory.

In the United States, there has been a kind of countermovement away from the growing involvement of the federal government in the fiscal and regulatory control of educational policy. However, this countermovement has been complicated, if not compromised, by the use of ideological brandishments by Department of Education officials to control educational policy indirectly. The aim, it appears, is not to move the central government out of the business of education entirely, as many of the architects of this conservative restoration claim, but to replace legal supervision with cultural control.

U.S. conservatives accept as an article of faith that there was a relationship between the increased involvement of the national government in local educational policy in the 1960s and 1970s and the declining levels of pupil achievement and social discipline. They believe they have a mandate to decentralize, deregulate, and to diminish the central government's role in schooling. Their goal is to return fiscal and regulatory control to state governments, local school boards, and the private sector. Periodic references to the high academic standards of the Japanese play an important part in their political maneuvering. Of course, what is rarely mentioned is that Japan achieved this standard within the framework of a highly centralized school system.

The irony in all this is that the political conservatives in the United States share the same views as liberal politicians in Japan in their opposition to tight control over education. Partially, this can be explained by the contradictory historical and cultural differences and similarities between the two nations. The United States tends to act out of a loose mix of classically antistatist, laissez-faire, bourgeois liberalism, whereas in Japan there is a postfeudal alliance of a strong state rooted in a centralized purpose. Because the state itself is considered a moral entity in Japan, there are fewer conflicts between public versus private goals and church versus state values than there are in the United States.

The political contradictions in the United States are well-expressed in the debate over the role of religion in public education, especially school prayer, and science curricula based on religious dogma. This contradiction becomes a little more understandable when it is realized that Americans in some ways are among the most traditional and religious people in the world. Seymour Martin Lipset points out that on a very fundamental level the United States and Japan, when viewed politically, have many conservative similarities. In terms of religion, he says that Americans have held onto a set of premodern and preindustrial values which are reflected in their religious belief systems and in the extent and scope of their religious activity.

Logically, the question could be raised as to what extent the centralized administrative structure of schooling in Japan is related to its high standard of academic achievement. Similarly, it could be asked, to what extent has the movement toward more centralization in the United States been responsible for lower achievement levels? Unfortunately, the level of scholarship in the politics of education is not comprehensive enough to answer these questions with any certainty at this time.

The Historical Context

In terms of Japanese history, there is some debate over the extent to which the dependence on central authority is the fixed, eternal and traditional value it is represented to be by some foreign scholars and by government officials. The debate turns on the question of the degree to which pre-Meiji Japan was a cohesive state, as opposed to an extremely loose collection of semiautonomous fiefdoms each struggling for its own interests and very loyal to its local lords.

Whatever was the case in the more distant past, we have a rather clear picture of the patterns for the last approximately 120 years in both the United States and Japan. From the beginning, control over education in the United States was vested in locally established boards of education which set educational policy and hired teachers. On the other hand, Japan evolved from a more centralized, highly nationalistic system borrowed from Europe during the Meiji Period.

The Meiji leaders, as Richard Rubinger has indicated, set goals and structures for Japanese education tied directly to the interests of the state, and these remained essentially unchanged until the post-World War II period. The goals included raising minimum academic standards, encouraging progress based on merit, and the use of the school as a primary agent of moral and political socialization.

On September 2, 1871, a Ministry of Education was established in Japan with a mandate to create a nationwide school system under its authority. By 1886, the outline of a national framework for schooling was in place with educational bureaucrats in the Ministry of Education making the kinds of decisions that individual teachers had made previously.

Although the Meiji Restoration is an important political turning point in the history of education in Japan, as Rubinger points out, some of the elements in its educational mandate were carried over from the earlier Tokugawa Period. Among these was private sector education, which to this day continues alongside the public system in a very significant and robust way in the *juku* and private high schools and colleges.

Another turning point in Japanese educational history was the post–World War II imposition of a program of "democratization" by the American Occupation Forces. On the administrative level, the aim was to reverse the hold of the central bureaucratic authorities in the Ministry of Education over the formulation and implementation of educational policy. This was to be achieved primarily through the popular election of local school boards with strong legal power.

Since the 1950s, the centralized bureaucracy in the Ministry of Education has effectively reversed the postwar liberalization efforts to decentralize educational control to local school boards. Politically this was possible because, except for the short-lived Socialist government in 1947–48, conservative rule at the national level has been virtually unbroken since the promulgation of the Meiji Constitution in 1889.

The Textbook Issue

The issues surrounding the centralization of educational control are dramatically represented in the textbook and curriculum controversies. As Tokyo Metropolitan University professor Masami Yamazumi has stated, the government has conducted a well-orchestrated and systematic plan to promote policies that cancel out the School Education Law of 1947 passed with the approval of the Occupation Forces. A major intent of the law was to open up the rigid state textbook approval process.

More recently, in a set of recommendations handed to Prime Minister Yasuhiro Nakasone in 1987 by the National Council on Educational Reform, there was a call for a simplified textbook screening system. Almost immediately, it drew negative reactions from almost all interested groups in Japan who viewed it as yet another effort to strengthen the Education Ministry's control over textbooks. The Japan Teachers Union (Nikkyoso), the largest teacher labor union, issued a statement criticizing the recommendations as designed to strengthen rather than lessen the already too tight control of the Ministry over school textbooks. Many other groups and individuals, as reported in the media when the recommendations were issued, reflected the view of Chiba University professor of educational administration, Sadanobu Minowa, that "the Council's proposal holds the public's involvement to a minimum."

The most persistent and antagonistic rival of the Ministry of Education over the process of textbook control as well as the appropriate historical image of Japan portrayed in the curriculum is Nikkyoso. This rivalry is an important factor in the political history of postwar Japan. Haruo Ota, in his recent study of this struggle, has concluded that the Ministry has successfully retained its near monopolistic control over every facet of education, leaving Nikkyoso with no direct access to the decision-making process.

Ota also concludes that Nikkyoso, in its struggle for control, has lost sight of matters directly related to the education of children. On the other hand, William Cummings has argued that more equilibrium exists with a split between the Ministry, which controls finances and curriculum, and the Union, which has autonomy over classroom practice characterized by humanistic and self-actualizing goals for pupils, in particular on the elementary school level.

As recent events in both the U.S.S.R. and the United States illustrate, neither Japanese government efforts to control textbooks and school curriculum nor the controversies resulting from these efforts are unique to Japan. Soviet leader Mikhail Gorbachev's promise to open up his society was reflected in a series of announcements that new textbooks were being published with a franker view of Soviet history dating back to the 1917 Russian Revolution.

The prediction in the Soviet press at the time was that texts would restore several old Bolsheviks and some modern Party officials, such as Nikita Khrushchev, to public approval. As anticipated, these pronouncements resulted in the usual resistance to this kind of critical change. Yegor Ligachev, a high-ranking official in the Kremlin hierarchy, warned historians not to abuse this freedom by writing of the country's past as "seven decades of mistakes, failure and disappointment."

In a 1987 speech, the United States Secretary of Education warned that part of the solution to the problem of U.S. children not learning must come from a revision in the process by which textbooks are adopted, and in their content. He expressed great dismay with the system of textbook adoption which, he felt, allows state and local jurisdictions to respond to demands by such constituencies as parents, publishers, elected officials, and other interest groups.

The implication was that the system as it has evolved gives too much attention to the interests of women, ethnic minorities, environmentalists, the elderly, the handicapped, and even nutritionists. The result, he argued, is a kind of national system of textbook adoption which "depressed quality; encourages dumbness, even falsehood; and gives us American books which are trivial, limp, and lacking in connective tissue."

In the United States' textbook battles of the 1980s, sectarian religious dogma played an equal, if not more important, role than the special interest groups mentioned by the Secretary of Education. The reality is that a good case could be made that there are two groups in conflict with each other for control over curriculum and textbook content. On the one side are the political moderates, largely representing the urban, professional middle class, who tend to favor disembodied competencies and test-taking information. On the other side is the so-called "New Right," which wants to eliminate from textbooks birth control advice, material on racism and militarism, and theories on scientific evolution. In its place they want school prayer and the Biblical teachings of Christian Fundamentalism.

Textbooks and curriculum development, as Michael Apple has pointed out, is a battleground over cultural authority. Finally, the textbook debate in Japan, the U.S.S.R., and the United States is over what is to be the dominant knowledge system or metaphysics in each nation. At the heart of these disputes are questions about the ends and means of schooling, appropriate pedagogy, and ethics and politics. For this reason, there are few areas of dispute that are more critical or more emotionally charged.

Democratic Education

The definition of democratic education in Japan is different than the one supported by U.S. educators. Benjamin Duke, speaking from over twenty-five years as an educator in Japan, argues that the difference can best be explored through examining the relative emphasis each nation places on educational equality and individuality.

Educational equality in Japan is defined in terms of a nationwide standard based on a common curriculum and textbooks approved by the Ministry of Education. Individuality is defined as the ability to work with others and to function harmoniously in a group. Thus, for the Japanese government, standardization, uniformity, and conformity embody the ultimate ingredients of democratic education.

What the Japanese model clarifies is that the concept of democratic education has different meanings in different cultural contexts. Historically, the fear generated by the large representation of communists, socialists, and teacher unionists in the 1950s on democratically elected school boards was used by the government to elevate the principle of educational equality over individual freedom. In bowing to the fear of long-term misuse of power at the local level, the Japanese rejected the concept of democratic education which had been put in place during the U.S. occupation. Ultimately, this returned Japan to a position of limiting the freedom of local communities over educational policy formulation.

Today, some comparative educators, including Benjamin Duke and Nobuo Shimahara, perceive a trend in the United States toward the adoption of the Japanese definition of educational equality with its stress on standardization and uniformity. The U.S. Congress and courts, they point out, are increasingly making decisions based on the need to provide "equal protection under the law" and thereby limit the freedom of state and local school boards to set policy.

The actual power of the over 15,000 school boards in the United States, for example, is compromised by the overlapping authority of local and state governments and the fragmentation of state authority among governors, legislators, state boards, superintendents and departments of education, and textbook committees. Equally formidable obstacles to educational reform exist in Japan. The Ministry of Education operates in a government managed by a political party in power for decades, and is locked in combat with a national teachers union which claims to speak for a large segment of teachers. At this point, each side has a vested interest in the status quo and has effectively played itself into the role of checkmating each other's reform agendas.

Patterns of Educational Reform

The proliferation of national educational task forces and study commissions in both Japan and the United States in the 1980s had generated new optimism that the climate for educational reform would become more favorable. In particular, the National Council on

Educational Reform, also called the Ad Hoc Council on Education, launched in 1985 as an advisory body to the prime minister of Japan, raised expectations that real reforms would be implemented.

The detailed media attention to the problems of Japanese schooling also fueled these expectations. As Shimahara states, the Commission was established as a response to the intense attacks on centralized control, standardized educational practice, and uniformity in schooling. Also, the adverse effects of the competitive college entrance examinations on secondary schooling and adolescents were subjected to wider scrutiny than ever before.

However, most critically, the gap between good and poor schools had escalated and had caused rising tensions in schools. Clearly, this was undermining the principles of educational equality around which the entire system was supposed to have been built. Whatever else, all these charges signaled that the system was entering a period of serious decline.

In reading the reports issued by the Ad Hoc Council on Education, it would be easy to conclude that reforms would be initiated which had the cultivation of student individuality as their overriding purpose. Clearly, the rhetoric of the reports was away from educational equality and toward individual freedom. The reports generated considerable discussion on how individuality could be developed in school along with harmonious adjustment in a group-oriented culture. Linguistic and cultural issues were raised focusing on the distinction between individualism (*kojinshugi*), which implies egotism and concern for self without regard to others, and individuality (*koseishugi*), which is less radical in its implications.

Does all this mean Japan is paving the way for the decentralization and diversification of education? The consensus among foreign analysts is that while the rhetoric is impressive, the resulting changes will not be. There is very little likelihood of a third great wave of educational reform in the immediate future. True, the pendulum of the rhetoric of educational discourse has swung toward decentralization, but the gravity toward centralization continues to be strong. The invariable historical force, as Shimahara argues, is always toward group orientation before the advocacy of individuals.

These events demonstrate once again how difficult it is to achieve anything but the narrowest of educational reforms in Japan. For example, the Council, in response to the criticism that the existing local school district system is too rigid, recommended such minor alterations as increasing the number of school districts in which parents can choose among two or three public schools and suggested that children be allowed to attend schools outside their districts.

As an editorial in *Nihon Keizai Shimbun* stated after the third set of recommendations had been presented by the Ad Hoc Council on April 1, 1987, to Prime Minister Nakasone: "[The recommendations] proved to be somewhat disappointing. Despite the extensive discussions of the Council, it failed to incorporate drastic measures for fundamental reform of the national educational system across the board."

Neither the council's recommendations nor other social indicators promise anything other than the continuation of the conservative direction of Japanese education. In fact, such factors as the emerging pattern of social stratification reflected in college-entry rates, and the real possibility of severe economic reversals in Japan, point to less, not more, progressive reform in the future.

The narrow and persistent conservative agendas in Japanese and U.S. schools represent a troublesome problem. The concerted effort among leaders in both countries to limit the debate over educational goals to a choice between national and economic priorities or individual freedom is archaic and ultimately dangerous. Our increasingly interconnected and interdependent world requires a broader and more humane vision of educational purpose.

17

Continuity and Change in Mid-Nineteenth-Century Japanese Education

Richard Rubinger

Although the Meiji Restoration of 1868 marks an important turning point in the political history of modern Japan, in education there were no sudden changes in 1868. In fact, many of the educational developments in the period following the Restoration had been underway for some time, considerably easing the adjustment to a modern system. By the end of the Tokugawa period (1600–1868) school institutions of all kinds had increased to impressive numbers. One important source estimates that there were as many as 17,000 schools by the end of the period.[1] Not only was the samurai leadership class fully literate but the spread of *terakoya* (parish schools), *gogaku* (local schools), and *shijuku* (private academies) to rural as well as urban areas provided considerable opportunities for commoners as well.[2] Thus, before the modern system was introduced in 1872 large numbers of students in Japan had been introduced to the basics of reading and writing, teachers had gained experience and developed methodologies, and numerous families had adjusted to a style of life that included schooling for their children.[3]

One of the best examples of modernizing functions within the framework of Tokugawa schooling practice is provided by the *shi-*

juku institution. These private academies were run by an individual scholar, usually in his own home, and were supported totally by students' fees. They were thus outside the feudal framework, unlike the domain and *bakufu* schools. They covered a vast array of institutional arrangements, from small and intimate tutorial types such as Yoshida Shoin's Shoka Sonjuku in Hagi to huge centers with elaborate administrative machinery and codified rules and regulations such as Hirose Tanso's Kangien in Hita and from simple writing schools scarcely different from *terakoya* to advanced research institutes. They can be distinguished as a school type, however, by the fact that they were privately run, they were free from official control, and they posed no geographical or class barriers to entrance. Consequently, they could attract a national constituency from the various social classes from all parts of the country.

At the academies students could study fields of learning strongly discouraged at the official schools: various nonorthodox brands of Confucianism, nativist studies (*kokugaku*), and areas of practical value—Western languages, medicine, astronomy, navigation, coastal fortification, cannonry, naval architecture, engineering, and so forth. In addition, it was in the academies that administrative and pedagogical practices developed that anticipated modern schools. At Confucian schools like Tanso's Kangien, as early as the beginning of the nineteenth century an elaborate, articulated school system was created through which students moved by merit and competitive performance. An emphasis on ability and talent, frowned on in official schools, became pronounced in the Dutch language academies.

In schools such as Ogata Koan's Teki Juku in Osaka both samurai and commoners were taught to read and translate Dutch works on science and technology. The provision of advanced training in technical fields and the open admissions policy enabled these academies to become agents of change from a traditional vocational pattern of hereditary succession to a more modern function of schooling—selecting and sorting students into occupational areas by ability and specialized training. The Dutch academies, in particular, became escalators of talent into official bureaucracies and mechanisms for increased upward mobility for commoners and lower samurai, decades before the modern system was proposed.

Although innovation and experimentation marked some aspects of late Tokugawa schooling, traditional patterns persisted. There continued to be wide disparities between the quality and quantity of education in urban and rural areas up to the end of the Tokugawa period. Schooling was widespread, as noted above, but was unevenly distributed throughout the country. In the cities, *ter-akoya* tended to be more numerous, larger, and more systematic in their training than the rural schools. The content of text materials differed also—the curriculum of the city schools catered to the interests of the merchant class while that of the rural schools provided useful information for farmers. The rural schools tended to be small and attendance was far less regular than in the city schools. The Dutch academies, which taught high-level Western studies and technical knowledge, were all in the main urban areas of Edo (Tokyo), Osaka, Kyoto, and Nagasaki.

There were wide disparities in the educational offerings for the samurai among the different feudal domains because of great diversity in the availability, quality, and level of domain school offerings. Some provided only the rudiments of learning, others only advanced stages. Some had no domain school at all for their samurai, others had only one or had several, and made attendance compulsory. By late in the Tokugawa period, Western studies was offered at some of the larger and more strategically placed domains, such as Choshu, Satsuma, or Saga. Others remained unenthusiastic and some specifically forbade it. By one estimate, one-quarter of all the domains at the end of the period had introduced Western studies of some kind in some degree, primarily in medicine, military affairs, and shipbuilding.[4] There is no evidence that any domain did away with neo-Confucianism as the core of the curriculum of the domain school. The *Four Books* and *Five Classics* remained the central texts in 95 percent of all domain schools.[5] Some domain schools began admitting commoners before the end of the Tokugawa period but most did not. Aizu and Hikone domains continued to forbid entrance of commoners to the end.[6] When commoners were admitted at all it was usually in a separate facility so that mixing of classes would not occur. Of 245 domains which left records of such things only seven indicated facilities for women.[7]

Education in Tokugawa Japan generally reflected the class distinctions of the larger society. Male members of the samurai class were probably fully literate and attended schools in systematic fashion. They were all exposed to the Confucian classics and some were introduced to Western learning as well, whether in their domain school or, more likely, in one of the private Dutch academies. Merchants in the cities sent their children to *terakoya* for the basics of reading, writing, and calculation. Children of the leadership levels within the farming class were well represented at rural *terakoya* and at some of the academies. Ordinary farmers, on the other hand, saw little need for formal schooling outside the home.

Education at the end of the Tokugawa period was characterized by arrangements that were generally unsystematic and private. Initiatives rested with consumers—individual families and students—rather than with public authorities. The questions of where, when, and how much education should be sought were individual matters. Thus, schooling was very much a patchwork of different teachers and a variety of institutions put together by individuals often in an ad hoc and idiosyncratic manner.

The Tokugawa legacy in education was both advantageous and detrimental to the establishment of a centrally controlled modern school system following the Meiji Restoration. Facilities and personnel were on hand; Western studies had been introduced; merit qualifications, comprehensive curricula, and articulated system had been tried. At the same time, education on the eve of the Meiji Restoration was marked by particularity among different regions and among different classes. It was characterized by discontinuity among institutions and a lack of articulation in the system as a whole.

Establishing a National School System

The Meiji government's first educational priority was to establish a system of higher education that would replenish the leadership group with the best talent in the country. The earliest proposals, which predated the completion of the Restoration wars, led to bitter disputes among the three groups with the most at stake in the outcome: the Confucianists, who had been the officially recognized scholars of the Tokugawa period; the Shintoists, who had found themselves suddenly in favor as the ideological supporters of imperial restoration; and the advocates of Western learning, whose skills were very much needed to deal with the problems of defense against and negotiation with the Western powers. By the summer of 1870, when the imperatives of the state had become clearer, the Confucian domination of higher education had ended and the Western scholars emerged triumphant, in uncontested control of the university.[8] The university became the government's central institution for assimilating advanced and practical knowledge from the West. Foreign instructors were hired in large numbers, students were sent abroad for study, and scholarships were established to encourage the most promising students to come to Tokyo.

On September 2, 1871, a ministry of education was established with a mandate to create a nationwide school system under its authority. On September 4, 1872, the Preamble to the Fundamental Code of Education was issued by the government.[9] On the same day all schools in the country were ordered closed. They were to reopen according to detailed provisions of the Code, copies of which were sent to the prefectures on the next day.

The Preamble made it clear that the goals of education under the new system were to be quite different from the stress on Confucian morality found in the official schools of the Tokugawa period. Instead there was to be a focus on individualism, equality among the classes, and self-improvement. The Code, as originally drawn, consisted of 109 articles providing a comprehensive outline of a national system of schools—the first in Japanese history. The country was divided into school districts with a designated number of universities, middle schools, and elementary schools in each. Compulsory education was set at four years. Local supervisors were appointed to enforce attendance, build new schools, and oversee the distribution of public funds. If the Code was overly optimistic it nevertheless reflected the hopes and ambitions of the newly formed leadership in the reforming powers of education under central guidance.

The decade of the 1870s witnessed intensive efforts by the Ministry of Education at both the higher and lower ends of the school plan of the Fundamental Code of 1872. Tokyo University was established in 1877 for the advanced training of future leaders, and over 20,000 elementary schools were hurriedly put in place throughout the country for lower-level mass education. Although the university was essentially something new—based on Western-style curricula and staffed with foreign instructors—the elementary schools continued to show their Tokugawa inheritance. The rapid construction of schools throughout the country depended heavily, through the 1870s, on buildings, facilities, personnel, text materials, and school equipment that had been used for the Tokugawa *terakoya* and academies. New buildings could not be built overnight and initially new elementary schools were primarily housed in Buddhist temples and teachers' homes, as was traditional. As a result, previously existing facilities and traditions of schooling played a critical transitional role in the period before public-supported facilities became available.

Textbooks, Teacher-Training, and School Finance

Once buildings were provided, and students enrolled, what did they learn? In October 1872, shortly after issuing the Fundamental Code, the Ministry of Education set out detailed guidelines for curriculum and textbooks for elementary schools but adopted a laissez-faire policy with regard to implementation. As a result, in the early 1870s there was a considerable mix of text materials used in elementary schools—readers, vocabulary lists, and copybooks from the old *terakoya* as well as newer texts based on Western translations disseminated by the new publication offices within the Ministry of Education. Local compliance with the new curriculum guidelines was at first weak, and local areas continued to emphasize reading and writing (as in the *terakoya*) as opposed to newly mandated courses such as geography, science, and Western-style calculation. A study of the contents of ethics and language texts used during the 1870s and 1880s has suggested that at least in these two areas there continued to be a good deal of mixing of Western, Japanese, and Confucian values for some time.[10]

In the 1870s there began a transformation in the preparation of teachers. Previously there had been no prescribed training for instructors at the numerous academies or *terakoya*. The *terakoya* teachers, unlike the Confucian scholars who taught at the *bakufu* and domain schools, were without official status or authority but nonetheless commanded considerable respect. By the late 1870s, the teachers who had been holdovers from the Tokugawa schools were gradually replaced by a new breed trained at prefectural normal schools. Later, in the 1880s, training of teachers became the centerpiece of Mori Arinori's nationalist reforms of the educational system. Military drill and uniforms became compulsory in the normal schools in order to instill in young teachers-to-be habits of obedience to higher authority.

Financially, the school plan of 1872 provided the government with the best of all worlds—national control and local support. The principle that schools should be supported by those who used them was written into the document itself. Thus, during the 1870s and 1880s, as government control grew, its financial contribution remained comparatively small. After 1873 the Ministry's support for elementary schools never went over 10 percent of total school income.[11] In 1882 government support was entirely withdrawn.

Thus, local areas had to develop schemes to support government-mandated schools. The approaches differed but most localities re-lied on some combination of tuition charges, interest from endowments, private donations, and locally collected tax revenues. This was a considerable burden for local communities and in some cases reached the point where schools were burned in protest over excessive taxation. Tuition charges for schooling, however, were nothing new. Such things had been commonplace in both *terakoya* and academies in the Tokugawa period. The difference was that schooling was not compulsory before 1872 and the methods of pay-ment had been much more flexible. Very often charges were made by the ability to pay, and gifts of clothing or food for the teacher could be used in place of cash, in the earlier period. It was only in 1900 that tuition for elementary schools was abolished, stimulating a sharp climb in enrollment.

Middle Schools and Mobility

From the early 1870s to the late 1880s, articulation between the lowest and highest levels of the school system continued to be pro-vided, as they had in the Tokugawa period, by a wide variety of independent institutions outside effective government control. These schools offered diverse opportunities to those best able to take advantage of them—namely, former samurai and the local leadership classes. As long as this situation persisted, the possibil-ities of commoner mobility through the system remained limited. Although the Fundamental Code of 1872 had mandated public mid-dle schools in each of 256 middle school districts, the prefectures, already strapped financially with expenses for elementary schools, were not able to comply with the law. Of a total of 389 middle schools in existence in 1877, only thirty-one were public.[12] At the private middle schools, students were mostly from the former sam-urai class, and support came from contributions of former daimyo. At the public middle schools the change in the content of the curric-ulum was far more dramatic than in the elementary schools. They followed a comprehensive course based on Western studies—science and foreign languages primarily. As early as 1872, Ministry of Ed-ucation guidelines suggested that middle schools, rather than being an extension from elementary levels, were for university prepara-tion. Thus, they were built into the system from the top not from the bottom.

The predominance of private middle schools through the 1870s meant that ambitious youths, like their Tokugawa counterparts, continued, largely on their own initiatives, to combine travel and the availability of private schools to fashion highly individualized sequences of learning. In the next decade this was no longer the case. In September 1879 the government issued a new law superseding the Fundamental Code which attempted to lessen some of the burdens placed on local areas. The unintended result was that when pressures were relaxed people began to desert the public schools for the more intimate and familiar *terakoya*-type schools which continued to thrive. The government responded in the 1880s with a reassertion of central power, redirecting the goals and content of learning away from what was perceived to be the Western excesses of the 1870s. Particular attention was paid to middle schools. The curriculum was standardized and less attention was paid to foreign languages and more to traditional subjects like ethics and literature. By the mid-1880s regulations had gone into effect which set rigorous standards for all middle schools and made it difficult for any school to receive the middle school designation without extensive reforms. The private schools, the mainstay of intermediate-level education up to that time, could not meet the heavy financial burden of such reforms and virtually disappeared. The public middle schools now became the prestige channel for those wishing to advance to the university.

Efforts to reform the school system culminated in 1886 with a series of laws drawn up by Mori Arinori, the first minister of education in the new cabinet system. The goals and structures of the comprehensive system of schools erected by these statutes remained essentially unchanged until the American-inspired Occupation reforms after World War II. The goals of schooling in the Mori system were tied directly to the interests of the state. Elementary schools were charged with inculcating proper character and patriotic loyalty and teachers were trained in normal schools run along military lines. The newly designed Imperial University was intended to train elites for government service. Between these two, functioning as an elite sorting mechanism, were the middle schools. Once the middle schools provided articulation between the lower levels, which were compulsory, and the upper levels, for elites, the possibilities for commoners to advance to higher education increased. By 1890 the proportion of commoners in the ordinary middle schools went over 50 percent for the first time; by 1898 the figure stood at 67.6 percent and continued to rise.[13]

Conclusion

By 1886 the outlines of a distinctive Japanese organization of schools had appeared. The system was not yet fully mature, however. School attendance did not reach near-universal levels until the turn of the century; vocational training was only in its infancy; opportunities for women lagged behind those for men; and there remained only a single officially recognized university. The basic framework, however, was in place. As we have suggested here, continuities with Tokugawa educational practice were strong in the opening decades of the Meiji period, and so changes were more gradual and their effects less wrenching than many writers have led us to believe.

It is also clear that the new Meiji leaders found the loose arrangements of Tokugawa schools inadequate to the needs of a strong, centralized state. They viewed uniformity as an essential value in the new system, not just because they sought to use schools as primary agents of moral and political socialization, but also because they were intent on raising minimum standards of education and encouraging progress based on merit and talent. And they planned to do this nationwide, eliminating the disparities that had characterized Tokugawa educational practice. Access to schooling at all levels was widened, mobility through the system was increased, qualifications of teachers were raised, ability was rewarded along more impartial lines, and the inequities stemming from class and geographical location were lessened.

But these considerable achievements were not gained without cost. By the late 1880s, educational professionals of the central bureaucracy in the Ministry of Education in Tokyo were making decisions that previously had been made by individual teachers. The Ministry now determined curricula, selected textbooks, set school hours and schedules, prepared examinations, decided what methods teachers would use, and so on. Teachers, who had embodied educational practice in the Tokugawa period, were turned into mere parts of a larger, national apparatus. The shift in the locus of educational authority from the teachers of domain schools, *terakoya*, and the academies to the centralized bureaucracy by the 1880s brought with it a diminishing of the possibilities for individual and local influence in the control and practice of education.

As the public system was put in place under the guidance of the Ministry of Education, functions that had earlier been carried out by individuals and by schools outside the framework of official control gradually were co-opted by the expanding public sector. Private schools continued to educate large numbers of students in Japan (as they still do), but they had lost their former independence. They no longer provided real alternatives to the public system, as they had in the Tokugawa period. The private schools were no longer outside the system but appendages of it. Although the policy of creating a strong public system and of imposing uniform regulations from the top achieved many desirable results, it also tended to stifle individual initiatives and to overlook the special requirements of local areas. The result was a lack of flexibility in the system as a whole—a legacy with which Japanese educational policymakers must still contend.[14]

Notes

1. Herbert Passin "Japan," in *Educational and Political Development*, ed. James S. Coleman (Princeton: Princeton University Press, 1965), 274.

2. Richard Rubinger, *Private Academies of Tokugawa Japan* (Princeton: Princeton University Press, 1982), 4.

3. For further elaboration of this point see Herbert Passin, *Society and Education in Japan* (New York: Teachers College Press, 1965), 50–61.

4. Kokuritsu kyoiku kenkyujo, comp., *Nihon kindai kyoiku hyakunen-shi*, vol. 3 (Tokyo: 1974), 448.

5. Fukaya Masashi, *Gakureki-shugi no keifu* (Nagoya: Reimei Shobo, 1969), 25.

6. Mombusho, comp., *Nihon kyoiku-shi shiryo*, vol. 1 (Tokyo: 1892), 373–74, 680.

7. Fukaya, *Gakureki-shugi*, 27.

8. The details of this development may be found in Kyoiku-shi hensan-kai henshu, comp., *Meiji iko kyoiku seido hattatsu-shi*, vol. 1 (Tokyo: Byuginsha, 1938), 239–40.

9. An English language translation of the Preamble is found in Passin, *Society and Education in Japan*, 209–11.

10. E. Patricia Tsurumi, "Meiji Primary School Language and Ethics Textbooks: Old Values for a New Society?" *Modern Asian Studies* 8:2 (1974): 247–61.

11. Murakami Toshiaki and Sakata Yoshio, eds., *Meiji Bunka-shi*, vol. 3 (Tokyo: Yoyo-sha, 1955), 372.

12. Fukaya, *Gakureki-shugi*, 125.

13. Kikuchi Joji, "Kindai Nihon ni okeru chuto kyoiku kikai," *Kyoiku shakaigaku kenkyu* 22 (1967): 136–37.

14. More extended treatment of many of these themes may be found in the author's "Education: from One Room to One System," in *Japan in Transition: From Bakumatsu to Meiji*, ed. Marius B. Jansen and Gilbert F. Rozman (Princeton: Princeton University Press, 1986), chap. 8.

18

State Control and the Evolution of Ultranationalistic Textbooks

Masami Yamazumi

When the national education system was first established in 1872, the government did not attempt to control textbooks but instead left their preparation and publication in the hands of private publishers. The system changed in 1880, when the government first drew up a list of unacceptable textbooks, then the following year formulated rules for teaching, which textbooks were obliged to follow. The teaching of world history, with which educators had attempted to broaden children's horizons and diffuse modern ideas, was banned. Only Japanese history could be taught. In the government's view, the sole purpose of teaching history was to foster reverence for the emperor; teaching children about the French Revolution or America's Declaration of Independence, and thereby acquainting them with such concepts as freedom, equality, humanism, and independence, could only work to the disadvantage of government. This was the government's first assault on textbooks.

The second assault came toward the end of the decade, when the government began promoting nationalism under the popular slogan

A version of this essay was published in *Japan Quarterly* Vol. 28 (1981), and in *Democracy in Contemporary Japan*, Gavan McCormick and Yoshio Sugimoto, eds. (Sydney: Hale and Iremonger, 1986). Reprinted by permission of M. E. Sharpe Publisher.

"increase the wealth of the nation and strengthen the army." In 1886 the minister of education stated: "If Japan is a third-rate power let us strive to be second-rate. If we are second-rate, let us strive to be first-rate. Education can and must play a part in this process." He then proceeded to lay down guidelines for schools at all levels. Concerning the university he declared, "If asked whether the university exists for the sake of learning or for the sake of the nation, I would reply that it exists for the nation." A system for carefully screening primary- and middle-school textbooks was established at this time. Furthermore, four years of elementary education were made compulsory. In this way the government further strengthened its control over education.

The third assault on textbooks came just before the Russo-Japanese War (1904–5). In 1890 the government promulgated the Imperial Rescript on Education, which was designed to bring to education the same system of thought control that had been instituted in the army, as a reminiscence of the prime minister at the time, Yamagata Aritomo, makes clear: "It seems to me that education ought to possess an imperial mandate just as the military." In this way education was made to serve the interests of the imperial line. "Should emergency arise, offer yourselves courageously to the State; and thus guard and maintain the prosperity of Our Imperial Throne." It was to remain the guiding principle of education in Japan until 1945. The promulgation of the Imperial Rescript on Education led to a lengthy discussion in the Imperial Diet concerning textbooks. Members argued that the textbooks then in use did not reflect the spirit of the Rescript and they urged the state to take over their preparation and publication. The chance to effect this change came in December 1902, when, as a result of a scandal involving bribes by textbook publishers, a number of people were arrested and the minister of education was forced to resign. On the pretext of putting an end to the bribery problem, the government decided the following April to assume all responsibility for the preparation and publication of textbooks. Indicative of the change in educational policy, the minister of education, a former physicist, was replaced by an army commander who, when hostilities with Russia commenced the next year, was appointed chief of general staff and sent to command the Japanese forces in Manchuria.

In the years that followed, textbooks were frequently rewritten to promote new government policies. The childhood of the renowned medical researcher Noguchi Hideyo (1876–1928) is a case in point. When Noguchi was one year old he burned his left hand so badly that it was deformed, and at school other children teased him about it. A passage in a 1937 ethics textbook reads: "Hideyo began to attend school. As one might expect, the other children made fun of his hand. Though it saddened him he decided to ignore them: 'So what if my hand is deformed. If I study hard I can succeed in life—I'll show them!' " For the 1943 version, the passage was revised to read: "So what if my hand is deformed. If I study hard I can do something great for my country—just wait and see!" The tide in battle had already turned against Japan, and the citizenry had been mobilized; now children were expected to do their part as well, and toward this end the childhood of this historical personage had been rewritten. Revisions of this sort were common during the war.

Wartime geography textbooks, too, were heavily revised. They began by calling attention to the curved shape of the Japanese archipelago and its strategic location on the eastern rim of Asia. "The shape of Japan is not without significance. We appear to be standing in the vanguard of Asia, advancing bravely into the Pacific. At the same time we appear ready to defend the Asian continent from outside attack." Obviously this passage was meant to convince children that the location and shape of Japan indicated that Japan's mission was to rule Asia.

The theory of Japan's divine origins was propounded most strongly in history textbooks. A 1943 edition began:

> The deep green of the pines within the Imperial Palace celebrates the prosperity of our emperor's reign, while the pristine waters of Isuzugawa speak to us clearly of Japan's primeval glory. Long, long ago in the Age of the Gods, the gods Izanagi and Izanami gave birth to these beautiful islands, which we now call the Eight Great Islands. These they arranged like a great floating fortress to be caressed by the warm Black Current. Next they gave birth to a multitude of gods. Finally, the Sun Goddess was born as the rightful ruler of Japan. It is she who laid the foundation of the Japanese state, she from whom our emperor is descended. The virtue of this most august of goddesses knows no bounds. As her name suggests, our country is awash with her blessings, which extend to the very ends of the earth.

The passages quoted above are by no means unrepresentative of wartime textbooks, which were consistent in their support for the mythological origins of Japan, impressing upon children how fortunate they were to live in the "Land of the Gods."

Postwar Reform and the Appearance of Free Textbooks

After accepting the terms of the Potsdam Declaration, the Japanese government repeatedly affirmed its intention to retain its national polity; however, from the late autumn of 1945 it stressed that the purpose of education was to promote world peace and the welfare of mankind. This was partly at the insistence of the Occupation forces, but another factor was pressure for democratic reform from indigenous groups kept silent during the war, including students.

There was no time to revise textbooks, so as a stopgap measure the government distributed old ones, after blackening out militaristic passages. Officials of the Occupation forces, however, decided the Japanese government efforts were inadequate, and, on December 31, 1945, forbade the teaching of ethics, Japanese history and geography, and recalled all textbooks.

In the fall of 1946, the first new Japanese history textbook was published. Entitled *Kuni no ayumi* (The Course of Our Country), it was the first Japanese history textbook since the issuing of the Elementary School Regulations of 1881 that began with a description of the Stone Age instead of mythology. Moreover, it contained the fruits of prewar research into Japanese history, hitherto excluded from primary- and middle-school textbooks. The debate over *Kuni no ayumi* that followed its publication is also of great significance, because under the prewar system all criticism of textbooks had been stifled.

The Fundamental Law of Education was enacted the following year. At the time, approval of the Occupation forces was needed to promulgate all laws, but as statements of those involved in its drafting, such as Nambara Shigeru, president of the University of Tokyo, make clear, it was the product of independent discussion within the Education Reform Committee, which was formed in 1946. Its ten articles set a new guiding principle for education and educational administration. Especially important was the resolve expressed in its preface to realize through education the ideals of the Constitution: the sovereignty of the people, the basic rights of the individual and the renunciation of war.

With the Fundamental Law of Education as their guide, educators groped toward a new system of education, rejecting in the process standardized education. This is especially clear in the first Course of Studies drawn up in March of the same year. Attached to it was a proposal that schools themselves decide basic educational policy.

This new policy was realized most clearly in textbooks for the newly created social studies course. The desirability of a social studies course had been debated from 1945, and it had gradually taken shape along the lines of its American model. The first classes commenced in September 1947. For these classes the Ministry of Education had prepared eight textbooks. At the same time, their relative importance in the classroom was lessened, as is readily apparent from the instructions for teachers and parents contained at the end of each volume, as, for example:

> The material in this book is not a collection of essential facts that must be taught to each and every sixth-grade student. To do so would be a biased approach both in terms of content and emphasis. You must not confuse this textbook with older ones. It is not meant to be systematically explained and committed to memory, nor should it be the only teaching material used.

Many teachers, used to relying solely on textbooks, had difficulty at first adjusting to the new policy. But before long, they were discussing local problems in class and using a variety of teaching materials.

The School Education Law, passed in 1947, returned the preparation and publication of textbooks to private hands, abolishing after more than forty years the state-run system. Free textbooks were in use from 1949. Aware of the problems connected with textbook selection, the Ministry of Education published a booklet on the subject in April 1948. School authorities, it said, were free, after consulting with teachers, to choose the textbooks they believed best for their schools. The prospectus for the 1949 textbook exhibition went even further: "Within different classes at the same grade level, it is permissible to use different textbooks." Teachers were thus given the greatest possible flexibility in their choice of teaching materials.

The Conservative Party Promotes
Textbook Revision

In the opinion of the distinguished British Japanologist George Sansom, who visited Japan in 1950, one of the most encouraging aspects of the new Japan was its attitude toward public education. Regardless of the perils ahead, education, he believed, held great hope for the future of the Japanese people. He warned, however, of the likelihood of a revival of authoritarianism once Japan had regained its independence, in view of its lack of an indigenous tradition of respect for individual rights and the people's willingness to follow orders.

Sansom's fears were justified. The reverse trend began the very next year, when, amid growing U.S.-Soviet tensions and the outbreak of the Korean War, the peace and security treaties were signed in San Francisco, thus bringing the Occupation to an end. In October the Advisory Committee for the Reform of Government Orders, which had issued reports on the depurging of war criminals, new economic and labor laws, and administrative reform, submitted a report covering education as a whole entitled "Recommendations Concerning Reforms in the Educational System." While admitting that postwar educational reform had been useful in rectifying past mistakes and in establishing a democratic system of education, it said, "By basing our system on that of a foreign country where conditions differ, and pursuing only ideas, we have incorporated in our system many undesirable elements." It recommended among other things that members of local educational boards be appointed by local and prefectural governments rather than be elected, that vocational education be stressed and more vocational courses offered, especially at the junior-high level, and that the Ministry of Education once again assume responsibility for the preparation and publication of textbooks. The Japan Teachers' Union and textbook publishers objected so strongly to the final proposal, on grounds that it was a revival of the prewar system, that the advisory committee was unable to implement it.

In 1955 the ruling Democratic party went on the offensive. In a booklet entitled "Deplorable Textbooks," it harshly criticized the content of social studies textbooks. This was the first time the ruling party had resorted to such tactics and the public was shocked. The booklet criticized the following four types of textbooks: those that supported teachers' unions and advocated their exercise of political power, those that depicted the life of workers as harsh and supported radical labor movements, those that praised the socialist systems of the Soviet Union and China while criticizing the Japanese system, and those imbued with communist ideology. Once again the Japan Teachers Union vigorously opposed what it regarded as an infringement on the right to free education, and it was joined by various educational and historical societies and the Science Council of Japan. They fought a losing battle, however, for with the merger of the Liberal and Democratic parties in the fall, the conservative forces gained a firm hold on the reins of power and were able to consolidate their control over the educational system.

In 1956 two bills were introduced in the Diet, one to change the system for selecting members of educational boards from an elective system to an appointive one as suggested earlier and the other to tighten the screening of textbooks. These bills, too, raised a storm of protest that was not confined to members of the Japan Teachers Union; ten university presidents, as well as the National Federation for Board of Education Members, denounced the bills. Only the first was passed, and only because the conservative party pushed it through the House of Councillors; in the process, several hundred policemen had to be called in to maintain order. Although the bill on textbooks was tabled, the government accomplished its objective later that year by making administrative changes in the Ministry of Education, whereby textbook inspectors were placed within the ministry. To the previous five-man team a sixth was added to inspect the new social studies textbooks. The last was notoriously strict.

The next year, the government attempted to break up the Japan Teachers' Union by instituting the Teachers' Efficiency Rating Plan, under which teachers were rated each year by principals. In 1958 it further strengthened its control by effecting a comprehensive revision of the curriculum. The proposal for textbooks attached to the Course of Studies drawn up in 1947, giving teachers free choice of texts, was abandoned. Furthermore, the new Course of Studies was published in the Diet's official "Gazette," by which it acquired strong official sanction.

In 1963 the government passed the Law Concerning Free Provision of Textbooks in Compulsory Education. Both the constitution and the Fundamental Law of Education state that textbooks should be provided free, so long as education is compulsory. This seems only reasonable. Until this time, however, the government had done everything in its power to subvert this policy, so, as might be expected, its motives in finally passing the law were not benevolent. For while it provided for the distribution of free textbooks, it also required textbook publishers to possess considerable capital. Also, textbook selection was transferred from the school to the municipal level. These stipulations gave large publishers a distinct advantage. As a result, the number of textbooks available for selection was greatly reduced.

The change in the level at which textbooks were chosen had a more direct effect on education than did the strengthened textbook authorization system. From then on few teachers attended the annual textbook exhibition; indeed, there was little point to it. The new system promoted standardized education, while at the same time dampening teachers' enthusiasm.

Government efforts to control textbooks are really but one part of a well-orchestrated, systematic plan to push the country to the right. While reestablishing its control over textbooks, the government has worked to rehabilitate the prewar national anthem *Kimi ga yo* (The imperial reign) and the rising sun flag to strengthen ethics education and to resuscitate the Imperial Rescript on Education.

Early in the century, the Christian leader Uchimura Kanzo (1861–1930) said that *Kimi ga yo* was not the national anthem. "Its purpose is to praise the emperor. A national anthem ought to express the feelings of the people." According to prewar textbooks it was a prayer that the emperor's reign last eternally, and it acquired unofficial status as the national anthem. Though it was discredited in the immediate postwar years, in 1950 the minister of education recommended it be sung at school gatherings on national holidays. In the 1958 edition of the Course of Studies for elementary schools, it was one of the songs in the curriculum for music class which all children were supposed to sing. Finally, in 1978, when the Course of Studies was again revised, *Kimi ga yo* was officially designated the national anthem.

But most disturbing are the government's attempts from the 1970s to revive the Imperial Rescript on Education. In 1974 the prime minister, Tanaka Kakuei, wrote: "Education today over-emphasizes intellectual development at the expense of moral development. While we fatten children's intellect their morals starve." Concerning the Imperial Rescript he has said: "Much of it expresses universal moral principles. It has qualities that transcend its form, that speak to us today as then." By "form" he no doubt meant its designation as an imperial rescript. In his opinion, its form was irrelevant, since it contains "universal moral principles." His opinion is shared by many government leaders today.

Surely, in light of our experience, it would be a grievous mistake to reinstate the Imperial Rescript. All the virtues expounded in it were meant to strengthen the emperor's control over the nation. Even its seemingly universal concepts, such as conjugal harmony and trust among friends, cannot be considered outside their context. It is sometimes pointed out that Westerners have praised the Imperial Rescript, but their evaluations are based on translations, which are misleading. The word *kokken*, for example, has been rendered "constitution" in English. Unlike Western constitutions, however, the Constitution of the Japanese Empire, promulgated along with the Imperial House Act, was an imperial edict. Such translations give the Imperial Rescript a specious modernity.

The question facing us today is how to avoid repressive government policies that stunt the individual's growth. We must help children to realize their full potential within their own districts, their own schools—where they live and grow. And by affording them contact with other cultures, we must endeavor to develop a Japanese culture that is at once universal and individual.

19

Political Teacher Unionism in Japan

Haruo Ota

Every facet of Japanese society was changed after World War II. Education was no exception. Under the slogan of "democratize education," the educational system was reformed. One of the most notable phenomena in the drastic change in postwar education was the emergence and development of large-scale teacher unionization.

Prior to the war, a teacher was assigned the role of "an obedient servant of the state, subject to the closest scrutiny of his personal life and placed at the lowest level of the civil service hierarchy."[1] Although there were some efforts to unionize the teaching force, those efforts were sporadic and isolated and, therefore, never successful in attracting the majority of teachers.

Shortly after the war, the dream of prewar teacher union activists came true; the Nihon Kyoshukuin Kumiai (Japan Teachers Union), better known as Nikkyoso, was formed, which organized almost all of the nation's elementary and secondary school teachers at that time. Since then, Nikkyoso had been a major educational and political force affecting not only the welfare of its members but also the governance and control of Japanese education.

There has been persistent antagonistic rivalry between Nikkyoso and the Ministry of Education, which holds the responsibility of

An earlier version of this essay was published in *The Politics of Teacher Unionism, International Perspectives*, Martin Lawn, ed. (London: Croom Helm, 1985).

implementing the policies of the conservative ruling government. The Ministry of Education has consistently insisted on strong governmental control over education. On the other hand, Nikkyoso, supporting the opposition Socialist party, contends that education should not be controlled by the government but by the people. This rivalry, which has exacerbated conflicts and confrontations between the two forces over virtually every facet of education, is a manifestation of the state of postwar Japanese education. It is for this reason that a study of Nikkyoso is "the key to an understanding of developments within postwar Japanese education."[2]

Nikkyoso, from the beginning, has been interested in professional aspects of teaching and Japanese education. Nikkyoso's platform, adopted as basic policy at its inaugural meeting, clearly states that its objectives are to establish democratic education and freedom of research as well as to raise the economic, social, and political status of its members and to contribute to the construction of a democratic nation devoted to peace and freedom.

To encourage democratic education and freedom of research, Nikkyoso has conducted various activities, among them the National Education Research Conference (Kyoiku Kenkyu Zenkoku Shukai), generally known as Kyoken. As one observer put it: "This is an attempt by Nikkyoso as a professional organization of educators to organize educational research systematically in order to develop democratic education."[3] The first conference was held in November 1951 with the theme of education for peace under the slogan, "Never send our students to the battlefield again." Over 3,000 teachers attended the three-day conference and discussed in eleven sectional meetings topics such as the efficiency of the newly introduced 6–3 school system, the decline in student achievement, special education, kindergarten programs, the content of textbooks, and the development of peace education.

Today, Kyoken has become established as a permanent and important part of Nikkyoso, attended by nearly 20,000 teachers with over twenty sectional meetings. The conference is open not only to teachers but also to parents and the general public. Scholars sympathetic to Nikkyoso make significant contributions to the conference. They give lectures and serve at sectional meetings as advisors. The tradition of inviting a group of scholars who share Nikkyoso's ideals lends "a certain degree of academic respectability to Nikkyoso's entire movement."[4]

There is no doubt that Kyoken has provided the opportunity for classroom teachers to examine and study the problems they encounter in their day-to-day activities and, consequently, to promote quality in teaching. However, it is important to note here that the goal of Kyoken is not to promote teachers' research activities merely for the sake of research, but, as the basic policy of Kyoken states, "to understand educational problems as they correlate with political, economic, and social problems, to democratically promote educational research activities in connection with the advancement of the livelihood and rights of teachers, and to establish an educational environment devoted to the freedom of the worker."[5]

Economic Unionism

Under the current legal system in Japan, public employees, including teachers, do not enjoy the basic rights of workers to bargain collectively and to strike. This has been a controversial issue in trade unionism in general and in teacher unionism in particular in postwar Japan.

During the early postwar years, the legal status of teachers was much different from what it is today. The policy toward labor unionization that was established during the American Occupation was very liberal for that period; the Occupation authorities encouraged the labor movement in order to advance their major goals of Japanese society. The newly adopted constitution guaranteed "the right of workers to organize and to bargain and act collectively" (Article 28). Moreover, the new Trade Union Law granted even the right to strike to employees in both the private and the public sectors. It was during this liberal period that teachers established Nikkyoso to take advantage of the Occupation authorities' liberal attitude toward labor unions and of the new constitution and law.

This liberal period, however, was very short-lived. With its perception of both the international and internal communist threat and the relationship of Japan's union leadership to communism, the Occupation authorities drastically altered their policy, moving from a prolabor to an antilabor position.

After General MacArthur's intervention in a general strike, a series of legislative acts intended to restrict public employees' right to bargain collectively and to strike were drawn up by the Japanese government. Among these acts was the Local Public Service Law (LPSL: Chiho Komuin Ho) of 1950, which is one of the most important acts for teachers because it defines their legal status.

Under the provisions of this law, teachers have been classified as local public servants, and their basic rights as workers, guaranteed by the constitution, have been restricted. Under the law, teachers can form organizations "whose purpose is to promote improvement of working conditions" (Article 52). Such organizations, however, may be formed only at the prefectural and/or local level where the teachers are employed (Article 53).

Teachers can still negotiate with the local government; however, there are some restrictions. First, the scope of negotiations is very narrow; only wages, hours, and other working conditions are negotiable. Other concerns, especially managerial issues, are nonnegotiable. Second, the term "negotiations" as used in the LPSL is different from the term "collective bargaining" used in labor relations in the private sector.[6] Third, teacher organizations cannot strike in the event that an impasse is reached in negotiations. Without the right of striking, which is the most effective bargain level available to any employee organization, a public employee union is a relatively weak "negotiator."

The implication of the Local Public Service Law (LPSL) for Nikkyoso is of great significance. Nikkyoso is not a national union but a federation of prefectural "personnel organizations" (*Shokuin Dantai*) of teachers. More precisely speaking, Nikkyoso is merely a voluntary organization which is not recognized by any law. As has previously been mentioned, teacher unions are public employee organizations that must be organized within the prefectures in order to be allowed to negotiate with the local governments. Thus Nikkyoso, legally speaking, is not eligible to negotiate with the national government since teachers are hired by the prefectural government. Only prefectural and local teacher organizations can negotiate with governments on this level.

The chief problem Nikkyoso has been facing as a union is how, without the critical right to bargain collectively and to strike, it can improve the economic condition of its members. We can identify three major approaches Nikkyoso has employed to cope with the problem. The first and most novel approach has been to appeal to international organizations, including the International Labor Organization (ILO), in an effort to win broad-based support. Nikkyoso began a strong campaign to "restore the fundamental rights of workers" on the stage of the ILO in 1960 immediately after an education minister's refusal to hold consultative meetings with them. Nikkyoso submitted a list of complaints to the ILO charging that: (1) the Japanese government defies trade union rights by denying public employees the right to strike; (2) the Japanese government interferes with Nikkyoso's organization and administration by discriminating against full-time union officials and union members; and (3) the Ministry of Education refuses to meet Nikkyoso representatives. Nikkyoso also requested that the ILO recommend that the Japanese government recognize Nikkyoso as a representative bargaining organization for teachers.[7]

In its testimony before a fact-finding commission appointed by the ILO, Nikkyoso explained why the union could not negotiate with the government at either the national or the local level. At the national level, Nikkyoso contended, the Ministry of Education had refused negotiations with the union on the ground that, under the LPSL, no national union could be recognized as a bargaining unit for teachers because they were local public servants appointed by local or prefectural school boards. Nikkyoso further charged that at the local level the school boards refused to negotiate with the local teacher unions, claiming that budgets, salaries, working conditions, class sizes, and so forth were decided by the Ministry of Education and that they had nothing to do with those matters. Thus Nikkyoso concluded that "there was no one with whom the union could negotiate."[8]

In the meantime, the government ratified a controversial resolution, Convention 87 of the ILO, and adopted several amendments to domestic labor laws. However, the government did not alter its basic position on the public employee unions even after hearing the recommendations of the Commission. The Ministry of Education resumed consultative meetings with Nikkyoso in 1965 but Nikkyoso still did not have the right to enter into negotiations. Even after the Commission's report, Nikkyoso has continually complained about the unfair labor regulations of the Japanese government to international organizations such as ILO, UNESCO, WCOTP, and IFFTU. Although Nikkyoso has been successful in obtaining international support for the restoration of the fundamental rights of workers in Japan, it has not been successful enough to get the Japanese government to recognize it as a labor union.

Nikkyoso's second approach to developing economic unionism has been through a wage struggle within the prevailing system. While on the one hand the LPSL deprived teachers of the right to bargain collectively and to strike, on the other hand it established the National Personnel Authority (NPA: *jinji-in*), whose duty is to make recommendations to the cabinet to bring the wages of public employees in line with wages earned in private industry. The cabinet, the ruling party in the government, then establishes the national wage scale for public employees, taking into account the NPA's recommendations. However, since the recommendations do not have binding power, the cabinet has the prerogative to adjust or even to ignore the recommendations. Once the national salary scale for teachers is set up in this way by the cabinet, it becomes a guideline for teachers' salaries throughout the country. Consequently, the salaries of public school teachers do not vary much among different prefectures.

Under the NPA's system for determining teacher salaries, the major tactics used in Nikkyoso's wage struggle have been to demand that the NPA submit an acceptable wage adjustment recommendation to the cabinet and to petition the cabinet to totally accept the NPA's recommendations. To this end, Nikkyoso has engaged in demonstrations in the NPA building and around the Diet (Japan's parliament) to put pressure on the NPA and the cabinet. In 1966, for example, Nikkyoso called mass vacations to demand from the government full implementation of the NPA's recommendations for a 6.9 percent salary increase. With the overwhelming approval of the action by the union members, over 130,000 teachers in twenty-three prefectures walked out of their classrooms for either half a day or two hours. This collective action was not strong enough to persuade the government to implement salary increases retroactively, but it was the greatest direct action taken by Nikkyoso in the wage struggle in its history to that point.

Thereafter, Nikkyoso used similar tactics almost every year and, year by year, it made progress toward its goal of obtaining full implementation of the NPA's recommendation within the present system. Finally, in 1971, the government agreed to implement the salary increase of public employees retroactively.

Through its successful wage struggle within the NPA system, Nikkyoso has come to realize the necessity of taking a more radical approach for the advancement of economic unionism. At its national convention in 1970, Nikkyoso reexamined the wage struggle within the NPA system and set forth a new approach aimed at replacing the present system of determining wages with direct negotiations with the government and restoring the basic rights of workers to bargain collectively and to strike. To develop this approach, Nikkyoso emphasized strike action under the slogan "Restore the right to strike by strikes." In April 1974, for example, Nikkyoso went out on a one-day strike along with workers in other parts of the public sector to press for their demands for restoration of their right to strike as well as for large wage increases. Approximately 330,000 teachers in thirty-four of Japan's forty-seven prefectures participated in the strike, which left 24,000 elementary and secondary schools disrupted and classes for 12 million students suspended. This strike was of great significance. First, it was the first one-day strike in Nikkyoso's history. Since the foundation of Nikkyoso, teachers had never failed to show up for work for a full day because of strike action. Second, the strike was undertaken under the slogan "Restore the right to strike by strikes." And that, Nikkyoso claimed, convinced teachers of the necessity of the restoration of their right to strike.

However, this strike-oriented approach was not without problems. It was countered by strong attacks and criticism from both within the union and from outside. On the same day of the strike, the police took action, investigating the union's headquarters, the prefectural headquarters, and the leaders' houses in nearly 900 different locations in twelve prefectures for evidence related to so-called "strike for the right to strike." Over 15,000 teachers were summoned by the police for investigation. One day later, the union's chairman Makieda was arrested in Tokyo.[9] Moreover, the new approach has been subject to criticism by the union's minority group, who supports the Communist party. Its contention, to be discussed shortly, is that teachers must realize that people have a high expectation for teachers and that teachers have an obligation to serve all the people as they educate students. The group has urged teachers to reconsider Nikkyoso's strike-oriented approach and to establish a new policy which is not contrary to the people's expectation for teachers.[10]

Political Unionism

It can be said that the history of education in postwar Japan is a history of confrontation between the conservative government and Nikkyoso struggling for control over education. From its beginning, Nikkyoso has been under the control of people closely associated with Marxist-oriented left-wing political forces such as the Socialist and Communist parties. Under their leadership, Nikkyoso has been concerned not only with the economic affairs of its members and their rights, but also with Japanese education in the political, social, and cultural contexts.

Based on such left-wing ideology, Nikkyoso's major educational goal has been to establish "democratic education." According to the union, democratic education is education for the people that aims for peace and truth in the world, based on the spirit of the Fundamental Law of Education.[11] To Nikkyoso, strong governmental control of education means education controlled by a conservative party and a bureaucracy which is backed by monopolistic, capitalistic organizations. Given such an ideology and the objectives of Nikkyoso, it is not surprising that the union has expended its energy mostly on the struggle with the government, especially with the Ministry of Education, for control over education. There have been numerous confrontations and conflicts between the Ministry of Education and Nikkyoso. Here, let us examine some particular confrontations which are of great significance in the development of postwar educational policy in Japan.

As was the case with labor union policy, the American Occupation took a very liberal position on educational policy. The Occupation put a great deal of emphasis upon educational reform to accomplish its major goals of demilitarization and democratization of Japanese society. To this end, the Occupation tried to reform Japan's highly centralized educational system, in which the Ministry of Education had monopolistic power.

Decentralization of the school system, therefore, was the most fundamental theme of the Occupation's reforms. Complying with the Occupation's policy, the Japanese government attempted to decentralize its system with the establishment of American-style locally elected school boards and curtailment of the power of the Ministry of Education. Behind the Occupation's educational reforms was the idea that it could take control away from the central government and turn it over to the people.[12]

The honeymoon period of Nikkyoso and the Ministry of Education came to an end in the early 1950s, just after Japan regained her independence with the signing of the San Francisco Peace Treaty, when the Japanese government began to revise the postwar educational system developed under the Occupation. The first attempted revision of the reformed educational system was to change the selection process of school board members from election to appointment. The government proposed a new law which would empower the prefectural governor and the local mayor to appoint the members of the board of education with the approval of the prefectural and local assemblies. The law also provided that the Ministry of Education would have the power of approval over the appointments of the prefectural superintendents of schools, and that the Ministry of Education and the prefectural school boards would have veto power over local board decisions.[13]

The conservative government rationalized the new system on the grounds that it would "insure the political neutrality of education, build a harmonious relationship between educational administration and local government and . . . consolidate educational administration into one body consisting of the national, prefectural, and local educational agencies for more efficient administration of education."[14] Among these reasons, the "political neutrality of education" was the most controversial issue.

Under the old system, since teachers were allowed to be board members, many Nikkyoso-supported candidates were elected and, in some cases, they dominated the boards. The conservative government came to realize that this development could pose a threat to their control over education because, under the elective board system, Nikkyoso, supported by the Socialist and Communist parties, could have great influence in local school governance. The government needed a system that would prevent these political factions from gaining power over school governance and that could preserve the "political neutrality of education."

From Nikkyoso's point of view, however, the proposed appointed school board system was not only an attempt to decrease the influence of Nikkyoso on school boards, but also an increase of political interference in education by the conservative government.

Nikkyoso organized nationwide rallies against the new system. In Tokyo, it held mass demonstrations with twenty-nine other organizations including the National Association of the Board of Education, the Japanese PTA, and the Federation of Housewives. However, the appointed school board system eventually replaced the elective system in 1956, when the conservative government succeeded in passing the law which authorized the new system, taking advantage of their majority in the Diet.

Coupled with the debate over the school board system was the so-called Teacher's Efficiency Rating System (*Kinmu Hyotei*). While the revision of the school board was a controversy over control in the local school governance, the institution of the rating system was a controversy over control in the school. In 1956, the Ehime Prefecture Board of Education decided to implement the rating plan in order to reduce its financial deficit. Under the plan principals would rate the efficiency of teachers without consulting with them, and only those teachers with high ratings would receive annual pay increases. One year later, the Ministry of Education proposed an extension of the system throughout the country. The Ministry of Education urged each prefecture to adopt the rating system for salary increases, promotion, and other administrative matters pertaining to teachers. It also developed an evaluation form which included such rating criteria as classroom management, lesson guidance, disposition of school duties, love of education, sincerity, sense of responsibility, impartiality, knowledge, ability, skills, and the like.[15] The Ministry of Education argued that administrative decisions on teachers' pay should be based on performance and capabilities because the seniority-based system was unjust in that it treated competent and incompetent teachers equally. The Ministry of Education also contended that the rating system would provide a rational basis for personnel administration.

Nikkyoso quickly responded by issuing a statement of "Warning to the Ministry of Education" which expressed its strong determination to fight against the rating system. The "Warning" further analyzed the underlying idea behind the rating system: "The main purposes of the system are to establish a school system that the Ministry of Education can control as it did in pre-war Japan, to implement the educational policies of the ruling government, to restrict teachers' autonomous behavior, and to undermine the teachers' union movement."[16]

Following Nikkyoso's widespread and defiant struggle, which included a series of nationwide mass vacations and demonstrations, the rating system was eventually implemented in all but two prefectures. However, the system did not function as originally intended; the rating results were not employed as the basis for determining salary increases and promotions. For one thing, school boards were reluctant to use the ratings for personnel administration due to the almost certain turmoil which would result from the ratings and the invalidity of the evaluation form. For another thing, Nikkyoso was successful in rendering the system meaningless. In one instance, teachers in Kanagawa prefecture undermined the system by getting their principals to give similarly favorable ratings to all of them.

A related issue in personnel administration was the government's attempt to institute the appointment of "head teachers" (*shunin*) in the school. The issue arose in 1971 in a final report prepared by the Central Council for Education—an advisory body to the Ministry of Education. The report recommended that there be established a well-organized intraschool administrative system so that educational activities could be developed under the leadership and responsibility of the principal. To this end, the report recommended the creation of managerial positions within the faculty. Following the report, the Ministry of Education issued an ordinance which authorized the position of "head teachers" and provided that "under the supervision of the principal, the head teachers will engage in liaison and coordination work and will also give guidance and advice on the formulation of educational plans and other school affairs." The Ministry of Education stressed the monetary and educational benefits of "head teachers" and deemphasized the managerial characteristics.[17]

Nikkyoso was opposed to the Ministry's action, claiming that since "head teachers" were to be appointed by school boards and receive allowances, the position of "head teachers" would crystallize the hierarchical power structure in schools, and that it would disrupt the unity of teachers and their union membership and strength. Although Nikkyoso was unsuccessful in preventing the institution of the plan, it has been trying to make the position of "head teacher" less attractive and less managerial by urging appointed head teachers to donate all or part of their allowances to the union so that it could use the money for the purchase of instructional aids and equipment. The exact effect at this writing is not ascertainable, but a recent study indicates that the position of "head teachers" has been gradually institutionalized as a managerial position in schools.[18]

Still another major issue in the confrontation between Nikkyoso and the Ministry of Education concerns the curriculum and textbooks, that is, the content of education. Nikkyoso has been claiming that the Ministry of Education should not be concerned with the content of education but only with "external matters" of education, such as the physical facilities of schools.

Under the current system, the basic framework for school curricula, including the objectives and standard contents to be taught in each subject, is outlined in the Course of Study prepared by the Ministry of Education. The controversy is as to whether the Course of Study is merely a guideline for the formation of each school's own curriculum or if it is to be the standard curriculum for all of the nation's schools. Under the former interpretation, individual schools and teachers have the right to develop their own curriculum. But under the latter, schools and teachers are required to comply with the standard curriculum. Although Nikkyoso has interpreted the Course of Study as a guideline, the Ministry of Education has increasingly gained greater power over the contents of education, claiming the right to standardize school curricula.

The underlying concepts of the current system for the selection of school curricula and textbooks assume that it would enforce and improve uniform educational standards, guarantee equal opportunity in education, maintain the appropriate content of education, and insure the political neutrality of education. However, there is no doubt that the system also decreases the influence of teacher unions on the content of education. In the eyes of Nikkyoso, therefore, the Course of Study and the textbook authorization system are obvious attempts by the Ministry of Education to mold the content of education in accordance with governmental policies.[19]

Major Problems Facing Nikkyoso

In recent years there has been a general acknowledgment that Nikkyoso is at risk. Two major problems facing the union are declining membership and bitter internal rivalry, threatening the breakup of Nikkyoso.

Size and membership are often used as indicators of union power. As far as the size of membership is concerned, Nikkyoso, as it approaches 600,000 members, is Japan's largest teachers' union and the second largest national union. The number of members in Nikkyoso has been increasing over the last decade. Absolute membership in a union, however, does not necessarily provide accurate information about the union's power; gains in absolute membership may simply indicate an expanding work force and the maintenance by a union of its share of that work force. This is the case with Nikkyoso. When founded in 1947, Nikkyoso claimed that it had organized nearly all of the nation's school teachers. Today, however, only a little over half of all personnel in elementary and secondary schools remain members of Nikkyoso. Gradually, and sometimes dramatically, year by year, the rate of membership has steadily declined.

According to statistics compiled by the Ministry of Education, the decline in membership has occurred as follows: 86.3 percent of all educational personnel were members in 1958; 74.0 percent in 1962; 63.3 percent in 1965; 56.2 percent in 1970; 55.9 percent in 1975; 52.0 percent in 1980; and 51.1 percent in 1982. However, these figures are somewhat misleading, as the numbers indicate the percentage of Nikkyoso's membership in the total work force in elementary and secondary schools, including principals, vice-principals, and other noninstructional staff. Nikkyoso claims that figures indicating membership as a percentage of the nonsupervisory, instructional work force provide a better indication of the organizational leverage of the union. According to Nikkyoso, in 1978, for example, the rate of membership was 73 percent, nearly 20 percent higher than indicated in the Ministry of Education's survey. Moreover, the union contends that in 1980 approximately two-thirds of forty-seven prefectural unions maintained a membership of over 70 percent of their elementary and secondary school teachers.

Nevertheless, it cannot be denied that there has been a downward trend in the enrollment of those eligible for membership. A number of factors have consistently been cited to account for this decline. The fierce struggles against the government and the compulsory withdrawal of principals and vice-principals from the union are probably two major factors responsible for the declining membership rate of the 1950s and 1960s. During its struggle against the Teachers' Efficiency Rating System, for example, Nikkyoso lost 80,000 members between 1957 and 1960. In Ehime prefecture alone, where the rating system was initiated, the union lost 2,000 members a year during that period, and, at present, only a small percentage of the prefectural teachers remain in Nikkyoso.

In addition, new revisions in the National Public Service Law in 1966 forced principals and vice-principals to withdraw from the union. Some 40,000 supervisory members gave up their membership in Nikkyoso after the implementation of the revisions. Until forced to withdraw, about 40 percent of the principals and over 60 percent of the vice-principals had remained members of Nikkyoso, despite various attempts by the government to discourage them from retaining their membership in the union.[20]

A more important factor in the contemporary decline in membership is the significant decrease in the number of new teachers who have joined Nikkyoso in the last decade. In 1970, 51.2 percent of all new teachers joined the union, while in 1982 only 35.7 percent did. Nikkyoso here again claims that the statistics of the Ministry of Education are misleading because they are compiled at the beginning of the academic year when some new teachers have not yet decided whether to join the union or not, and because some new teachers are required by school boards not to join the union when they are hired.

However, a recent survey, conducted by Nikkyoso itself, confirmed the trend among new teachers of standing off from the union. Nikkyoso's survey of 3,391 new educational personnel, from twenty to twenty-four years of age, revealed that most of the teachers surveyed were not sufficiently motivated to get involved in union activities.[21] Although eight out of ten recognized the necessity of teachers' unions, they did not feel they had serious enough problems to seek help from unions, nor did they feel they would look to unions for help even if they did. Five of ten were satisfied with their salaries and fringe benefits, and four of ten had no complaints about their working conditions or rights. Among those who were dissatisfied with salaries and working conditions, very few took their grievances to unions. In addition, only three of ten had negative attitudes toward the educational policies of the government, which Nikkyoso had always opposed.

There has been persistent internal rivalry in Nikkyoso between the groups which support the Japan Socialist Party (JSP) and the Japan Communist Party (JCP). The rivalry extends back to the early postwar period before Nikkyoso was formed and has become so bitter in recent years as to threaten the very existence of the union.

Probably the most bitter controversy involving these two political groups has been over the issue of formal affiliation with political parties. The political activism of labor unions in Japan is well known; Japanese unions have overtly supported particular political parties, including the JSP and JCP. Close relationships with political parties have provided "the instruments through which unions have been able to participate in government, albeit as part of the opposition."[22] Nikkyoso, being no exception to this, has given support to both the JSP and JCP up until the early 1960s. That policy was changed at the 1961 annual convention. Taking over the union's national leadership from the Communist group, the Socialists proposed a motion to give exclusive support to the JSP on the ground that the JSP had broad support from the working class.

The motion to support only the Socialist party was eventually adopted one month later, but the issue has still remained controversial. Since that time, the Communist faction has proposed a motion at every annual convention that the policy of exclusive support for the Socialist party should be amended to one of support for both the Socialist and the Communist parties. Although the motion has failed to be adopted to date, the margin of the vote has been getting as narrow as one-third in favor of the motion. The narrower the margin, the bitterer the dispute between the two factions. It is not unusual that a bitter debate on political affiliation dominates the union's annual convention.

The bitter rivalry between the two forces also can be seen in their disagreements about strike action and the definition of "teacher." The latter controversy stems from the JCP's announcement of a new definition of "teacher" immediately after Nikkyoso's unified one-day strike in April 1974. In the announcement, the JCP contended that it was wrong to define teachers merely as laborers and thus neglect a professional and sacred aspect of their role. The announcement was extremely controversial because it was an affirmation of the concept of the "holiness" of teaching, which Nikkyoso has traditionally denied because that concept has been used by the government in its attacks on Nikkyoso.

This theoretical difference carries over to the debate on strike tactics. As has already been mentioned, since 1970 Nikkyoso has adopted strike action as an important means of promoting its concerns. The Socialist faction, the majority in the union, supports and promotes the policy on the grounds that the strike is the most effective weapon laborers can use to win concessions from the government. On the other hand, the Communist faction, stressing the professional aspects of teaching, proposes an alternative strike policy which they believe could be supported not only by teachers but also by principals and parents. Only limited strike action is acceptable to this faction.

In 1973 the Tokyo prefectural union, under the leadership of the Communists, went on strike. During the strike action, the union let some teachers stay at each school to supervise the children. This action was taken because the union thought that teachers should not ignore their responsibilities to children and parents even while on strike. Although the Communists have remained a minority faction in Nikkyoso, their negative attitude toward strikes has had great impact on the union's strike policy. Since the historical one-day strike of 1974, Nikkyoso has been unsuccessful in achieving nationwide unified strikes due to the opposition of Communist groups in several prefectures. It seems that the internal conflicts between the two factions, having stemmed from the debate on the definition of "teacher," have now weakened the leverage of the union, and perhaps threatened to destroy the union itself.

Conclusion

Nikkyoso and the Ministry of Education, the two major actors on the scene of postwar Japanese education, have been fighting each other for unilateral control of educational policy. It appears in retrospect that the consequences of their battles have been unfortunate for postwar Japanese education for two reasons.

In the first place, the end result is that a policy-making structure has been established which gives the Ministry of Education monopolistic power over every facet of education, leaving Nikkyoso, which represents the majority of Japanese teachers, no direct access to the decision-making process.

Secondly, in the course of the all-out battles between Nikkyoso and the Ministry of Education, little consideration has been given to the education of children; educational questions have been subordinated to the issue of control. Consequently, Japanese education has developed the testing system, under which high priority is put on the selective function of education rather than on the educational function itself.

It seems that Nikkyoso is now both at a crossroads and in a crisis. Nikkyoso could continue pursuing the path which it has traveled for the last three decades. It could still seek political unionism and continue asserting that only through changes in the existing political and educational order can the general problems of education be resolved. However, traveling this path would mean that Nikkyoso would remain an outside force, without any significant voice in the formal decision-making structure of Japanese education.

But there is another path available for Nikkyoso to take. Traveling this path would require Nikkyoso to carry dual goals, to aim for fundamental changes in the existing political and educational system as a long-term and ultimate goal, while at the same time, as a short-term goal, attempt to improve the quality of education within the prevailing structure. This would necessitate, for example, that Nikkyoso be willing to accept the task of rescuing the children suffering under the current testing system. Pursuing this path would certainly demand greater social and educational responsibilities from Nikkyoso; however, it could possibly give Nikkyoso a greater chance to unite teachers once more around fundamental issues which focus on the educational needs of children and the responsibilities for building a peaceful world.

Notes

1. Solomon B. Levine, "Japan," in *Teacher Unions and Associations: A Comparative Study*, ed. Albert A. Blum, (Urbana, Illinois: University of Illinois Press, 1961), 148–99.

2. Benjamin C. Duke, *Japan's Militant Teachers: A History of the Left-Wing Teachers' Movement* (Honolulu: University of Hawaii, 1973), xiii.

3. Mitsuru Yuasa, *Sengo Kyoiku Rodo Undo no Rekishi*, (A history of the educational labor movement in postwar Japan) (Tokyo: Shin Nihon Shuppansha, 1982), 70.

4. Duke, 108.

5. Nikkyoso, *Nikkyoso Sanjunenshi* (Thirty year history of the Japan Teachers Union) (Tokyo: Rodo Kyoiku Senta, 1977) 52.

6. Donald R. Thurston, *Teachers and Politics in Japan* (Princeton, N.J.: Princeton University Press, 1973), 181–82.

7. Nikkyoso, 219.

8. Duke, 169.

9. "Nikkyoso" (The Japan Teachers Union), *Japan Quarterly* 21, no. 4 (October-December 1974): 329–32.

10. Hiroshi Egawa, *Nikkyoso wa Ima* (The Japan Teachers Union today), (Tokyo: Rodo Kyoiku Senta, 1977), 159.

11. Masahiko Saito, "Nikkyoso no Soshiki-kiko Unei to Tatakai" (The Japan Teachers Union: its organization, administration, and movement), *Kyoiku Hyoron* 390 (April 1980): 41–43.

12. United States Education Mission to Japan, *Report* (Tokyo: The Mission, 1946). Mimeographed.

13. Takashi Ota, *Sengo Nihon Kyoikushi* (A history of postwar Japanese education) (Tokyo: Iwanami, 1978), 258.

14. Duke, 130.

15. Ibid., 141–42.

16. Nikkyoso, 113.

17. Ibid., 155, 616.

18. Hajime Shincharo, "Sonogono Shunin Teate Kyoshutsu Undo: Kyoshutsu-ritsu no Teika ga Imisurumono" (The movement to donate head teacher allowances: the implications of declining donation rates) *Gekkan Rodo Mondai* 254 (November): 66–71.

19. Motofumi Makieda, "Kyoiku no Jiyu o Mamore" (Protect the freedom of education), *Gekkan Rodo Mondai* 218 (February 1976): 68.

20. Duke, 181.

21. Nikkyoso, "Shinki Saiyo Kyoshokuin Ishiki Chosa Hokokusho" (A survey report on the attitude of new educational personnel), *Gekkan Kyoiku no Mori* 4, no. 10 (October 1979): 51–63.

22. Thurston, 222.

20

Variations on Democratic Education: Divergent Patterns in Japan and the United States

Benjamin C. Duke

Following the end of World War II, democratic education became virtually a universal concept underlying the momentous movements to reform national systems of education throughout the world. The definition and application of it, however, encompassed widely varying interpretations from country to country. What one nation espoused as democratic education another branded as totalitarianism. What a third considered democratic education, a fourth rejected as chaotic license. Consequently, as many varieties of democratic education evolved as there were nations who claimed to practice it.

One of the most revealing ways of appreciating how democratic education has assumed divergent forms between nations even with vital historical relationships and intimate commercial and political ties, is to compare it in Japan and America. Both of these economic superpowers are justifiably ranked among the leading democratic nations of the world. Both employ an open electoral system with

An earlier version of this essay was published in the *International Review of Education*, Vol. 24 (1983). Copyright © 1983 by Martinus Nijhoff Publishers and UNESCO, Institut für Pädagogik. Reprinted by permission of Kluwer Academic Publishers.

that widespread suffrage which is fundamental to Western-style democracies. And both scrupulously preserve the so-called "four freedoms" of speech, assembly, worship, and press, ingredients considered essential to a genuinely democratic form of government. In other words, both Japan and the United States are committed to the common ideals underlying a democratic society.

Democratic education, however, represents a strikingly different matter. Even though most Japanese presume their school system is patterned closely after the American as a result of the postwar occupation, Japanese democratic education follows a dissimilar pattern from the American. Analysis of the differences not only reveals how two democratic nations so closely allied can pursue contrasting paths to democratic education; it also exposes the difficulties inherent in attempting to transplant a particularized version of democratic education from one nation to another.

The focal point of this comparison concerns the original educational goals of the American Occupation of Japan as outlined in the Report of the United States Education Mission to Japan, 1946, and the fate of those reforms in the 1980s. The significance of this well-known Mission Report is that it summarizes in a relatively few pages the ideals of American democratic education: it sets the pattern for the great American democratic reforms of Japanese education; it provides an instrument for comparing democratic education in Japan and America; and, finally, it serves as a yardstick to evaluate the basic assumptions underlying the American ideals of democratic education at the end of the war in comparison with contemporary trends in the United States.

When General MacArthur was confronted with the initial task of demilitarizing and democratizing Japanese education in 1946, he promptly turned to Washington for civilian assistance. The American government responded by assembling a unique mixture of educators, religious leaders, and other fairly distinguished Americans. Few, if any, members had direct experience of Japan until they were thrust into an incredibly hectic schedule in early 1946, just a few months after the war.

During a period of one month, these twenty-seven Americans toured several major Japanese cities, interviewed through interpreters a number of Japanese educational leaders, and visited schools in ruins. Further, and quite remarkably, the team found time before returning home to prepare the celebrated Mission Report, which established the framework for the democratization of Japanese education and, as it was hoped, of Japanese society. Little wonder, then, that this most crucial of American Occupation educational documents faithfully articulates American egalitarianism in education. There was little inclination nor time to do otherwise.

The Report of the Education Mission summed up the fundamental American attitude toward democratic education accordingly: "If the schools are to become effective instruments of a strong democracy, they must be kept close to the people."[1]

This brief passage embodies the very heart of the American commitment to construct a "new Japan" based on the American model. Education "close to the people" in order to build a "strong democracy" succinctly describes the American ideal of "grassroots democracy." Having just experienced victory over the Germans and the Japanese, the Americans held an unbounded faith in their style of democracy and the locally controlled school system which supported it. Predictably, the Mission recommended democratic reforms of Japanese education patterned directly after that as idealized in America.

In another section, the American democratic tradition in education was expressed from a different angle:

> A system of education for life in a democracy will rest upon the recognition of the worth and dignity of the individual . . . [which] cannot be promoted if the work of the school is limited to prescribed courses of study and to a single approved textbook in each subject. The success of education in a democracy cannot be measured in terms of uniformity and standardization.[2]

This assertion stems from historical circumstances in which the new American republic was initially sewn together from thirteen existing colonies whose leaders were apparently unwilling to relinquish control of education to the new central government since the matter of education was not included in the Constitution. Thus, the new United States came into existence without a ministry of education, technically placing educational control in the hands of the various states. As the nation developed, the immense diversity of American society and the high regard for individualism in the westward expansion of the frontier inculcated within the American character the fundamental belief that diversity and democracy are synonymous. Conversely, uniformity and standardization under a central ministry of education were incompatible with democracy, according to the American way of thinking.

In still another passage, the basic American theme was characterized again in a slightly different manner. "Schools should be integral parts of the community they serve" reflects the American tradition in which the local community assumes responsibility for the operation of its schools through a locally elected school board. This board of laymen, reflecting the general will of the community, serves the local citizenry by establishing educational policies acceptable to it. In the process, American-style democracy functions at the local level. It represents "grassroots democracy," a cherished principle of American democratic education.

Following the advice of the Mission Report, the Occupation authorities, working through the Japanese Ministry of Education, drafted one of the most important laws during the American era, entitled simply *The Board of Education Law, 1948*. Among the multitude of educational ordinances enacted during the Occupation, the School Board Law merits particular consideration because perhaps no other American reform of Japanese education better typifies the very foundation of the American democratic tradition in education. No other educational reform more accurately characterizes what the totality of the American reformation of Japanese education and society was all about. Its intent was the massive transfer of control of the schools from the central government to the local level. It exemplifies grassroots democracy in the American tradition.

The initial plan was to implement the school board system down to the village level from 1948. However, the concern of certain Japanese leaders as well as the economic exigencies of the time brought about the postponement of board elections at the local level. Only the five major cities and all prefectures elected school boards in 1948. The elections in 1950 and 1952 extended coverage to include a total of over 10,000 locally elected school boards.

Opposition to the School Board Law from within Japanese educational circles, in retrospect, was a harbinger of the controversy which was to transpire after the American Occupation ended. The late Vice-Minister of Education Daishiro Hidaka at the time reiterated his opposition to the rapid implementation of such a radical reform. According to him, local Japanese society was inexperienced in the decision-making process and consequently was unprepared for such responsibility traditionally assumed by the Ministry of Education.

Hidaka argued that local control of education could become as undemocratic as the central control of education which had degenerated under the Japanese militarists. He contended that local powerful individuals, meaning landowners, would dominate the boards at the village level. At the city level, he predicted that labor unions would ultimately position themselves to exert undue influence. Consequently, the results of the School Board Law in both the urban and rural areas would eventually nullify the democratic intent of the American reform, according to this Japanese educator.

What transpired was contrary to the expectations of the American Occupation authorities. The school boards from the outset became embroiled in partisan politics, presaging a fierce struggle for the control of Japanese education. Left-wing forces, led by a socialist-communist coalition dominating the newly formed Japan Teachers Union, realized early on that organizations influencing the school board could substantially shape local education policy. This is, of course, precisely how the school board system can function. The Americans were appalled, however, when the Union launched powerful national political campaigns to capture local school board seats for union teachers and leftist sympathizers.

Japan entered the new era of postwar independence in 1952 with a school system already locked in a bitter struggle between left-wing and conservative powers over the control of education. The American model had become the focus of the conflict. Ironically the left championed the American democratic reforms, specifically the new school boards where Teacher Union candidates had gained one-third of all school board seats in the 1952 elections, defying previous warnings by American officials.[3] Simultaneously, the Union in concert with other left-wing forces attacked American capitalism, American foreign policy, and the continuation of American military bases in Japan. In contrast, the ruling conservative party carved out a close military and commercial relationship with the United States, simultaneously expressing deep concern with the left-wing influence in education. Powerful politicians within the governing party increasingly criticized the postwar American educational reforms which they felt provided a fertile field for left-wing activities that could upset the social order.

The entire slate of Japanese reform of the American reforms was carried out in the name of democratic education. The late Minister of Education Araki Masao, one of the most powerful postwar politicians and instrumental in bringing about these revisions, interpreted the Ministry's position accordingly. The government was invested with the mandate under the Constitution, prepared during the American Occupation, to assure that "all people shall have the

right to receive an equal education correspondent to their ability."
In order to provide every child from Hokkaido to Kyushu with an
equal education, the Ministry of Education maintains the responsibility to set uniform national standards through a mandatory curriculum, and to authorize textbooks to comply with it. It's
democracy in education.[4]

In contrast, the U.S. Education Mission presented the diametri-
cally opposite viewpoint: "The success of education in a democracy
cannot be measured in terms of uniformity and standardization."
On the other hand, to the Japanese government, uniformity and
standardization embody the very essence of democratic education. A
nationwide educational standard based on a common curriculum
and common textbooks approved by the central Ministry of Education is specifically designed to ensure equal educational opportunities for all, the ultimate goal of democratic education.

The American tradition of local control of education, in which the
will of the community is reflected in the schools through the locally
elected lay school board, was intended to respond to the diversity of
American society. Freedom meant the fulfillment of the individual
in a plural society. Uniformity meant restriction of the individual.
Democratic education to the American, therefore, implies the absence of a central authority prescribing a standardized curriculum.

The critical difference between the American and Japanese interpretation of democratic education rests essentially on the degree of
emphasis placed on these two goals: the development of individualism and equal educational opportunities for all. In comparison to
the American tradition, the Japanese have placed far greater emphasis on the latter, as expressed by former Minister Araki, in their
efforts to build a democratic society. Their centralized school system
with its uniform curriculum, approved textbooks, standard classroom setting and seating arrangements, widespread use of school
uniforms, and so forth are, when contrasted with the American
school, manifestations of an endeavor to minimize the differences
among individuals.

The full cycle from the American interpretation of democratic education to the Japanese interpretation has been a natural evolution-
ary process in postwar Japan. It was predictable from the
beginning. When the Americans arrived in 1945, the control of education was posited at the center in the Ministry of Education. The
determination of course content, textbooks, teaching methods, and
so forth was the responsibility of the central government, considered undemocratic by the Americans. When the Americans de-

parted in 1952, 10,000 locally elected school boards legally assumed much of that responsibility, which was considered democratic by the Americans.

Today, in the 1980s, the Japanese Ministry of Education essentially determines what is to be taught in the classrooms through its national curriculum and the officially approved textbooks. High school and university entrance examinations are based on that set curriculum, which effectively permeates the entire school system. The pendulum has thus completed its swing. The fundamental question remaining, then, is "Which represents democratic education, the American or the Japanese model?" Or, "Could both be democratic?"

This question holds considerable relevance for America today. There appears to be a trend in the United States away from local control of education. Since the 1950s, the central governmental organs, both the Congress and especially the courts, have been increasingly setting standards and rendering decisions for the local community that were traditionally made by each individual state and/or the locally elected lay school board. Although the Americans have no Ministry of Education as traditionally understood, federal governmental bodies in a multiplicity of instances (for example, court-ordered school busing, or congressional funding for specified programs) have been encroaching upon local control of education. Thus, the assumption of the 1946 U.S. Mission to Japan that "if the schools are to become effective instruments of a strong democracy, they must be kept close to the people" appears to contradict trends underway in postwar America.

Can one conclude that centralization of educational power is an eternal threat to the well-being of a democracy, as the American Mission expressed in 1946: "A highly centralized educational system, even if it is not caught in the net of ultra-nationalism and militarism, is endangered by the evils that accompany an entrenched bureaucracy"? The Americans were clearly warning the Japanese that the power of the Ministry of Education must be checked at all times.

To test the validity of the American assumption, the Japanese model is worthy of consideration. Employing the conventional European and North American standards for judging democracy, such as broad-based opposition political parties, including a robust communist party, open elections, an independent judicial system, a probing press, and so forth, the form and substance of Japanese political institutions can be categorized just as democratic as the

American. Japan has its share of political abuses but no greater, and in some instances less, than the Americans. Nearly four decades after World War II, Japan's democracy is alive and well, in spite of the concentration of educational power at the central governmental levels.

What the Japanese model clarifies is that there are multiple paths to democratic education and that the traditional American education model was not necessarily the best for Japan in the long run. The irony is manifest in the fact that the Japanese government, elected through a democratic process initiated during the American Occupation, has rejected the democratic pattern of educational control also initiated by the Americans.

This leads, then, to the ultimate possibility: "Could the Americans learn anything from the Japanese version of democratic education?" Consider again a comparison. One major distinction between education in these two countries is that in Japan, centralization of educational authority relates in part to the interpretation of delicate subject matter. The analysis of Japanese history—the causes of World War II, the role of the emperor, all controversial issues between the left and right—is of vital significance to the Japanese government. The Ministry contends that these teachings must be impartial and fair, as judged by the duly elected government, subject to national referendum representing the majority of the people.

The contentious issues in American education revolve around civil rights of minorities and equal protection under the law, racially, religiously, financially, and academically. To the American government, particularly the federal courts, equality of educational opportunity means placing all races together in school. What transpires in the racially integrated classroom, as long as it is religiously neutral, is left to the teacher—usually within very broad guidelines set by the local and state governments, not the federal government. From this aspect, Japan has perhaps little to offer the Americans.

However, the other major difference between the two countries is that in contrast to America, devoid of a Ministry of Education, equality of educational opportunity to the Japanese Ministry of Education means establishing a uniform national academic standard through a standardized curriculum with its accompanying textbooks, and a set teacher's guide to equalize the teaching methods as much as possible. All the children then theoretically have an equal opportunity to learn. When you begin with the Japanese assumption that national standards depend on the equalization of local educational opportunities, then local control on the American pattern appears incongruent. Only under a nationally controlled system can national norms be effectively established, according to the Japanese governmental interpretation. The logic proved consistent in the courts when the Japanese supreme court in a critical decision constitutionally recognized the Japanese educational reform of the American educational reforms.[5]

If you begin with the American assumption that in a strong democracy education must be "kept close to the people," then you encounter certain disparities in American developments in the postwar era. The courts, especially the federal, have been ruling in a variety of cases that local control of education has failed to provide equal protection under the law on racial and religious grounds. If the courts remain consistent, this interpretation could be extended to cover social inequalities related to the academic and financial areas, the latter having already been tested in several state cases. Hence, the courts have been both directly and indirectly intervening in many local communities in order to render the schools constitutionally democratic.

The irony in these developments should not be overlooked. The basic principles of democratic education introduced into Japan by the American Education Mission in 1946 and expressed in the role of the local school board are now being subjected to judicial review in the United States. The locally elected lay school board is gradually relinquishing its authority to render local decisions about such issues as Bible-reading in the classroom, school ceremonies, which school a child should attend in his community, modes of school transportation, and school financing. The trend is significant. Local control of American education, in effect, has been increasingly judged undemocratic through a variety of judicial decisions in a host of local communities on the fundamental constitutional issue of equal protection under the law, precisely the theoretical base underlying Japan's centralized interpretation of democratic education.

The U.S. Mission to Japan in 1946 specifically attempted to "prevent the possible misuse of the power" of the central government by recommending the transfer of educational control from the Ministry of Education to the prefectural and local levels. The Americans never wavered for a moment in their faith in the grassroots democracy of local control of education. The Japanese, however, recognized the potential "misuse of power" at the local level early on and revised the American reforms in accordance with a Japanese interpretation of democratic education, emphasizing "equal educational opportunities" with the Ministry of Education playing the central role.

Slowly, and perhaps inexorably, the Americans have been moving toward more educational power and influence at the center, in part as a result of the new interpretation by the federal courts of equal protection under the law and its dramatic application in the areas of religion in the classroom and racially segregated schools. Although the present administration in Washington is endeavoring to reverse the centralizing tide of events, the trends indicate that the Americans have been edging closer to the Japanese interpretation of democratic education in which central organs of government set certain national guidelines to insure equality at the local school level. An irresistible conclusion is that, in one sense, the former student in the matter of democratic education may someday become the teacher.

Notes

1. Report of the United States Education Mission to Japan: Submitted to the Supreme Commander for the Allied Powers (Tokyo, 20 March 1946), 30.

2. Ibid., 65.

3. *Nippon Times*, 3 June 1956.

4. Interview, Araki Masao, Tokyo, 21 August 1968.

5. Benjamin C. Duke, "The Japanese Supreme Court and the governance of education," *Pacific Affairs* (Spring 1980).

21

Japanese Education Reforms in the 1980s: A Political Commitment

Nobuo K. Shimahara

School reform movements in Japan and the United States are developing in opposite directions. On the one hand, the American movement is seeking greater national uniformity in curriculum, student performance, fiscal standards, teacher certification, and other areas.[1] As the movement progresses, the state's role in schooling will loom larger and become more critical than ever.[2] On the other hand, Japanese reformers are currently interested in eliminating the rigid uniformity and standardization that epitomize the Ministry of Education's central control of the school system. They are attempting to pave a way to diversifying education and decentralizing administration. Keeping in mind that Japanese education has been centralized since the nineteenth century, one can justifiably ask to what extent Japan is committed to altering its current system. Similarly, one might ask to what extent the Americans will be able to achieve the national standards they believe necessary.

These relevant, empirical questions are to be tested in two nations distinguished by sharply contrasting cultural orientations. One is the group orientation of the Japanese, which lends cultural support to centralization; and the other is American individual-

A version of this essay appeared in *Issues in Education* (American Educational Research Association), Vol. 4, No. 2 (1986).

ism, which has dictated the development of all social institutions in the United States including the school. We are often unaware that educational evolution is in significant measure molded by cultural orientation, what Kluckhohn calls the "covert culture," which unconsciously governs the way we think and how we approach problems.

Japan is one of only a few nations that relies so extensively on formal education to advance modernization and industrialization, to develop character, and to cultivate the moral and cultural sensitivity of its citizens. Thus formal education has been uniform and centrally controlled since it was established nationwide in 1886, except for several years immediately after World War II. Japan developed a meritocracy shaped by educational competition, a predominant form of competition dictating social mobility since the Meiji period.

Today, however, some consider uniform schooling inadequate to meet the increasingly divergent individual and social needs. The pronounced absence of diversity in Japan's schools and the adaptability needed to meet emerging needs and demands is said to be a cause of rising tension in schools.[3] Moreover, the high school and university examination system, the centerpiece of Japanese education, which generates what the Japanese characterize as "excessive" competition, is viewed as becoming dysfunctional.

Educational Reform as a Political Commitment

Reviewing the pertinent literature suggests that two factors are politically more significant than others in the current reform movement. One is economic and the other social, but both are part and parcel of the political concerns of the Japanese government. The government is controlled by the Liberal Democratic Party, a conservative force that has dominated the nation's politics for more than three decades; it is the political arm of Japan's dominant industry.

As has been so in the past, Japan is concerned with developing its role in the world market in the twenty-first century and stabilizing its economic and social order as it undergoes a qualitatively significant transition from this century to the next. That concern is articulated in a report, "Japan in the Year 2000," prepared by the Economic Council of the government's Economic and Planning Agency.

The National Council on Educational Reform (NCER), the moving force in the present school reform movement, draws upon the

Economic Council's report to articulate the urgent needs for reforms. In brief, the Economic Council foresees a drastically different industrial structure in Japan, one that will be increasingly dominated, by the year 2000, by the fast-emerging high-technology industry based on sophisticated information and knowledge.[5]

According to the Economic Council's predictions of the competitive international market in 2000, Japan will be a leading exporter of capital and a leading manufacturer of advanced software. To remain competitive in the modern world of the highly complex information industry, biotechnology, lasers, and fifth-generation computers, the Council stresses, Japan must have long-range plans to restructure her research and development policies and especially to train her human resources. The proposals for reforming Japanese education under consideration by the NCER are in significant measure a political response to Japanese industry's call for developing the human resources it expects to be crucial to its future.

One of the premises underlying the NCER's deliberations is that Japan's long-standing fixation with the West as the source of all things modern has been reversed in the past decade or so. The West has served as the model for industrialization since the Meiji Restoration in 1868, and during the ensuing century catching up with the West became Japan's national obsession. But in the 1970s and 1980s Japanese development gradually shifted from industrialization guided by the "catch-up" ideology to unprecedented technological advancement for which there is no ready-made model.[6]

The nation is avidly seeking a new model. As pointed out by the Economic Council, this is an unparalleled historical development for which Japanese government and industry have not adequately prepared.[7] In short, the educational reform movement of the 1980s is promoted by Japan's political concern with industrial development in the next several decades. To express that concern, the national government established the National Council on Educational Reform and determined its mandates.

Concerning social factors, the NCER points out that Japanese education currently suffers from a "grave state of desolation" caused by pathological conditions of society and schools.[8] The development of such conditions, in its view, has led to increasing public criticism and distrust of public education.[9] The Japanese term for desolation is *kohai*, referring to a state of desertedness and deterioration, and it is used to render an emotionally charged indictment of education. Obviously the Japanese are highly critical of their education, in contrast to foreign observers who more often than not uncritically admire Japanese educational accomplishments. That reveals Japan's deep concern with the emerging "crisis" in education. The state of desolation, according to NCER, is manifest in a persistent syndrome of students' deviant behaviors—especially bullying, "school violence," refusal to attend school, and increasing juvenile delinquency—and excessively intense competition in entrance examinations, which hinders the adolescent's creativity and intellectual and personality development.

Although intense competition in entrance examinations has been a perennial problem in Japan for decades, its adverse effects on secondary education and adolescents are greater currently than previously, as more students prepare for entrance examinations. Meanwhile, bullying has become a serious national concern, as it occurs rather tenaciously in early adolescent years in various forms involving individual victims and the gangs that bully them. To explain such deviant behaviors as bullying, NCER cites the ill effects of economic affluence; an increase of centrifugal forces in society, which resulted in declines in social bonding and interdependence; a decline of group life among school children, which is a context of their moral life; and rigid uniform schooling that permits little individual freedom.[10] These are what NCER considers the negative effects of modern civilization upon character formation and self-control.

To summarize, at a time when both industry and the public are concerned about the present state and the prospects of Japanese education, it is politically astute and timely to launch a school reform movement. Prime Minister Nakasone capitalized upon the nation's ripening mood as he audaciously took the lead in calling for sweeping school reforms in his message to the Diet in February 1984.[11] Indeed, he made school reform one of his three major political commitments.[12] What by now should be obvious to all is the unique nature of this particular reform movement; unlike its predecessors, this one is directed from above.[13]

NCER's Proposed Reforms

Beginning its work in September 1984, NCER presented its first report in June 1985 and its second in April 1986. Because the news media extensively covered the NCER's entire deliberations, the reports captured the nation's attention and stimulated public reactions. Thus far, however, the reports have generated more questions for further inquiry and public debate than specific reform proposals.

Careful review of the reports reveals that they are marked by at least three characteristics. First, NCER envisioned a sweeping reform of formal and informal education at all levels and in all categories, including the home and the community. Second, NCER addressed an extraordinarily broad range of issues, and, perhaps because of that, its deliberations remained at a general and conceptual level. Third, the specific proposals considered for implementation were relatively limited.

The salient features of the specific and the relatively general proposals are:

1. Replacement of the Joint First-Stage University Entrance Examination now required for all applicants for national and other public universities by a "Common Test," an improved examination used by both public and private universities as the first entrance examination prior to the second entrance examination given by individual institutions;

2. Introduction of six-year secondary schools as an alternative to the current three-year lower and three-year upper secondary schools to provide continuity in secondary education;

3. Introduction of an alternative high school education whereby students may complete the required credits at schools of their choice;

4. New provisions that will enable individual schools to gain greater freedom in the use of the course of study; diversification of the curriculum to meet individual needs; greater emphasis on moral education and instruction in basic knowledge and skills; improvement of instruction of foreign languages and programs for Japanese returnees from abroad;

5. Promotion of decentralized control of education, so that local boards of education and schools may establish greater autonomy and responsibility leading to the development of unique programs and identities;

6. Improvement of the professional training of teachers with emphasis on student teaching and a requirement of one-year internship for newly employed teachers; liberalization of certification requirements to recruit competent teachers from a broader spectrum of applicants;

7. Broadened standards for the establishment of the institutions of higher education to provide greater diversity; provisions for de-

veloping distinctive and diverse institutional structures and programs; improvement of graduate programs and increased access to training at the master's and doctoral levels; enhancement of research at the university through the creation of "flexible research structures and organizations";

8. Establishment of a University Council that will oversee the quality of institutions of higher education.[14]

In brief, all these proposals share common underpinnings: NCER's emphasis on what it calls diversification of Japanese educational structure intended to loosen uniformity and central control. But conspicuously, NCER failed to attack the entrenched entrance examination system, a most persistent source of tension and anxiety in Japanese education and, according to the NCER itself, a cause of the desolation of Japanese education. Although NCER proposes a common test, that is not likely to affect the system significantly. Nor is the proposed six-year secondary school likely to alleviate tangibly the general pressure for high school entrance examinations as long as it remains a small-scale alternative, which appears to be NCER's initial intention.

Another observation refers to NCER's critical concern with *gakureki shakai*, the social practice that overemphasizes school backgrounds as a qualification for employment at the expense of other qualifications. It is exactly this emphasis on school credentials that generates intense and prolonged competition for admission to those universities that provide the credentials needed for attractive employment. Although this was a major topic in NCER's deliberation, the council stopped short of recommending that this hiring practice be changed. Aware that it is a deep-seated and extremely difficult problem that exists outside the domain of education, NCER merely issued a moral appeal to work organizations.

Central Controversy and Paradox

NCER proposes to replace the present rigid uniform system of formal education with an alternative marked by flexible diversity. As NCER boldly states in its first report, "Most important in the educational reform to come is to do away with the uniformity, rigidity, closedness and lack of internationalism, all of which are deep-rooted defects of our educational system."[15] "Individuality" is identified as a central concept underlying the consideration of reforms in all areas. One of the noteworthy aspects of NCER's proceedings is that it is dealing with perhaps the most complex tension between two forces in the Japanese cultural system: the tension between the group and the individual.

Japan is known for its dominant group orientation, a pervasive centripetal force governing social relations in the work place, the patterns of social mobility and promotion in work organizations, and cultural premises underlying schooling and socialization. The development of individual potential in Japanese society is mediated through imposition of group norms upon individuals—a culturally induced mode of meeting individual needs and aspirations. The group generally takes precedence over the individual.[16] Yet the reformers boldly propose to place greater emphasis on the fulfillment of individual needs and potentials, a plausible response only to the potential demands of a far different social structure still to emerge. Although such a proposal appeals to the Japanese as an abstraction, especially to those who are often beset by constant group pressures, it challenges the basic ethos of group primacy, which serves in face-to-face social interaction as a guide for individual behavior and attitudes.

Individuality as an abstract concept is invariably stressed in such official documents as the Course of Study and the Fundamental Law of Education. But that concept, as commonly understood in America, marked by its cultural stress on individualism and self-actualization, is rather foreign to most Japanese, who seek personal and social identity with the group.[17] Nonetheless, reformers insist that promoting individuality is unusually important at a time when Japan is working toward a new horizon and that it should be a primary commitment of schooling.

One of the four divisions of NCER, the one that considered the educational system for the twenty-first century, initially focused on "liberalization" of the nation's school system as it now exists under control of the Ministry of Education.[18] This division attributed educational desolation to the uniform schooling maintained by the ministry in the interest of providing equal education throughout the nation. The division contended that uniformity was effective as long as Japan needed a well-trained population with uniform education to catch up with the economic and technological development in the West, but that time has now passed. At the outset of its deliberation it concentrated on a frame of educational liberalization and debated such radical issues as parental freedom to choose any school and eliminating the school district system, the freedom to establish new schools with little governmental interference, the freedom to publish textbooks without the ministry's authorization, the chartering of good *juku*, and eliminating the ministry's control over the curriculum.[19] These are totally unconventional ideas that demote the authority of the ministry to secondary importance, even though the Japan Teachers Union, a radical trade union, has subscribed to them for years.[20]

But such radical liberalization of schooling immediately met outright opposition from the ministry and from the chairman of the NCER division on reforms in elementary and secondary education. Understandably, public confrontation between the heads of two divisions of the reform council proved embarrassing, although both eventually agreed that the rigid uniformity of schooling must give way to greater diversity. Subsequently the division on education for the twenty-first century went on retreat to produce a considerably compromised position paper more or less acceptable to the other parties.[21]

Tension between the group and the individual is explicit in the fact that individuality is said to be a central guiding concept of reform, but simultaneously NCER is deeply concerned with what it regards as the weakening of traditional values and norms that constitute the moral framework of the individual and social bonding.[22] In other words, tension is inevitable between the new stress on individuality, characterized by centrifugal orientation, and the need for preserving the traditional values and norms, characterized by a centripetal direction, that is, group-centeredness. NCER's second report addresses this paradoxical problem: "In the process of modernization and the resulting weakening of traditional values and norms, society loses its strength as a unit, and the role of the home is lessened, and this in turn brings about a failure to provide basic discipline or instruction in manners and customs."[23] NCER further warns that "a collapse of the sense of social solidarity and interdependence, and deterioration of a shared sense of norms" is occurring in contemporary Japan. The school's failure to promote "sound character formation," it suggests, is a contributing factor.[24]

Therefore, "it is necessary," emphasizes the second report "that the schools make efforts to enrich moral education. . . . In elementary education, emphasis should be attached to teaching basic manners and customs, as well as the development of both self-restraint and willingness to follow social norms in daily life."[25] Moral education has become a major topic even for election campaigns. In June 1986, Prime Minister Nakasone's first campaign speech stressed his interest in improving moral education and specifically referred to character development, whose main attributes include perseverance and self-restraint.[26]

That the Japanese attach importance to moral education is reflected in its prominence in the school's formal and informal curricula and the responsibilities they impose upon teachers. Strongly influenced by Confucianism, moral education attained its central position as early as 1880, just twenty-three years after the Meiji Restoration.[27] The new moral education developed in the postwar period is quite different from the moral training, or *shushin*, that existed before the war. Nevertheless, it responds to the needs the Japanese have articulated from the Meiji Restoration to the present day: basic discipline, sound character development, and sensitivity to social bonding and interdependence. However, the problem that NCER sees is that "moral education is not effectively provided."[28]

The Japanese emphasis on moral education apparently elevates adaptability to group norms to an imperative. In contrast, the development of individuality is inherent in identity formation in the Western cultural context, of which Erik Erikson speaks eloquently.[29] In the West, developing individuality is a process of active interaction between individual and environment, a process that creates tension and challenge—a series of experiences that must be challenged and assimilated by an individual as an independent person. In contrast, Japanese socialization typically lacks a dialectical self-process undergoing tension and assimilation.[30] In a word, NCER's stress on both individuality and moral education is paradoxical. It is addressing a fundamental conflict between the group and the individual and a conflict between traditional and emerging values.

A Final Remark

Although Japan's education reform movement is a particular case, it does offer general evidence that enables the reader to gain a broad understanding of the nature of the education enterprise beyond Japan. Education is, to an appreciable extent, a function of political and economic interests in industrialized nations, including Japan and the United States. For example, school reforms have been invariably initiated and advanced by political and industrial groups in both nations in the past, as they are today.[31] As pointed

out above, the Japanese reform movement in the 1980s has its
roots in political and economic interests. The Carnegie Forum on
Education and Economy, which proposes education reforms, is the
latest example in the United States. The Forum's purpose is to link
education policies with economic growth.[32] In contrast, Japanese
teachers and administrators have neither initiated such a movement nor participated actively in it. Although intellectual leaders of
the Japan Teachers Union, a powerful trade union, have proposed
reforms, they have not received enough public support or funding in
a nation where the school system is firmly controlled by the Ministry of Education.

Japanese school reforms since the Meiji era have vacillated relative to their goals. Until a series of Meiji reforms culminated in the
establishment of the centralized school system at the end of the
1890s, the goals of reforms changed considerably, from centralization to decentralization and back to centralization again. Likewise,
as discussed earlier, this pattern of pendulum swinging recurred in
the postwar period, and now the pendulum is swinging back toward
decentralization and diversity. But gravity toward centralization
has always been far stronger than the reactions to it. That reflects
Japanese group orientation, an invariable cultural and historical
force governing the evolution of Japanese social institutions. That
NCER's reform deliberations tend to remain at an abstract level reveals the influence of the tradition that NCER is trying to change.

NCER faces dichotomous forces: advocacy of individuality, however abstract it may be, and adherence to traditional values and
norms. Although its reform campaign must be appreciated in the
context of new sociopolitical trends, the acceptance of its proposals
is significantly contingent upon their compatibility with Japan's
value system.

Notes

1. See United States Department of Education, *The Nation Responds* (Washington, D.C.: U.S. Government Printing Office, 1984).

2. Denis Doyle and Chester Finn, "American Schools and the Future of Local
Schools," *The Public Interest* 77 (Fall 1984): 77–95.

3. Provisional Council on Educational Reform, *First Report on Educational
Reform* (Tokyo: Government of Japan, 1985), 18–19; The National Council on Educational Reform, *Outline of Proceedings* (Shingikai no gaiyo) part 3 (Tokyo: Government of Japan), 3–46. Rinji Kyoiku Shingikai is the Japanese name of the

reform council under discussion in this paper. Its English translation varies and is confusing. The Provisional Council on Educational Reform or the National Council on Educational Reform is the typical identification of the council in English. Throughout this paper it is identified as the National Council on Educational Reform.

4. The Economic Council, *Japan in the Year 2000* (Tokyo: Japan Times, 1983).

5. Ibid., 69–76.

6. The National Council, *Outline*, 25–32.

7. The Economic Council, *Japan*, 1–90.

8. The National Council, *Summary of Second Report on Educational Reform* (Tokyo: Government of Japan, 1986), 1–2.

9. The National Council, *Summary of Second Report*, 6.

10. Ibid., 22.

11. Yasuhiro Nakasone, "The 1984 Annual Message to the National Diet at the 101st Session" (Shisei Hoshin Enzetsu), in *Materials on First Report of the National Council on Educational Reform* (Rinkyoshin Dayori), ed. The National Council on Educational Reform (Tokyo: Government of Japan, 1985), 162–67.

12. Ibid., 163.

13. Takashi Ohta, "A Critique of Educational Reforms Proposed by the National Council on Educational Reform" (Rinkyoshin no Kyoiku Kaikaku o Hihansuru), in *All About the National Council on Educational Reform* (Rinkyoshin no Subete), ed. Eideru Kenkyujo (Tokyo: Eideru Kenkyujo, 1985), 36–47.

14. The National Council, *First Report; Second Report on Educational Reform* (Kyoiku Kaikaku ni Kansuru Dainiji Toshin) (Tokyo: Government of Japan, 1986).

15. Ibid., 26.

16. See Chie Nakane, *Japanese Society* (Berkeley: University of California, 1970); Takie Lebra, *Japanese Patterns of Behavior* (Honolulu: University of Hawaii, 1976); Nobuo Shimahara, *Adaptation and Education in Japan* (New York: Praeger, 1979).

17. See Robert Bellah et al, *Habits of the Heart* (Berkeley: University of California, 1985).

18. The First Division of the National Council on Educational Reform, *Memorandum* (Shingi Memo), in *All About the National Council on Educational Reform*, ed. Eideru Kenkyujo, 128–38.

19. Benjamin Duke, "The Liberalization of Japanese Education," *Comparative Education* 22 (1986): 39.

20. Japan Teachers Union, *Educational Reform in Present Japan: Report of the Second JTU Council on Educational Reform* (Tokyo: Japan Teachers Union, 1983).

21. Kuroba, *Rinkyoshin* 27–32.

22. See the National Council, *Second Report*.

23. The National Council, *Summary of Second Report*, 6.

24. Ibid.

25. Ibid., 16.

26. *Asahi Shimbun*, 8 June 1986.

27. See Tomitaro Karasawa, *Japan's Modernization and Education* (Nippon no Kindaika to Kyoiku) (Tokyo: Daiichi Hoki, 1976).

28. The National Council, *First Report*, 20.

29. See Erik Erikson, *Identity, Youth, and Crisis* (New York: W. W. Norton, 1969).

30. Shimahara, *Adaptation*, 31–43.

31. For example, the following works support this thesis: Michio Nagai, *Modernization and Education* (Kindaika to Kyoiku) (Tokyo: Tokyo University, 1969); Samuel Bowles and Herbert Gintis, *Schooling in Capitalist America* (New York: Basic Books, 1976).

32. Carnegie Forum on Education and the Economy, *A Nation Prepared: Teachers for the 21st Century* (New York: Carnegie Corporation, 1986), 10–21.

Part IV

Works in English on Japanese Education, 1970–1988: A Selected Bibliography

James J. Shields, Jr.

The purpose of this bibliography is to provide a comprehensive and effective research tool for scholars and educational policymakers with an interest in Japanese education. With this in mind extensive bibliographic searches were undertaken between 1982 and 1988 by the author at Teachers College, Columbia University and Harvard University, School of Education in the United States, and at the Ministry of Education, Science and Culture (Mombusho), the National Institute of Educational Research, The Japan Foundation, and International House in Tokyo. In addition, bibliographic reviews were held with university scholars and government officials in Japan and the United States during the same period.

Insofar as this bibliography is representative of a broad range of books and reports published in English in the 1970s and 1980s, it provides a guide and measure of the shifting currents of thought on Japanese education among scholars, journalists, government officials and special interest groups. Clearly, for instance, in the 1970s, issues related to university student protest, educational history, especially in the Meiji period, the teachers movement, higher education, and the relationship of schooling modernization and westernization attracted considerable attention.

In the 1980s, other issues moved into the foreground including: equity matters, notably those focused on women and the handicapped; social, cultural and psychological factors related to education in the home and the early levels of schooling; Occupation educational history; teacher education; and lessons Japanese schooling hold for other national systems.

Beyond these shifts in focus, two other patterns become evident in this bibliography. The first has to do with the important areas of concern which have been largely neglected in both decades. These include critical studies of the philosophical and ideological foundations of Japanese education, issues of personal and academic freedom, the junior high school level and adolescence, the academically and artistically gifted, and community colleges and vocational education. The other pattern has to do with the range and the level of analysis found in different kinds of publications, for instance, in government documents as compared to those of university scholars or freelance writers.

The over 200 English language sources listed here constitute not only a surprisingly large but also a very respectable research base for those interested in studying Japanese education, especially those with little or no Japanese language skills. However, even though this is probably the most comprehensive bibliography of English language sources on Japanese education it is by no means complete. There is, in addition, a vast body of journal, magazine, and newspaper articles on Japanese education, many of which can be identified through the sources listed here. Beyond this there exists a good number of widely scattered and mostly uncatalogued sources which await recognition by diligent bibliographic researchers, particularly in the more specialized areas of educational studies.

Books, Pamphlets, and Nongovernmental Reports

Adams, Don. *Education and Modernization in Asia*. Reading, Massachusetts: Addison-Wesley, 1970. Chapter 2.

Allen, George C. *Appointment in Japan: Memories of Sixty Years*. London: Athlone Press, 1983. 196 pp.

Amagai, Isao. *Higher Education in Japan: Problems and Prospects*. Tokyo: Japan Society for the Promotion of Science, 1977. 42 pp.

Anami, Virginia S. *Nishimachi: Crossroads of Culture: A Historical Sketch of Nishimachi International School*. Tokyo: Nishimachi International School, 1982. 80 pp.

Anderson, Ronald S. *Education in Japan: A Century of Modern Development*. Washington, D.C.: U.S. Government Printing Office, 1975. 412 pp.

Aso, Makoto, and Ikuo Amano. *Education and Japan's Modernization*. Tokyo: The Japan Times, 1983. 111 pp.

Association of International Education. *Japanese Colleges and Universities 1987: A Guide to Institutions of Higher Education in Japan*. Tokyo: Maruzen, 1987. 711 pp.

Beauchamp, Edward R. *An American Teacher in Early Meiji Japan*. Asian Studies at Hawaii Series, no. 17. Honolulu: University of Hawaii Press, 1976. 154 pp.

———. *Education in Contemporary Japan*. Fastback 171. Bloomington, Indiana: Phi Delta Kappa Educational Foundation, 1982. 38 pp.

———, ed. *Learning to Be Japanese: Selected Readings on Japanese Society and Education*. Hamden, Connecticut: Linnett Books, 1978. 408 pp.

Beer, Laurence Ward. *Freedom of Expression in Japan: A Study in Comparative Law, Politics, and Society*. Tokyo: Kodansha International, 1984. Chapter 7.

Bereday, George Z. F., and Shigeo Masui. *American Education through Japanese Eyes*. Honolulu: University Press of Hawaii, 1973. 279 pp.

Bethel, Dayle. *M. Makiguchi: The Value Creator: Revolutionary Japanese Educator and Founder of Soka Gakkai*. New York: Weatherhill, 1973. 174 pp.

Bettelheim, Ruth, and Ruby Takanishi. *Early Schooling in Asia*. New York: McGraw-Hill, 1976. 202 pp.

Bonet, Vicente M., ed. *Religion in the Japanese Textbooks*. 3 volumes. Tokyo: Enderle Book, 1973–74.

Bowman, Mary Jean, Hideo Ikeda, and Yasumasa Tomada. *Educational Choice and Labor Markets in Japan*. Chicago: University of Chicago Press, 1981. 367 pp.

Bunka Shinkokai. *Higher Education and the Student Problem*. Tokyo: Japan Cultural Society, 1972. 309 pp.

Burkman, Thomas W., ed. *Occupation of Japan: Education and Social Reform*. Norfolk, Virginia: McArthur Memorial, 1982. 529 pp.

Burks, Ardath W., ed. *The Modernizers: Overseas Students, Foreign Employees and Meiji Japan*. Boulder, Colorado: Westview Press, 1985. 450 pp.

Burn, Barbara, Philip Altbach, Clark Kerr, and James A. Perkins. *Higher Education in Nine Countries*. New York: McGraw-Hill, 1971. Chapter 9.

Chiba, Akira. *Japan's Programs for Gifted and Talented Education*. Tokyo: International Society for Intelligence Education, 1980. 66 pp.

Chuo Seishonen Dantai Renraku Kyogikai. *The Role of Education for Development Seminar, Tokyo, November 7–21, 1975*. Tokyo: National Council of Youth Organizations in Japan, 1975. 175 pp.

Cleaver, Charles Grinnel. *Japanese and Americans: Cultural Parallels and Para-doxes*. Tokyo: Charles E. Tuttle, 1978. Chapter 8.

Cummings, William K. *Education and Equality in Japan*. Princeton, New Jersey: Princeton University Press, 1980. 305 pp.

————, Ikuo Amano, and Kazayuki Kitamuri. *Changes in the Japanese University: A Comparative Perspective*. New York: Praeger, 1979. 288 pp.

———— et al., eds. *Educational Policies in Crisis: Japanese and American Perspectives*. New York: Praeger, 1986. 308 pp.

DeVos, George A. *Socialization for Achievement: Essays on the Cultural Psychology of the Japanese*. Berkeley: University of California Press, 1973. 597 pp.

Dore, Ronald P. *The Diploma Disease Education, Qualification and Development*. Berkeley: University of California Press, 1976. Chapter 3.

————. *Education in Tokugawa Japan*. Ann Arbor, Michigan: Center for Japanese Studies, The University of Michigan, 1984. 346 pp. (Reprint: London: Athlone Press, 1965, edition with new preface.)

Dowsey, Stuart, ed. *Zengakuren: Japan's Revolutionary Students*. Berkeley, California: The Ishi Press, 1970. 271 pp.

Duke, Benjamin C. *Japan's Militant Teachers: A History of the Left-Wing Teacher's Movement*. Honolulu: University Press of Hawaii, 1973. 246 pp.

————. *The Japanese School: Lessons for Industrial America*. New York: Praeger, 1986. 242 pp.

Eckstein, Max A. *A Comparative Review of Curriculum: Mathematics and International Studies in the Secondary Schools of Five Countries*. Washington, D.C.: National Commission on Excellence in Education, 1982. 115 pp.

Forbis, William H. *Japan Today: Peoples Places, Power*. New York: Harper and Row, 1975. Chapter 7.

Freund, William C., and Eugene Epstein. *People and Productivity: The New York Stock Exchange Guide to Financial Incentives and the Quality of Work Life*. Homewood, Illinois: Dow-Jones-Irwin, 1984. Section 2.

Fukurai, Shiro. *How Can I Make What I Cannot See*. Trans. Margaret Haas and Fusako Kobayashi. New York: Van Nostrand Reinhold, 1974. 127 pp.

Gross, Carl. *Sokagakkai and Education*. East Lansing: Institute for International Studies, Michigan State University, 1970. 76 pp.

Gumbert, Edgar B., ed. *In the Nation's Image: Civic Education in Japan, the Soviet Union, the United States, France and Britain*. Atlanta: Center for Cross Cultural Education, Georgia State University, 1987. 130 pp.

Hall, Ivan Parker. *Mori Arinori*. Cambridge, Massachusetts: Harvard University Press, 1973. 535 pp.

Hall, Robert K. *Education for the New Japan*. Westport, Connecticut: Greenwood Press, 1971. 503 pp.

Hendry, Joy. *Becoming Japanese: The World of the Pre-School Child*. Honolulu: University of Hawaii Press, 1986. 194 pp.

Hiroshima University, Research Institute for Higher Education, ed. *Higher Education Expansion in Asia*. Hiroshima: The University, 1985. 167 pp.

————. *Japanese Patterns of Institutional Management in Higher Education*. Hiroshima: The University, 1974. 43 pp.

————. *A National Survey of Opinion among Foreign Teachers at Japanese Universities and Colleges*. Hiroshima: The University, 1979. 18 pp.

Holmes, Brian, ed. *Equality and Freedom in Education: A Comparative Study*. London: George Allen and Unwin, 1985. Chapter 6.

Hough, J. R., ed. *Educational Policy: An International Survey.* New York: St. Martin's Press, 1984, 100–135.

Imamura, Anne E. *Urban Japanese Housewives: At Home and in the Community.* Honolulu: University of Hawaii Press, 1987. 193 pp.

International Society for Educational Information. *The Modernization of Japanese Education.* 2 volumes. Tokyo: The Society, 1986.

Iriye, Akira, ed. *Mutual Images: Essays in American-Japanese Relations.* Cambridge, Massachusetts: Harvard University Press, 1975. 169–87.

James, Estelle, and Gail Benjamin. *Public Versus Private Education: The Japanese Experiment.* New Haven, Connecticut: Institution for Social and Policy Studies, Yale University, 1984. 160 pp.

Japan Association of Universities of Education. Committee for Facilitating Research. *Teacher Training in Japan.* Tokyo: Dai-ichi Hoki, 1986. 53 pp.

Japan Center for International Exchange. *Japanese Philanthrophy and International Cooperation.* Tokyo: The Center, 1985. 170 pp.

Japan Teachers Union. *Educational Reform in Present Japan: Report of the Second JTU Council on Educational Reform.* Tokyo: The Union, October 1983. 50 pp.

———. *History of Peace Education Movement in Japan—30 Years of JTU Educational Research Activities.* Tokyo: The Union, n.d.. 70 pp.

———. *How Should Education in Japan Be Reformed Now? The First Draft of the People's Educational Reform Plan.* Tokyo: The Union, April 1984. 22 pp.

———. *Japan Teachers Union: Its Organization and Movement.* Tokyo: The Union, 1983. 27 pp.

———. People's Education Research Institute. *Teaching Materials for Peace Education: Theory and Practices.* Tokyo: The Union, n.d.. 30 pp.

Kaneko, Motohisa. *Enrollment Expansion in Postwar Japan.* Hiroshima: Research Institute for Higher Education, Hiroshima University, 1987. 111 pp.

Katai, Tayama. *Country Teacher.* Honolulu: University of Hawaii Press, 1984. 210 pp.

King, Edmond J. *Other Schools and Ours.* 5th ed. New York: Holt, Rinehart, and Winston, 1979. Chapter 11.

Kinmouth, Earl H. *The Self-Made Man in Meiji-Japanese Thought: From Samurai to Salary Man.* Berkeley: University of California Press, 1981. 385 pp.

Kiyooka, Eiichi, ed. and trans. *Fukuzawa Yukichi on Education: Selected Works.* Tokyo: University of Tokyo Press, 1986. 280 pp.

Kobayashi, Tetsuya. *Society, Schools and Progress in Japan.* Oxford, England: Pergamon Press, 1976. 185 pp.

Koike, Ikuo, ed. *The Teaching of English in Japan.* Tokyo: Eichosha, 1978. 917 pp.

Krauss, Ellis A. *Japanese Radicals Revisited: Student Protest in Postwar Japan.* Berkeley: University of California Press, 1974. 192 pp.

———, Thomas Rohlen, and Patricia Steinhoff, eds. *Conflict in Japan.* Honolulu: University of Hawaii Press, 1984. 417 pp.

Kuroyanagi, Tetsuko. *Totto-Chan—The Little Girl at the Window.* Tokyo: Kodansha International, 1982. 229 pp.

Kusuyama, T., A. Sumida, and T. Asada. *12 Aspects of Children of Japan.* Tokyo: Akishobo, 1980. 127 pp.

Lawn, Martin, ed. *The Politics of Teacher Unionism.* London: Croom Helm, 1985. Chapter 4.

Lee, Changsoo Lee, and George De Vos. *Koreans in Japan: Ethnic Conflict and Accommodation.* Berkeley: University of California Press, 1981. Chapter 9.

Lynn, Richard. *Educational Achievement in Japan: Lessons for the West*. London: The Macmillan Press, 1988. 157 pp.

Massey, Joseph A. *Youth and Politics in Japan*. Lexington, Massachusetts: D. C. Heath, 1976. 233 pp.

McCormack, Gavan, and Yoshico Sugimoto, eds. *Democracy in Contemporary Japan*. Sydney, Australia: Hale and Iremonger, 1986. 272 pp.

Morooka, Kazufusa. *Recurrent Education Policy and Development in O.E.C.D. Member Countries: Japan*. Paris: OECD, 1976. 59 pp.

Murray, Geoffrey. *Mariko-Mother*. Tokyo: PHP Institute, Inc. International, 1976. 124 pp.

Nagai, Michio. *Education and Indoctrination: The Sociological and Philosophical Bases*. Tokyo: University of Tokyo Press, 1976. 118 pp.

———. *Higher Education in Japan: Its Take-off and Crash*. Tokyo: University of Tokyo Press, 1971. 264 pp.

Najita, Tetsuo. *Visions of Virtue in Tokugawa Japan: The Kaitokudo Merchant Academy of Osaka*. Chicago: The University of Chicago Press, 1987. 334 pp.

Nakayama, Shigeru, ed. *Academic and Scientific Traditions in China, Japan and the West*. Tokyo: University of Tokyo Press, 1974. 337 pp.

Narita, Katsuya. *Systems of Higher Education: Japan*. New York: International Council for Educational Development, 1978. 142 pp.

Nihon, Hoiku Gakkai, ed. *Early Childhood Education and Care in Japan*. Tokyo: Child Honsha, 1979. 111 pp.

Nishi, Toshio. *Unconditional Democracy: Education and Politics in Occupied Japan, 1945–1952*. Stanford, California: Hoover Institution Press, 1982. 367 pp.

Notehelfer, Fred G. *American Samurai: Captain L. L. Janes and Japan*. Princeton, New Jersey: Princeton University Press, 1985. 386 pp.

OECD. *Classification of Educational Systems in O.E.C.D. Member Countries, Finland, Germany, Japan*. Paris: OECD, 1972. 72 pp.

———. *Educational Expenditure in France, Japan and the United Kingdom*. Paris: OECD, 1977. 334 pp.

———. *Educational Policy and Planning: Japan*. Paris: OECD, 1973. 282 pp.

———. *New Patterns of Teacher Education in Canada and Japan*. Paris: OECD, 1975. 88 pp.

———. *Reviews of National Policies for Education: Japan*. Paris: OECD, 1971. 162 pp.

Okamoto, Natsuki, and Miyoaki Shimizu, eds. *Javanese and Japanese Children; Comparative Studies on Psychological Development in Two Cultures*. Kyoto: Department of Psychology, Kyoto University, 1980. 195 pp.

Passin, Herbert, *Society and Education in Japan*. Tokyo: Kodansha International, 1982. 347 pp. (Reprint: New York Teachers College Press, 1965.)

Pempel, T. J. *Patterns of Japanese Policymaking: Experience from Higher Education*. Boulder, Colorado: Westview Press, 1978. 248 pp.

Radio-TV Education Association. *Radio and Television: Role in the Education of Handicapped Children in Japan*. Tokyo: The Association, 1982. 111 pp.

Robins-Mowry, Dorothy. *The Hidden Sun: Women of Modern Japan*. Boulder, Colorado: Westview Press, 1983. 370 pp.

Roden, Donald T. *Schooldays in Imperial Japan: A Study in the Culture of a Student Elite*. Berkeley: University of California Press, 1980. 300 pp.

Rohlen, Thomas P. *Japan's High Schools*. Berkeley: University of California Press, 1983. 363 pp.

Rubinger, Richard. *Private Academies of Tokugawa Japan.* Princeton, New Jersey: Princeton University Press, 1982. 282 pp.

Shimahara, Nobuo K. *Adaptation and Education in Japan.* New York: Praeger, 1979. 190 pp.

——. *Burakumin: A Japanese Minority and Education.* The Hague: Martinus Nijhoff, 1971. 102 pp.

Shimazaki, Toson. *The Broken Commandment.* Trans. Kenneth Strong. Tokyo: University of Tokyo Press, 1974. 249 pp.

Shimizu, Takeski. *Intelligence Education Materials for Primary School Children.* Tokyo: International Society for Intelligence Education, 1980. 75 pp.

Singleton, John. *Nichu: A Japanese School.* Irvington, New York: George and Spindler, 1982. (Reprint New York: Holt, Rinehart and Winston, 1967.)

Smith, Henry DeWitt II. *Japan's First Student Radicals.* Cambridge, Massachusetts: Harvard University Press, 1972. 341 pp.

Stevenson, Harold, Hiroshi Azuma, and Kenji Hakuta, eds. *Child Development and Education in Japan.* New York: W. H. Freeman, 1986. 315 pp.

Thomas, J. E. *Learning Democracy in Japan: The Social Education of Japanese Adults.* London: Sage Publications, 1985. 153 pp.

Thomas, R. Murray, and T. Neville Postlethwaite. *Schooling in East Asia.* Oxford, England: Pergamon Press, 1983. Chapter 2.

Thrush, John, and Philip R. Smith. *Japan's Economic Growth and Educational Change, 1950–1970.* Lincoln, Nebraska: EBHA Press, 1980. 90 pp.

Thurston, Donald. *Teachers and Politics in Japan.* Princeton, New Jersey: Princeton University Press, 1973. 337 pp.

Trainor, Joseph C. *Educational Reform in Occupied Japan: Trainor's Memoir.* Tokyo: Meisei University Press, 1983. 427 pp.

Tsurumi, E. Patricia. *Japanese Colonial Education in Taiwan—1895–1945.* Cambridge, Massachusetts: Harvard University Press, 1977. 368 pp.

Tsurumi, Kazuko. *Social Change and the Individual.* Princeton, New Jersey: Princeton University Press, 1970. Chapters 3, 9–11.

Umetani, Shun'ichiro. *Education and Vocational Training in Japan.* Hamburg, Germany: Das Institut fur Asienkunde, 1980. 108 pp.

UNESCO. *Case Studies in Special Education: Cuba, Japan, Kenya, Sweden.* Paris: UNESCO Press, 1974. 195 pp.

U.S. Department of Education. *Japanese Education Today.* Washington, D.C.: Government Printing Office, 1987. 93 pp.

U.S. Education Mission to Japan. *Report of the United States Education Mission to Japan: Submitted to the Supreme Commander for the Allied Powers, Tokyo, March 30, 1946.* Westport, Connecticut: Greenwood Press, 1977. 62 pp.

Vogel, Ernest F. *Japan as No. 1. Lessons for America.* Cambridge, Massachusetts: Harvard University Press, 1979. Chapter 7.

White, Merry W. *The Japanese Educational Challenge: A Commitment to Children.* New York: The Free Press, 1987. 210 pp.

——. *The Japanese Overseas: Can They Go Home Again.* New York: The Free Press, 1988. 179 pp.

Wolfe, Robert, ed. *Americans as Proconsuls: United States Military Government in Germany and Japan, 1944–1952.* Carbondale: Southern Illinois University Press, 1984. 536 pp.

Wordell, Charles B., ed. *A Guide to Teaching English in Japan.* Tokyo: The Japan Times, 1985. 343 pp.

Woronoff, Jon. *Japan: The Coming Social Crisis.* 4th ed. Tokyo: Lotus Press, 1982. Chapter 4.

Government Publications: Japan

Bunkacho. *Outline of Education in Japan.* Tokyo: International Cultural Relations Division, Agency for Cultural Affairs (The Japan Foundation), 1970. 47 pp; 1972. 60 pp; 1975. 60 pp.

Bunka Shinkokai. *Higher Education and the Student Problem.* Tokyo: Japan Cultural Society, 1972. 309 pp.

Chuo Kyoiku Shingikai. *Basic Guidelines for the Reform of Education for the Development of an Integrated Educational System Suited for Contemporary Society: Report of the Central Council for Education.* Tokyo: Mombusho, 1972. 219 pp.

————. *The Master Plan for the Reform of Higher Education: Interim Report.* Tokyo: Mombusho, 1970. 59 pp.

Foreign Press Center. *Education in Japan.* Tokyo: The Center, 1978. 32 pp.

Kodama, Taketoshi. *Pre-school Education in Japan.* Tokyo: NIER, 1983. 23 pp.

Mombusho. *A Brief Outline.* Tokyo: Mombusho, 1985. 90 pp.

————. *Community and Culture: Report of the Central Council for Education.* Tokyo: Mombusho, 1979. 11 pp.

————. *Course of Study for Elementary Schools in Japan.* Tokyo: Mombusho, 1976. 226 pp.

————. *Course of Study for Lower Secondary Schools.* Tokyo: Mombusho, 1976. 246 pp; 1983. 131 pp.

————. *Course of Study for Upper Secondary Schools In Japan.* Tokyo: Mombusho, 1976. 490 pp; 1983. 188 pp.

————. *Education in Japan: A Graphic Presentation.* Tokyo: Mombusho, 1971. 124 pp; 1978. 127 pp.; 1982. 127 pp.

————. *Educational Standards in Japan.* Tokyo: Mombusho, 1971. 255 pp.; 1975. 378 pp.

————. *Educational Statistics in Japan.* Tokyo: Mombusho, 1971. 93 pp.; 1974. 85 pp.; 1977. 86 pp.

————. *Higher Education in Japan.* Tokyo: Mombusho, 1972. 13 pp.

————. *Japan's Modern Educational System: A History of the First Hundred Years.* Tokyo: Research and Statistics Division, Mombusho, 1980. 473 pp.

————. *Life-Long Education, Report of the Central Council for Education.* Tokyo: Mombusho, 1981. 30 pp.

————. *The Ministry of Education, Science and Culture.* Tokyo: Mombusho, 1975. 56 pp.; 1981. 88 pp.

————. *Outline of Education in Japan.* Tokyo: Mombusho, 1979. 60 pp.; 1987. 97 pp.

————. *Physical Education and Sports in Japan.* Tokyo: Physical Education Bureau Mombusho, 1970. 25 pp.; 1981. 28 pp.

————. *Pre-School Education in Japan.* Tokyo: Mombusho, 1981. 21 pp.

————. *Social Education and Its Administration in Japan.* Tokyo: Mombusho, 1972. 40 pp.

————. *Statistical Abstract of Education, Science and Culture.* Tokyo: Research and Statistics Division, Mombusho, 1978. 195 pp.; 1979. 217 pp.; 1981. 185 pp.

——. *A Survey of the Demands of Life-Long Education: Interim Report.* Tokyo: Research and Statistics Division, Ministry of Education, 1972. 48 pp.

——. *Survey of Schools.* Tokyo: Foreign Press Center, 1983. 30 pp.

——. *Women and Education in Japan.* Tokyo: Social Education Bureau, Ministry of Education, 1972. 34 pp.; 1975. 22 pp.; 1980. 36 pp.; 1983. 34 pp.

Mombusho. Japanese National Commission for UNESCO. *Development of Modern System of Education in Japan.* Tokyo: The Commission, 1971. 96 pp.

——. *Elements of the Structure and Terminology of Agricultural Education.* Paris: UNESCO Press, 1975. 62 pp.

——. *Guidebook for the Teaching of Arithmetic in Elementary Schools in Japan.* Tokyo: The Commission, 1972. 96 pp.

——. *Guidebook for the Teaching of Industrial Arts and Homemaking in Lower Secondary Schools.* Tokyo: The Commission, 1973. 184 pp.

——. *Guidebook for the Teaching of Mathematics in Lower Secondary Schools in Japan.* Tokyo: The Commission, 1973. 117 pp.

——. *Guidebook for the Teaching of Mathematics in Upper Secondary Schools in Japan.* Tokyo: The Commission, 1974. 133 pp.

——. *Guidebook for the Teaching of Science and Mathematics in Upper Secondary Schools in Japan.* Tokyo: The Commission, 1974. 65 pp.

——. *Guidebook for the Teaching of Science in Elementary Schools in Japan.* Tokyo: The Commission, 1972. 104 pp.

——. *Guidebook for the Teaching of Science in Upper Secondary Schools in Japan.* Tokyo: The Commission, 1974. 57 pp.

——. *Nature and Use of Instructional Media.* Tokyo: The Commission, 1972. 54 pp.

——. *Revised Course of Study for Upper Secondary Schools in Japan.* Tokyo: The Commission, 1971. 490 pp.

——. *Standard Facilities and Equipment for Industrial Upper Secondary Schools in Japan.* Tokyo: The Commission, 1970. 217 pp.

——. *Teaching Materials and Equipment for Elementary and Secondary Schools in Japan.* Tokyo: The Commission, 1971. 155 pp.

——. *Technical and Technological Education in Japan.* Tokyo: The Commission, 1972. 198 pp.

——. *Training of Science Teachers in Japan.* Tokyo: The Commission, 1970. 216 pp.

——. *The Use of Audio-Visual Teaching Materials in Schools in Japan.* Tokyo: The Commission, 1971. 124 pp.

——. *The Use of Modern Media in Adult Education.* Tokyo: The Commission, 1972. 31 pp.

National Institute for Educational Research. *Audio-Visual Instruction in Asia: Workshop Report.* Tokyo: NIER, 1971. 167pp.

——. *Basic Facts and Figures about the Educational System in Japan.* Tokyo: NIER, 1982. 43 pp.; 1983. 73 pp.; 1986. 89 pp.

——. *A Brief Outline.* Tokyo: NIER, March 1985. 24 pp.

——. *Comparative Study of Curriculum Development at the Stage of Elementary Education in Asian Countries.* 3 volumes. Tokyo: NIER, 1970.

——. *The Development of Secondary Education in Japan After World War II.* Tokyo: NIER, 1982. 13 pp.

——. *Educational Goals, Aims and Objectives: Report of a Study by a Working Group in Asia.* Tokyo: NIER, 1974. 114 pp.

———. *Educational Research Workshop on Science Teaching in Asia: Final Report.* Tokyo: NIER, 1971. 82 pp.

———. *Educational Statistics in Japan.* Tokyo: NIER, 1985. 26 pp.

———. *In-Service Training for Teachers in Japan.* Tokyo: NIER, 1985. 17 pp.

———. *Modernization of Education in Japan.* Tokyo: NIER, 1978. 85 pp.

———. *Programme at Hyogo University of Teacher Education.* Tokyo: NIER, 1982. 17 pp.

———. *School Lunch Programme in Japan.* Tokyo: NIER, 1982. 18 pp.

———. *School Management in Japan.* Tokyo: NIER, 1984. 19 pp.

———. *The School Textbook System in Japan.* Tokyo: NIER, 1984. 15 pp.

———. *Standard of Education in Japan.* Tokyo: NIER, 1983. 21 pp.

———. *The Teaching Materials System in Japan.* Tokyo: NIER, 1984. 14 pp.

———. *The Use of Computer Education in Japan.* Tokyo: NIER, 1984. 19 pp.

Ogamo, Hideo. *A Master Plan for the Education of the Disabled by Tokyo Metropolitan Government.* Tokyo: Mombusho, 1974. 56 pp.

Okundo, Shinjo. *Improvement of Curriculum Standards in Japan—Revision and Enforcement of the Course of Study.* Tokyo: NIER, 1983. 22 pp.

Prime Minister's Office, National Council on Educational Reform. *The Council.* Tokyo: The Council, April 23, 1986. 12 pp.

———. *First Report on Educational Reform.* Tokyo: The Council, June 26, 1985. 84 pp.

———. *Summary of Second Report on Educational Reform.* Tokyo: The Council, April 23, 1986. 48 pp.

Shakai Kyoiku Shingikai. *Report on Social Education in a Rapidly Changing Society.* Tokyo: Social Education Bureau, Ministry of Education, 1972. 81 pp.

Tokyo Metropolitan Government. *Education in Tokyo.* Municipal library no. 14. Tokyo: Tokyo Metropolitan Government, 1979. 358 pp.

Tsujima, Yasuo. *Compulsory Education System of the Handicapped in Japan.* Yokosuka: National Institute of Special Education, 1980. 17 pp.

Bibliographies

An Introductory Bibliography for Japanese Studies: Social Sciences, vol. V, part 1, 1979–80. Tokyo: Bonjinsha, 1986. 161–82; vol. VI, part 1. 1988. 380 pp.

Center for Academic Publications. *Current Contents of Academic Journals in Japan 1984–1985. The Humanities and the Social Sciences.* Tokyo: The Center, 1986. 459 pp.

Japan Foundation. *Catalogue of Books in English on Japan 1945–1981.* Tokyo: The Foundation, 1986. 726 pp.

Masao, Terasaki. "Education." In *An Introductory Bibliography for Japanese Studies.* Volume IV, Part 1, Social Science 1970–1978. Tokyo: University of Tokyo Press, 1982. 169–91.

Passin, Herbert. *Japanese Education: A Bibliography of Materials in the English Language.* New York: Teachers College Press, 1970. 135 pp.

Teichler, Ulrich, and Fredrich Voss. *Bibliography on Japanese Education; Postwar Publications in Western Languages.* Munchen, Germany: Verlag Dokumentation, 1974. 294 pp.